State Repression and the Domestic Democratic Peace

Does democracy decrease state repression in line with the expectations of governments, international organizations, nongovernmental organizations, social movements, scholars, and ordinary citizens around the world? At present, most believe that a domestic democratic peace exists, rivaling that found in the realm of interstate conflict. Based on an investigation of 137 countries from 1976 to 1996, this book seeks to shed light on this question. Specifically, three results emerge. First, even though different aspects of democracy decrease repressive behavior, not all do so to the same degree. Human rights violations are especially responsive to electoral participation and competition. Second, although different types of repression are reduced, not all are limited at comparable levels. Personal integrity violations are decreased more than civil liberties restrictions. Third, the domestic democratic peace is not bulletproof; the negative influence of democracy on repression can be overwhelmed by political conflict. This research alters our conception of repression, its analysis, and its resolution.

Christian Davenport is an Associate Professor of Political Science at the University of Maryland–College Park, as well as Director of the Radical Information Project (RIP). He is the author of more than 25 articles appearing in the *American Political Science Review*, the *American Journal of Political Science*, the *Journal of Politics*, the *Journal of Conflict Resolution*, *Political Research Quarterly*, *Comparative Political Studies*, and the *Monthly Review* (among others). He is the recipient of numerous grants (including five from the National Science Foundation) and awards, including the William J. Fulbright Foreign Scholarship Award, the Pi Sigma Alpha Best Paper Award from the Midwest Political Science Association for 2005, 1 of 50 Leaders of Tomorrow by *Ebony Magazine* in 1995, and the Malcolm X Lover's Keeper of the Flame Award in 1992. The editor of two books, *Paths to State Repression* and *Repression and Mobilization*, Davenport is currently completing another book entitled *The Rashomon Effect: Contentious Politics, Data Generation and the Importance of Perspective*. For the 2006–7 academic year, he is a visiting scholar at the Russell Sage Foundation in New York City. For the 2007–8 academic year, he will be a visiting scholar at the Peace Research Institute in Oslo at the Center for the Study of Civil War.

Cambridge Studies in Comparative Politics

General Editor

Margaret Levi   *University of Washington, Seattle*

Assistant General Editor

Stephen Hanson   *University of Washington, Seattle*

Associate Editors

Robert H. Bates   *Harvard University*
Helen Milner   *Princeton University*
Frances Rosenbluth   *Yale University*
Susan Stokes   *Yale University*
Sidney Tarrow   *Cornell University*
Kathleen Thelen   *Northwestern University*
Erik Wibbels   *University of Washington, Seattle*

Other Books in the Series

Continued after the Index

State Repression and the Domestic Democratic Peace

CHRISTIAN DAVENPORT

University of Maryland–College Park

CAMBRIDGE
UNIVERSITY PRESS

CAMBRIDGE UNIVERSITY PRESS
Cambridge, New York, Melbourne, Madrid, Cape Town, Singapore,
São Paulo, Delhi, Dubai, Tokyo, Mexico City

Cambridge University Press
The Edinburgh Building, Cambridge CB2 8RU, UK

Published in the United States of America by Cambridge University Press, New York

www.cambridge.org
Information on this title: www.cambridge.org/9780521168717

First published 2007
First paperback edition 2010

A catalogue record for this publication is available from the British Library

Library of Congress Cataloguing in Publication Data

Davenport, Christian, 1965–
State repression and the domestic democratic peace / Christian Davenport.
    p. cm. – (Cambridge studies in comparative politics)
Includes bibliographical references and index.
ISBN-13: 978-0-521-86490-9 (hardback)
ISBN-10: 0-521-86490-9 (hardback)
1. Political persecution. 2. Democracy. I. Title. II. Series.
JC585.D33   2007
323.4'9–dc22   2007008932

ISBN 978-0-521-86490-9 Hardback
ISBN 978-0-521-16871-7 Paperback

The problem of taming (coercive) power is a very ancient one. . . . To anyone who studies history or human nature it must be evident that democracy, while not a complete solution, is an essential part of the solution.

Bertrand Russell (1938)

Contents

Figures

Tables

Preface

For about thirteen years, I have been trying to understand why governments use political repression. By this, I am referring to very specific types of government activity: restricting civil liberties (for example, political bans and instances of censorship) and violating personal integrity rights (for example, torture, disappearances, and mass killings). Along this quest, I was initially influenced by literature on authoritarianism, but later I became interested in the connection between democracy and state-sponsored coercive behavior. The reason for my transition was clear. Increasingly over the past few decades, the world has become enamored with democratic political institutions. Within academic literature, social movements, human rights organizations, think tanks, governments, and even pop culture, it is clear that democracy is heralded as a solution to many problems confronting human beings, including state repression. Given the varied quality of this discussion and the importance of the subject matter, I decided to explore the topic more rigorously.

Although my initial investigations into the subject were somewhat more narrowly defined (focusing on the influence of national elections, constitutions, and diverse cumulative indices), as my awareness of existing scholarship increased, several weaknesses were revealed. In this context, the scope of the work enlarged. My interest was further piqued, once I realized that some of the most influential thinkers in the social sciences had similarly grappled with the subject (e.g., Hobbes, Madison, Montesquieu, and Dahl). Given the normal marginalization of human rights and state repression within mainstream political science, such an acknowledgment was particularly important, not just intellectually and professionally but personally as well. I am generally of the opinion that although political scientists profess an interest in power, the form that power takes is severely circumscribed.

When one considers the history of political thought more seriously, however, it is clear that this is simply not the case.

As with any scholarly effort, I have accumulated many debts along the way. I owe thanks to a large number of people, who have served as advisers, counselors, sounding boards, devil's advocates, fans, inspirations, trainers, and critics. But always (always) they have served as friends and colleagues: Mark Lichbach, Charles Tilly, Will Moore, Ron Francisco, Matthew Krain, Steve Poe, Claudia Dahlerus, Jillian Schwedler, Mike Ward, Robert Goldstein, Eduard Ziegenhagen, Manus Midlarsky, Kenneth Bollen, Zehra Arat, David Cingranelli, and David Richards. I wish to acknowledge the assistance of my graduate student and friend, David Armstrong, whose statistical capabilities were extremely helpful. Ilene Cohen proved to be a marvelous copy editor and Margaret Levi's support and insight were invaluable. Repeatedly I was guided by Lew Bateman in a positive direction. I also thank Steely Dan, Public Enemy, and Pink Floyd for sporadic moments of calm and motivation. Lastly, I want to thank my family – the inner sanctum of sanity, serenity, and hot tea: Nejla Yasemin Yatkin, Juliet ("Ndidi") Seignious, Rodney and Barbara Williams, John Sparagana, Katie Kahn, Marina (formerly "Lil M") Sparagana, Hannah Sparagana, Darren Davis, James Gibson, Ray Duch, Wycuie Bauknight and Gloria Marcus, Quinn and Sylvia Rhone, Kysha Harris, Amilcar and Demetria Shabazz, Tunda and Ado, Assata Richards, as well as Michael and Lisa Lane. As you have all taught me, it takes a village to raise a child, but it takes a major metropolitan city to raise a professor, a fine piece of scholarship, and a decent human being. Peace to all of you. Standard with all such exercises, I alone take all responsibility for brilliant insights and unforgivable errors.

Christian Davenport
Washington, D.C.

State Repression and the Domestic Democratic Peace

Introduction

Rwanda   For Francois Xavier Byuma, the vice president of Rwanda's premier human rights organization – The League for Promotion and Defense of Human Rights (LIPRODHOR)[1] – July 15, 2004, could not have been more puzzling. On that day, as he issued a statement to diverse news agencies, the government of Rwanda officially closed the doors of his thirteen-year old organization, accusing it of "divisionism" and promoting mass killing. What made the closing of LIPRODHOR especially puzzling was the fact that after having survived civil war, genocide, and dictatorship, it was shut down once the "minimal" establishment of democracy had been achieved.

The fate of LIPRODHOR was not what one would have expected. One year following the onset of civil war in 1990, the Hutu organization was created in an effort to monitor the repressive practices of the then Hutu-led government. Its initial denunciations of human rights violations were directed against diverse authorities: specifically, between 1990 and 1993, they targeted the authoritarian government of President Juvenal Habyarimana[2] and from April 9 to July 19, 1994, the transitional government of President Theodore Sindikubwako and those associated with it such as Colonel Theoneste Bagosora and the Interahamwe. During this period, LIPRODHOR was heavily criticized and received numerous threats from the government. Indeed, it appeared that the organization would be eliminated at any time, but this was not the case. Rather, its efforts were delayed and disrupted but never fully ended.

---

[1] The group was formerly known as the "Christian League for Human Rights."
[2] Many influential members of LIPRODHOR are from Cyangugu, an area known as being hostile to former President Habyarimana.

After the installation of the new government following the political events of 1994, LIPRODHOR continued and expanded its work. At first, the human rights group concerned itself with the activities of the moderate Hutu and heavily Tutsi influenced government of Pasteur Bizimungu (from July 19, 1994, to March 23, 2000), but later, after Paul Kagame assumed power in 2000, the focus shifted to the first Tutsi-led government since independence.

During this time, LIPRODHOR's efforts were quite ambitious. In 1994, the organization compiled detailed reports about the violence that occurred over the previous four years. These were distributed to diverse government ministries as well as to the Rwandan population. Additionally, LIPRODHOR conducted "sensitization" sessions with local authorities and citizens to educate them about previous violent activity, it created and distributed newspapers (*La Verdict*, which focused on the genocide as well as the then experimental truth and reconciliation effort – Gacaca[3] – and *Umukindo*, which focused on general information about human rights in Rwanda as well as relevant international issues), it developed special re-search units, and it presented theatrical performances throughout the coun-try to inform citizens in a more informal and entertaining manner about what had happened. In 1995, the organization initiated a program to mon-itor prisoners (identifying the number of detainees and minors being held by the government, the general health of the incarcerated, and the progress made with individual cases); and in 1996, it opened a center for the doc-umentation of the Gacaca process – compiling eyewitness testimony (who did what to whom) and investigating the factual nature of the claims made during open sessions. In 2000, LIPRODHOR conducted a survey of how Rwandans felt about the Gacaca process and provided it to the Rwandan National Assembly in an effort to assist the deliberations about how well things were going and whether the program should be extended. That same year, the organization began identifying and monitoring complaints from ordinary Rwandans about human rights violations (for example, the impo-sition of political restrictions, land seizures, and disappearances).

Throughout this period of military control and state-building, the Rwandan government essentially left LIPRODHOR to do what it wanted. Toward the end of 2000, however, the context changed dramatically, seem-ingly for the better. For example, in March 2001, Rwanda held its first district-level elections with a participation rate of approximately 90 percent

---

[3] Literally translated, this means "truth (or justice) in the grass."

of eligible voters (half of the eight million individuals in Rwanda). During 2003, on May 26, the nation held its first constitutional referendum, with 95 percent of the eligible voters participating. On August 26, Rwanda held its first presidential election, which gave the incumbent, Kagame, a resounding victory over Faustin Twagiramungu, a Hutu and his sole competitor.[4] Finally, between September 29 and October 2, Rwanda held its first parliamentary elections, in which 74 percent of Rwandans cast their ballots for the president's party. These events represented a watershed in Rwandan history, signaling the last stages of a political transition that had been outlined in the Arusha accords of 1993, before the country descended into large-scale political violence.

Paradoxically, the "opening" also revealed a shift in repressive practices. In the postdemocratic context, LIPRODHOR was closed down and human rights practices slowly deteriorated, with opponents being banned or disappearing, the press being severely censored, and ordinary citizens being picked up and/or held for lengthy periods without clearly defined charges. In many ways, this was an improvement over the time of dictatorship (1994–2001). Between 1994 and 1998, the Rwandan government used extensive violence against citizens involving mass killing, torture, and beating. Between 1999 and 2000, a policy of forced "villagification" (relocation) physically removed large numbers of people and placed countless others in jail for resisting these efforts. Restrictions on political and civil liberties increased after the elections and the constitutional referendum but, violations of personal integrity decreased – diminishing the overall lethality of repressive behavior.[5]

---

[4] Twagiramungu was the leader of a political party that was banned during the election (the MDR – Mouvement Démocratique Républicain).

[5] This repressive climate was clearly not in line with statements made by the Rwandan government following the events of 1994 about how they wished to develop their political system and society. Indeed, after coming into power, political authorities consistently discussed a transition process of the first five (and then nine) years, during which time they planned to achieve numerous objectives including political democracy, economic development, and military security. By the time of the election for local-level leaders in 2003, one would not have anticipated that the regime would still be engaged in repressive behavior and that organizations like LIPRODHOR would be eliminated. Such an understanding was shared by those extending financial and political assistance to Rwanda. For example, one of the largest supporters of the postgenocide government, the United States, has consistently maintained that *a* and perhaps *the* major objective of Rwandan assistance programs was the development of a democratic government that respected human rights. Similarly, the United Nations High Commission for Refugees (UNHCR), another major financial supporter of Rwanda, consistently maintained that a democratic and nonrepressive government

Q [How can one explain the continued repressive activity in a situation of democratization?] Perhaps something about the very nature of the government and the "opening" itself undermined the ability to put a damper on the use of coercion. For example, prior to local elections, the Rwandan government maintained strict control over the electoral process using bans on expression, an excessive military presence, and strict supervision of voter identification that intimidated the population (see, for example, Reyntjens 2004). Moreover, the Rwandan government designed the constitution in such a way that executive power was largely insulated from mass opinion/ pressure, as well as from the checks and balances commonly associated with democracy (see, for example, Reyntjens 1996).[6] Finally, prior to the presidential elections, the Rwandan government engaged in another round of restrictions and intimidation. Although the quality-of-democracy argument explains the persistence of repression, it does not explain its frequency, scope, or form. To do this, one must consider another factor that has loomed over all aspects of Rwandan life since 1994: political conflict both at home and abroad.

The postgenocidal Rwandan government has faced a variety of challenges and challengers. Most prominently featured in the news, in Northern Rwanda and the Democratic Republic of Congo (the DRC), the government confronts the last residues of the military organization that perpetrated the state-initiated violence of 1994. In addition to this, throughout Rwanda, authorities confront the potential resistance of everyday Rwandans. As most now understand, the events of 1994 saw widespread participation, including not only political officials, members of the military, police (gendarme), and militia but also clergy, teachers, students, and farmers. Once the violence subsided and the new government came to power, many of these same perpetrators returned to Rwandan society. Given the skewed nature of the demographic situation – 85 percent Hutus and 15 percent Tutsi – and the fact that the ideological foundation as well

was the objective of economic assistance. The reality of Rwanda after democracy, however, was very different from the vision conceived years earlier. Although following through with the political transition and establishing a minimal level of democracy as well as limited state-sponsored political violence, the behavior of the Rwandan government was somewhat different from what most anticipated.

[6] Some even found the referendum process problematic. According to one study by the International Crisis Group, "There was no real possibility to reject (the constitution) because there was no campaigning to explain why it [was] bad. It was a state-managed referendum, and we have a state-managed result" (Ngowi 2003).

4

as the organization behind the violence remained intact, the possibility of contentious behavior in the future persisted. Especially troubling for the Rwandan government, it was not clear that the Tutsi inside the country, before the violence began, accepted the government of the Rwandan Patriotic Front (RPF)-influenced regime. Indeed, several cross-ethnic organizations created outside of the country comprising of disaffected Tutsi and Hutu sought to mobilize all Rwandans throughout the world against "the autocratic regime of President Paul Kagame" (Reyntjens 2004).[7]

In this context, the Rwandan government embarked on an ambitious plan to repress its citizens under the banner of "national unity," with the result that the pacifying influence normally associated with political democracy has not had an opportunity to flourish. Indeed, it seems likely that, despite the "opening" of government institutions, participation of citizens in the political process and clear separation of powers, repressive behavior in some form or other will be applied for quite some time.

The United States Within hours of the 9/11 terrorist attacks in New York and Washington, D.C., Attorney General John Ashcroft and Defense Secretary Donald Rumsfeld were working the telephones, discussing the necessity for a quick response to the threat directed against America and what they (as well as others in the Bush administration) thought was required to do so. Their plan was sketchy and hastily put together. Up to the last few moments, staffers were working on the text prior to congressional vote. Regardless of the particulars, however, everyone knew that the proposed changes in law, behavior, and resource allocation would be ambitious, addressing past inadequacies as well as future concerns. Timing was of the utmost importance. As Ashcroft stated on September 24: "The American people do not have the luxury of unlimited time in erecting the necessary defenses to future attacks. Terrorism is a clear and present danger today.... The death tolls are too high, the consequences too great.... Each day that passes [before some action is taken] is a day that terrorists have a competitive advantage. Until Congress makes these changes, we are fighting an unnecessarily uphill battle" (Ashcroft 2001a).

By and large, the public, the media, and U.S. political leaders went along with this fast-track counterterrorist response. Forty-five days after

---

[7] These alliances emerged following successive waves of migration out of Rwanda undertaken by leaders of the former Hutu government, genocide survivors who disagreed with the policies of the current government, and dissatisfied members of the ruling party (the RPF) itself.

the attacks, Congress passed the Patriot Act (the Uniting and Strengthening America Providing Appropriate Tools Required to Intercept and Obstruct Terrorism Act). From most accounts, the legislation presented a major reversal in American state repressive power. Simultaneously, it relaxed restrictions on wiretaps, searches of personal records (for example, medical, library, and financial), and seizures of financial resources; it created a new crime – "domestic terrorism" – with which a wide variety of dissidents could be charged (any actors that threatened the U.S. government with intimidation and coercion); it effectively suspended the writ of habeas corpus in a variety of circumstances; it allowed the CIA and the FBI to employ a wide range of overt as well as covert powers against both foreign and domestic targets with little to no oversight; it facilitated the seemingly limitless accumulation and sharing of information across diverse government organizations; and it created an environment within which coercive agents felt they could operate freely without fear of repercussion. In a relatively brief period, the federal government had reestablished and extended powers that Americans had not seen for decades – powers that were swept away by Attorney General Edward Levi following the series of break-ins, impromptu disclosures, scandals, hearings, apologies, and forced retirements stretching from local police departments around the country to the office of the president during the late 1960s and through the 1970s.[8] Those aware of this history had no interest in seeing coercive power in the U.S. increase, but right after 9/11 it was not the time for arguing. In the words of Ashcroft (2001b), such actions would "give ammunition to America's enemies and pause to America's friends."

Behaviorally, the government's response to threat was swift. Immediately after 9/11, for example, thousands of individuals were detained, interviewed, and registered.[9] This continued throughout the rest of 2001, including the effort to identify and catalogue all noncitizens in the United States coming from twenty-five countries. In support of this effort, airports around

---

[8] Important limitations established by Attorney General Janet Reno were overturned as well.
[9] The reason was simple: "In the days after the attacks, Attorney General Ashscroft told FBI Director Robert Mueller 'that any male from eighteen to forty years old from Middle Eastern or North African countries who the FBI simply learned about was to be questioned and questioned hard" (Bovard 2003, 107). Additionally, as *Newsweek* columnist Steven Brill noted, Ashcroft told FBI and INS agents that the goal "was to prevent attacks, not prosecute anyone. And the best way to do that was to round up, question, and hold as many people as possible" (Bovard 2003, 107).

the country (along with diverse other targets) were effectively militarized, reducing traffic as well as facilitating searches; protest permits were denied; money transmittal services were raided, assets were frozen, and these organizations were required to register with the federal government. All the while, access to information about what the government was doing was severely limited. Declarations of national security and reclassification of information effectively masked what was taking place.

The U.S. government's activities were in many respects constrained. Restrictions on civil liberties were drawn with consideration of the highly institutionalized nature of U.S. democracy. For example, Ashcroft's first attempt, the Mobilization against Terrorism Act (MATA) – an ambitious plan with even fewer restrictions and oversight than the Patriot Act – was not well received, and, indeed, the Patriot Act was constructed as a compromise to head off resistance. Additionally, acknowledging America's historical concern with centralized coercive power, the government established "sunsets" for several important provisions (contained within Title II of the Patriot Act) whereby specific elements of the government's power would expire unless renewed. Even in a time of domestic threats of unprecedented scale, the government of the United States had to concern itself with how much repressive power would be vested in the hands of political authorities. Furthermore, the range of possible repressive responses was severely curtailed: nowhere in public statements or other records was there precise discussion of provisions for violent activity; congress granted the executive the right to use "all necessary force," but this was not addressed in detail. Of course, we now know that plans involving violent behavior were being made (as Abu Ghraib and Guantanamo Bay revealed), but these were not part of the discourse about the larger domestic strategy that would be aimed at the American population.

Two years later, as the government attempted to further bolster its capacity to fight the "Global War on Terror," the parameters of U.S. repressive power were once more openly contested, more explicitly revealing the non-repressive tendencies of democracies. At this time, Patriot Act II (that is, the Domestic Security and Enhancement Act – draft legislation obtained and circulated by the Center for Public Integrity in 2003) was being discussed. The effort was again ambitious.

If passed, the act would bar Justice Department disclosure of information about alleged terrorism-related detainees; virtually eliminate public access to industry "worst case scenario" documents prepared for the Environmental Protection

Agency; create a "suspected terrorist DNA database that could include citizens as well as noncitizens and allow government inclusion of people merely suspected of "association" with "suspected" terrorists; codify the presumption of pretrial detention for citizens or noncitizens suspected of terrorist activity; and allow the U.S. government to "expatriate. . . . citizens associated with terrorist groups, an association that might be so broadly defined as to include participating in legal activities of a designated terrorist group, such as demonstrations. . . . The Patriot Act II would also allow secret detention of citizens and noncitizens suspected of terrorism for up to fifteen days without informing courts or lawyers; permit wiretapping of citizens and noncitizens for fifteen days entirely on the authority of the attorney general and without requiring court approval; terminate court-approved or court-mandated restrictions on police surveillance and spying on political activists that date from the abuses committed by the FBI and local police departments in the 1960s; and impose the death penalty for a range of protests that "involve acts or acts dangerous to human life," a broad definition that might encompass, for example, Greenpeace operations if a death resulted from such protest. (Sidel 2004, 31)

With distance from the attacks of 9/11 and no additional terrorist behavior, however, things had changed in the United States. By the time Patriot Act II was being discussed in early 2003, the reaction of the media and citizenry was quite different. Immediately upon the disclosure of the draft, different individuals and organizations, including many conservatives (such as Bill O'Reilly and William Safire as well as think tanks such as the Libertarian Cato Institute), openly criticized the government's efforts. Not only were these challenges coming from these rather isolated sources, but there was also the emergence of a grassroots movement with city ordinances/resolutions being passed in 408 communities in forty-three states (as of September 2005) that took stands against components of Patriot Acts I and II (American Civil Liberties Union 2005).[10] Even the Supreme Court, which had earlier opted not to hear cases relevant to the government's activity, began to take it upon itself to consider specific aspects of what was taking place, bringing the most important body of judicial review to bear on the topic.

Political conflict prompted a repressive response by the U.S. government, but the shape of this effort was initially as well as subsequently influenced by political democracy. In a sense, 9/11 structured the repressive practices advanced by the U.S. political system, but it did not dismiss them.

---

[10] This is available at the following URL: *www.aclu.org/safeandfree/safeandfree.cfm?id=11294&c=207.*

Introduction

Understanding and Ending Repressive Action

Although the activities within Rwanda and the United States are clearly an unlikely comparison, they motivate the current investigation. I believe that they are representative of broader issues confronting citizens and political authorities around the globe. The similarities are clear: in both cases, specific aspects of the government associated with democracy decreased the lethality of state repression, but the nature of that influence was determined by the level of the characteristic under discussion, the type of repressive behavior considered, and the magnitude of domestic and international conflict confronted.[11] The differences between Rwanda and the United States are also instructive. In the case of Rwanda, it is shown that in a context of continued large-scale violent behavior, even the smallest amount of democracy (elections and constitutional referenda) improves human rights conditions – albeit only certain aspects and not as much as one would expect. In the case of the United States, it is shown that even a country heralded as one of the most developed democracies in the world will resort to specific forms of repressive behavior when threatened with a single act of violent political conflict. Therefore, even though the pacifying influence of democracy is crucial for decreasing state repressive behavior, it is conditional.

Are all types of repression equally responsive to the influence of diverse democratic characteristics? Should all aspects of democracy be supported if one is interested in reducing the lethality of repressive behavior? Are pacifying influences robust across diverse forms of political conflict (that is, which versions of domestic democratic peace are bulletproof)? The current book addresses these questions.

The issues here are by no means new to students of politics. Since the origin of the nation-state, those subject to the coercive power of government have been trying to decrease this behavior, shifting its application away from the most lethal techniques. Although the solution to this problem has generated diverse ideas, debates, social movements, and public policies, over the last fifty years one answer has emerged that is at once simple, compelling, and widely accepted. Viewing authoritarianism ("closed" and unaccountable political systems) as the primary reason for

---

[11] It should be noted that I acknowledge there are a wide variety of democratic types and sub-types (Collier and Levitsky 1997); what I focus on in this book are particular characteristics of political systems that are generally associated with democracy.

9

state coercion (see, for example, Dallin and Breslauer 1970; Linz 2000; Walter 1969),[12] democratic political institutions have come to be seen as the ultimate answer to the problem of repressive behavior (see, for example, Dahl 1989, 223; Rummel 1997; Shapiro 2003). Throughout the world, individuals and groups increasingly look to elections, the representation of diverse political parties, and limitations on executive discretion to reduce state-sponsored bans, censorship, arrests, torture, disappearances, and mass killing.

[handwritten margin note: 3 things linked typically to repression]

The logic of this position is straightforward. It is generally believed that political leaders in authoritarian systems use repression for three reasons: (1) they lack viable alternatives for political control, (2) they suffer no consequences for taking such action, and (3) there are generally no effective mechanisms for countering/"checking" the coercive power of authorities within such governments.[13] Understanding this, those interested in reducing state repression have concluded that the best way to diminish this behavior is to create a political system that is the opposite of an authoritarian one. In short, they have concluded that democracies must be built and sustained. The reasons are again threefold. Leaders within these governments are generally less likely to apply coercion because (1) they have alternative mechanisms of control available to them (for example, normative influence), (2) they potentially suffer great consequences for engaging in this behavior (for example, being removed from office or being sent to jail), and (3) these political systems contain numerous institutional mechanisms for countering/checking the coercive power held by political authorities (for example, rival political organizations within the existing government and civil society).[14] Through an alteration of incentives and the very functioning of the process by which policies are enacted, democracy makes the political system more accountable to constituents and decreases the likelihood that repressive behavior (especially the most lethal forms) will be used.

---

[12] Others highlight human nature (Hobbes 1950; Sidanius and Pratto 1999), the nation-state (Levene 2005; Van den Berghe 1990), and political-economic relationships (Lopez and Stohl 1989; Pion-Berlin 1989; Stanley 1996).

[13] It is common for discussions of power mechanisms (especially within nondemocratic regimes) to be reduced themselves to coercion (Wintrobe 1998, 38). It is also common for discussions of power mechanisms within democratic regimes to highlight the diversity of strategies available to political leaders beyond those of coercive behavior.

[14] In addition to this, democratic political systems also socialize government personnel to believe not only that is repression difficult to apply but also that it is "wrong" to do so. This is not frequently highlighted in the literature.

Introduction

For about thirty-five years, quantitative research has been overwhelmingly supportive of this argument.[15] In almost every analysis, democracy is seen to decrease state repression. The research here directly complements a similar finding in the international relations literature regarding the pacifying influence of democracy on interstate coercion (war), popularly referred to as the "democratic peace" (Crescenzi and Enterline 1999; Gleditsch and Ward 2000; Hegre et al. 2001; O'Neal et al. 1996; O'Neal and Russett 1999; Rousseau et al. 1996; Russett 1993).[16] Accordingly, this book concerns itself with what I label the "domestic democratic peace" (Davenport 2004).

Existing work has been clear about the fact that institutions associated with democracy play an important and perhaps *the* major role in decreasing state repressive behavior; however, three challenges to existing research have recently emerged and potentially undermine this finding as well as the policy/approach to peace affiliated with it.

① First, democratic political institutions may influence only certain aspects *CHALLENGES* of repression. At present, statistical analyses focus on only one form of repression while ignoring others (see, for example, Davenport 1995a, 1995b, 1999; Hibbs 1973; Poe and Tate 1994).[17] This is likely inappropriate,

---

[15] This includes numerous authors (Bueno de Mesquita et al. 2005; Cingranelli and Richards 1999; Davenport 1995a; 1995b; 1996a; 1996b; 1997; 1999; Davenport and Armstrong 2004; Fein 1995; Franklin 1997; Harff 2003; Henderson 1991, 1993; Hibbs 1973; Keith 2002; King 1998, 2000; Krain 1997; Mitchell and McCormick 1988; Poe and Tate 1994; Poe, Tate, and Keith 1999; Regan and Henderson 2002; Richards 1999; Timberlake and Williams 1984; Zanger 2000; Ziegenhagen 1986).

[16] Additionally, it is similar to research on civil war – less popularly referred to as the "civil peace" (Hegre et al. 2001).

[17] There are good reasons for this practice. There is a certain moral imperative within this work where it is maintained that scholarship should be dedicated to the eradication of all phenomena that threaten human life without differentiation. Most individuals would characterize "genocide" (Charny 1999; Schmid 1991) and "politicide" (Harff 2003; Harff and Gurr 1988) as falling into this category. Indeed, to classify an event as genocide or genocidal is to levy one of the harshest condemnations available to us. In a sense, this behavior is important in that it defines the dimensions of repression; the rest of the conceptions and labels for the relevant state action are essentially affixed from this point. Also, within this category, but slightly less so because of the sheer difference in magnitude of violence involved is "state terror" or "state-sponsored terror" (De Swann 1977; Mason and Krane 1989; Moore 1954; Sloan 1984; Walter 1969) and "human rights violation" or "personal integrity rights" (Monshipouri 1995).

Another explanation for this practice is the fact that the rigorous investigation of human rights/state repression is still relatively new. Most effort in this field has been directed at defining the subject of interest, identifying relevant explanatory factors, and selecting appropriate methodological strategies for investigation. This makes sense because, without this groundwork, there would be no cumulative understanding or analysis. As Kuhn

11

however, and instead distinctions between types of coercive behavior need to be drawn. This is because the benefits and costs of relevant action are likely to vary with the strategy considered.

For example, as state violence eliminates challengers/challenges, it diminishes government resources and reduces the legitimacy of political authorities, which is costly for the regime.[18] By contrast, restricting civil liberties may drain more resources than would violent activity, but it does not result in the same loss of political legitimacy, with either domestic or foreign audiences. This is important, for democracies would likely wield greater influence on violent behavior than restrictions on civil liberties. Important differences also exist regarding what repression accomplishes. For example, political leaders who opt to use violence (eliminating citizens) completely deny the victims and those associated with them a place within the political system. But constraining or hindering political actors is not by definition a negation of a citizen's place in society. To the contrary, it could be seen as reflective of the citizens' place, as it protects them and others through the rule of law (see, for example, Della Porta and Reiter 1998; Franks 1989; Keith 2002; Levin 1971). Restrictive activities also differ from state-sponsored violence in other ways: (1) they can be reversed, (2) they can easily follow some transparent and legal process, and (3) they do not embody the ultimate form of state power – the taking of human life.

To conduct a proper examination of the influence of democracy on repression therefore requires a thorough analysis of the range of forms and values of repressive behavior. Preliminary analyses do support my contention that democracy is more effective in limiting violence than in limiting

(1962, 4) suggests, "Effective research scarcely begins before a scientific community thinks it has acquired firm answers to questions like the following: What are the fundamental entities of which the universe is composed? How do these interact with each other and with the senses? What questions may legitimately be asked about such entities and what techniques are employed in seeking solutions?" The community with which I am concerned has not addressed the second of these questions, but the others are fairly well developed. This fundamental research has detracted from explorations of other questions. The habits and dominant practices within the literature provide yet another explanation for the limitation. For example, most indicators of repression and democracy have taken a more aggregate approach and ignored the importance of disaggregation. In the case of repression, aggregation is likely favored because information is so hard to come by that disaggregation would leave the researcher with very little variation across time and/or space. Different aspects of repression are thus combined to facilitate investigation.

[18] This is in line with Arendt's (1951) point, that applied coercion signifies a loss of power and indicates a weakness (and not a strength) in the regime.

restrictions (Davenport 2004). Although this suggestion that combining distinct aspects of repression is inappropriate for it leads us to misunderstand the influence of democracy, it is clearly the case that additional investigation of this argument is necessary.

② The second challenge to the peace proposition concerns the possibility that certain democratic political institutions might be better than others at decreasing state repression. Reflecting a long-standing split in political theory, public policy, and social activism, some highlight the pacifying influence of elections and the representation of diverse political orientations (see, for example, Dahl 1966; 1971; 1989; Powell 2000; Schumpeter 1962) – which I call *Voice*. The objective in this context is to change the incentives of those wielding coercive power by indirect means. It is thought that the vote forces leaders to concern themselves with constituents (that is, those upon whom they depend for their jobs) and also provides a diversity of interests within government itself through the representation of different parties/beliefs, with the result that political authorities would be less inclined to restrict and violate citizens' rights. For a politician to violate these rights is essentially to ask to be thrown out of office. Others highlight the pacifying influence of checks and balances, executive constraints, and veto points/players (see, for example, Gurr 1974; Keefer and Stasavage 2003; Montesquieu 1989; Tsebelis 2002) – which I call *Veto*. The causal dynamics involved here are very different. In this context, the objective is to directly reduce the amount of freedom held by those wielding coercive power, hemming it in so to speak. It is thought that political authorities would have second thoughts about repressing citizens if they had to worry about potential resistance from other authorities, outright denial of approval for relevant behavior, and/or the possibility that some sanction might be imposed for attempting to employ such behavior (for example, having some desirable legislation blocked in the future).

Existing research is generally unclear about which aspects of democracy are most effective at decreasing repression. In the past, researchers have either collapsed different aspects of democracy together (see, for example, Davenport 1995b; Hibbs 1973; Mitchell and McCormick 1988; Poe and Tate 1994; Ziegenhagen 1986) or focused on only one aspect while ignoring others: Davenport (1998) and Richards (1999) focus on elections/electoral behavior and representation; Davenport (1996a) and Keith (2002) focus on constitutional structure and emergency powers. While Davenport and Armstrong (2004), by far the most rigorous investigation of the subject, do consider *Voice* and *Veto* separately, only one aspect of democracy (*Voice*) is disaggregated and thus the study is only of limited utility.[19] Bueno de Mesquita et al. (2005) offer another attempt at disaggregation, but – utilizing the same data that Davenport and Armstrong employed for *Veto* – they end up capturing diverse aspects of only one democratic component.[20] Further limiting this research, no studies look at different types of repressive behavior, and thus the robustness of the pacifying influence across coercive strategies is not considered.

(3)   The third challenge to existing literature concerns the fact that democratic political institutions may be able to decrease specific forms of repression only within certain contexts. Reflecting a long-standing debate in political theory [for example, "states of exception" (Agamben 2005), political order (Hobbes 1950)] and public policy [protest policing, crime control and, more recently, counterterrorism], questions have arisen about the effectiveness of democracy in decreasing repressive behavior in situations of political conflict. On this issue, opinions vary. For example, implicitly most maintain that democracy always diminishes repression, regardless of violent dissident activity and civil as well as interstate war (see, for

[19] The Davenport and Armstrong (2004) study investigated nonlinear influences of democracy on repression, and therefore it was directed toward a completely different issue. In contrast, Bueno de Mesquita et al. (2005) were clearly interested in tapping distinct components of democracy. Unfortunately, however, they assumed that disaggregating the Polity measure tapped distinct aspects of democracy. As found by Gleditsch and Ward (1997), however, not all components of the Polity measure are important. For instance, they discuss whether the component of the measure that carries the most weight empirically concerns executive constraints. This reduces the importance of the other subcomponents.

[20] Bueno de Mesquita et al. (2005) examine the influence of a variable that does not readily fit into my *Voice* or *Veto* distinction – a measure that captures the scope of the selection available to members of each country's legislature and several measures that capture diverse aspects of the coalition required for victory. While the second represents a clear indication of *Veto*, the first does not clearly represent *Voice*. For example, there is no consideration given to the actual involvement of the population. My conceptualization also tends to ignore those elements of democracy concerning individual public opinion as well as the activities/capabilities of civil society. The first is ignored on practical grounds. There are simply no relevant data across the number of countries and years with which I am interested. The second is ignored on conceptual grounds. The activities and quality of conditions for civil society, while highlighted in the democratic peace literature, is ignored within the repression literature, and it is too closely connected with the dependent variable. This follows literature in democratic theory where some juxtapose "hamstringing" political authorities – establishing accountability – others highlight "walling them in" with the development of a "robust public sphere" (Shapiro 2003, 56). The latter is problematic, however, because it is precisely the "robust public sphere" that would likely be targeted by state repression.

example, Davenport 1999; Hibbs 1973; Keith 2002; Krain 1997; Mitchell and McCormick 1988; Poe and Tate 1994; Poe, Tate, and Keith 1999). Here, the negative influence of democracy on repression identified previously is held intact. Others, however, maintain that when confronting political threats, democratic authorities (like all others) apply repressive behavior in an effort to eliminate challenges because of the presumed responsiveness of these political systems to the needs of its constituents (see, for example, Goldstein 1978; Rapoport and Weinberg 2001). In this case, the normally pacifying influence of democracy on incentives and the political process is weakened and/or moved in the direction of coercion.

It is further acknowledged that democracy might be limited in its pacific capabilities in a different way. It may be the case, for instance, that when a state considers using large-scale violent activity in conjunction with large-scale political restrictions (the ultimate form of repression), in situations of political conflict, democracy becomes irrelevant. A regime considering such a severe response is likely already beyond considerations of political legitimacy and electoral responsiveness, as it is concerned with issues such as political survival. By contrast, states considering less lethal and less extensive repressive activity, because they face less dire circumstances, may be more concerned with political legitimacy and electoral responsiveness.

Existing research sheds essentially no light on these issues, because they have been neglected. Those within the relevant body of scholarship ignore the fragility of the domestic democratic peace as well as the interactive effect of political institutions and contentious behavior. Instead, they focus on the direct, independent influence of democracy and conflict on human rights violations without considering the interaction between the two independent variables.

Toward an Investigation of Domestic Democratic Peace

In addition to addressing the limitations with the existing literature as identified earlier, essentially I have three reasons for investigating the influence of democracy on repressive behavior and the conditions that facilitate the former's reduction of the latter: in turn, these address empirical, practical, and theoretical issues.

Empirical Reasons   My initial motivation for conducting this study was the recent acknowledgment that democracy and state coercive practices do not always move in tandem. Research on this phenomenon – "illiberal

15

democracy" (see, for example, Zakaria 2004)[21] – has begun to acknowledge that the existence of a democratic institution does not preclude the existence of repressive behavior.[22] Related to this, my own research (Davenport and Armstrong 2004) shows that the type of political system and the use of repressive behavior employed by authorities are largely independent of one another until the highest levels of "democracy" are reached. Many movements up the scale of political democracy are thus unlikely to yield any influence on repressive behavior. After reaching a threshold, however, there is a notable shift downward in relevant activity. This is similar to the arguments of numerous other scholars (see, for example, Bueno de Mesquita et al. 2005; Dahl 1971).[23]

An additional motivation concerns timing. Within much political science research, the influence of liberalization (that is, decreased repression) on democracy is taken as the most common, important, and natural relationship. However, the historical sequence commonly investigated is not uniformly accepted, even for the most frequently cited cases in support of this argument. Sartori (1987, 382), for example, notes that part of the difficulty with the liberalization-to-democracy proposition is that even the English case is different from the French. As he states,

[i]n the former case it was Lockean liberalism that was transplanted to the New World and produced there the first modern democracy. But if we consider what happened in France (as well as neighboring countries), this genealogical line can be reversed, since the liberal element was imported, whereas the native element was a democratic rationalism à la Rousseau. However, if the anglophile Montesquieu came

[21] Similarly, there is the idea of "liberal autocracy" where a fundamentally "closed" regime relaxes its use of state repression.

[22] As Zakaria (2004, 17) notes, "today the two strands of liberal democracy, interwoven in the Western political fabric, are coming apart across the globe. Democracy (that which concerns institutions) is flourishing; liberty (that which concerns repressive behavior) is not."

[23] My interest in the topic was further prompted by the fact that those who suggested democracy and repression were related to one another conceptually were not clear about how much repression needed to be relaxed before one could have a democracy (e.g., Linz 2000, 58). Diamond (1996, 20), for example, identifies that "[c]ontemporary minimalist conceptions of democracy...commonly acknowledge the need for minimal levels of civil freedom in order for competition and participation to be meaningful." But exactly how much liberalization is needed? We don't know. Further complicating the issue, some research identifies that despite the significant relaxation of political repression, many citizens do not participate in democratic political systems. Regardless of how little expression, association, or assembly are restricted, many ignored information, campaigns, and political discussions, and even when they participated, they frequently misunderstood what was intended. This tends to make the connection between democracy and repression a bit more complex.

before the anglophobe Rousseau, afterward the roles were exchanged: Rousseau is older, Constant and Tocqueville are more modern. In effect, liberalism was accepted on the Continent and showed its best results after learning its lesson from the Jacobin democracy that preceded it. . . . So, while it is true – according to the main genealogical line, the Anglo-American one – that liberalism came first and democracy followed, it is equally true that in the nineteenth century liberalism was restated and refined on the basis of a previous democratic experiment that quickly went off course.

Many others share such an opinion. For example, Zakaria (2004, 51) prompts us to relax our unidirectional conception of the relationship between democracy and repression, arguing that historically "constitutional liberalism led to democracy, which led to further liberty (decreasing repression)" and so on.[24] Related to this, O'Donnell, et al. (1986, 6) explicitly point out that liberalization and democracy often proceed independently and at different speeds.

Finally, I examine the influence of democracy on repression because it continues a thirty-five-year-old tradition in conflict studies that explores the relationship between repression, regime type, and political conflict. At present, research highlights parts of the puzzle: the influence of conflict on repressive behavior (see, for example, Davenport 1995b; Hibbs 1973) or the influence of democracy on repression (see, for example, Bueno de Mesquita et al. 2005; Davenport and Armstrong 2004; Fein 1995; Poe and Tate 1994; Regan and Henderson 2002), but the intersection between democracy and conflict as it influences state coercive activity has not yet received attention. My investigation is thus a natural evolution of the conflict literature.

Practical Reasons The second reason for examining the influence of democracy on repressive behavior concerns the fact that the existence and robustness of such a relationship is important to citizens throughout the world. By most accounts, modern governments are the most lethal political entities in history. According to one study, from 1900 to 1987, "fifteen (states) . . . wiped out over 151 million people (within their own countries), almost four times the almost 38,500,000 battle dead from all this century's

---

[24] We should not really be surprised by any of this. For example, Sartori (1987, 384) argues that "[i]n the final analysis, equality has a horizontal urge, whereas liberty has a vertical impetus. Democracy is concerned with social cohesion and distributive evenness, liberalism esteems prominence and spontaneity. Equality (the essential aspect of political democracy) desires to integrate and attune, liberty is self-assertive and troublesome. Democracy has little feel for (pluralism), liberalism is its offspring. But perhaps the fundamental difference is that liberalism pivots on the individual, and democracy on society."

international and civil wars (combined)" (Rummel 1997, 92). This does not even include the last 18 years of violent activity, 105 years worth of lower-level state behavior such as torture and disappearances, or the influence of nonlethal repressive action such as political bans, mass arrests, and instances of censorship. Attempting to understand how to reduce behavior is therefore one of the most important topics of our age.

Democracy is especially important here because so many individuals believe that it is inextricably bound up with decreasing repressive behavior. Democratic social movements see this as one of their primary objectives (see, for example, Ekiert and Kubik 1999; McAdam 1982; Wood 2000); nongovernmental organizations (NGOs) around the world fund such efforts because of these influences (see, for example, Diamond 1995); and policymakers have attempted to build democracies as a way of reducing restrictions on civil rights as well as violations of personal integrity (U.S. State Department 2001). The pacifying influence of democracy on repressive behavior has become especially important for U.S. and Western foreign policy (see, for example, Bush 2005; Diamond 1995; Goldman and Douglas 1988). In this case, however, we find a major source of complexity over time.

For example, during the Cold War, U.S. policymakers gave priority to stability (political quiescence) over democracy; that is, the concern was more that a government not be subject to political challenge than that the state power be created, sustained, and legitimated for citizens. For the current Bush administration, this formula has been reversed (see, for example, McMahon 2005) as democracy is now given priority over stability. In this context, it is more important that a government be moved along a political continuum toward full democracy than that existing political challenges be eliminated.

The new strategy is extremely problematic when it comes to the consideration of state repression. Specifically, the U.S. government has expressed an interest in promoting democracy and human rights (that is, decreased repression), yet democracy, conflict, and repressive behavior appear to be related to one another. According to the position of the Bush administration, democracy and human rights can be pursued simultaneously, regardless of conflict: it is believed that the two generally move together. Existing research suggests, however, that while democracy decreases repression, repressive behavior is increased by political conflict. Thus, a question arises: what happens to repression in situations like Iraq when democracy and conflict exist at the same time (that is, when democratic transition takes place during a period of insurgency and domestic terrorism)? Can the peace normally brought by democracy withstand the disruption brought by political conflict? In other words, is the domestic democratic peace bullet-proof?

In many respects, this issue is new. During the Cold War, it was not a problem, as efforts to obtain stability were considered to be intimately connected to state repressive practices. In an effort to achieve the desired end, therefore, repressive behavior was deemed necessary, and regimes seeking stability employed it in large amounts. The new situation is less clear. Repression seems to be associated with efforts to achieve stability, but it is not readily apparent what happens to repressive behavior when democracy is attempted in the midst of political conflict. By focusing on the pacifying influence of democracy on state coercion, therefore, I explicitly acknowledge one of the most widely heralded outcomes associated with democratic government but consider the very real possibility that this outcome is potentially undermined by threats to political order.[25]

Theoretical Reasons The third and last reason for exploring the topic concerns the historical debate about the government's concentration of coercive power. Since the beginning of the nation-state, individuals have been aware that political authorities kept at their disposal weapons of immense power that could be unleashed against those within their territorial jurisdiction – techniques of rule that were held monopolistically (Held 1996; Weber 1946, 173) – and used with often devastating effects (e.g., Elliot 1972; Rummel 1997). The justification was clear: the state needed coercion in order to establish order domestically and to fend off aggression abroad (Hobbes 1950; Tilly, Ardant and SSRC 1975; Walter 1969).[26] Once developed, however, this capacity immediately raised the issue of how to prevent

---

[25] It should be noted that I do not use the often employed phrase "arbitrary uses" because it is never quite clear what this includes. Rather, I assume that throughout history, the interest is with reducing repression in general. At its root, this aspect of freedom is perhaps one of the most basic of human impulses – especially since the mid-twentieth century after which the potential for state coercion had never been greater.

[26] It is irrelevant for my discussion whether or not this coercive power was willingly handed over to authorities (Weber 1946) or accumulated by conquest (Tilly, Ardant, and SSRC 1975). Faced with the situation of concentrated coercive power, citizens were still left to ponder what to do next.

its abuse. Held (1996) identifies this as the central problem of liberal political theory. As he states,

> how was the "sovereign state" to be related to the "sovereign power" who were recognized as the legitimate source of the state's powers? Most liberal and liberal democratic theory has been faced with the <u>dilemma of finding a balance between might and right, power and law, duties and rights</u>. For a while the state must have a monopoly of coercive power to provide a secure basis upon which "free trade," business and family life can prosper, its coercive and regulatory capacity must be contained so that its agents do not interfere with the political and social freedoms of individual citizens, with the pursuit by them of their particular interests in competitive relations with one another. (p. 75)

On this question, answers have varied. In the nineteenth century, there were essentially three: (1) anarchists wished to eliminate the problem entirely – by destroying the state; (2) communists and socialists wanted to use the mechanisms of coercion for their own purposes – to build a new and better society; and (3) liberals sought to rein in coercive power – allowing those within the territorial jurisdiction to have the security that they desired but, at the same time, having a way of dealing with any abuses that might occur (Dahl 1989, 41, 50). By the mid-twentieth century, the first approach had essentially been dismissed as impractical, leaving the other two to battle it out, which they did both literally and figuratively. By the end of the twentieth century, almost all agreed that the liberals had won, and most discussions within academia, government, and civil society revolved around how one could best rein in coercive power. This led to yet another debate – albeit one where the differences were less stark.

Although diverse mechanisms of democratic control exist (for an overview, see Rosato 2003; Rummel 1997), by far the most compelling involves the principle of <u>accountability</u> – limiting the use of political power and sanctioning abuses (Fox 2000, 3).[27] The degree to which governing officials are made responsive to those subject to this power has long been of interest to democratic theorists such as Madison, Bentham, Schumpeter,

---

[27] According to Rosato (2003, 586), who discusses the international democratic peace, there are five different ways that accountability can lead to diminished coercion: as public constraint (responding to popular aversion to conflict), as group constraint (responding to anticonflict advocates), as slow mobilization (which impedes conflict behavior), as militating against surprise attacks (because of the fact that democratic deliberations take place within a public setting), and through the provision of information (which avoids conflict because it provides important cues to adversaries that preclude the necessity for fighting as this normally results from misunderstanding). In line with the literature on state repression, I focus on the constraint versions of the argument.

Axtmann, Dahl, and Held. Although the historical progression linking these diverse individuals together is contested (see, for example, Isaac 1998; Pateman 1970), it is reasonable to argue that none would advocate handing the means of coercion over to political authorities without some mechanism for regulating this behavior and subjecting it to some form of oversight as well as approval. Even advocates of such an approach, like Hobbes, appeared to have some reservations, conceding that when authorities overstep and engage in excessive repression, citizens had the right to challenge (and even overthrow) government leaders. Such a principle lies at the core justification for democracy itself. As noted by Dahl (1989, 95); "[a] democratic government provides an orderly and peaceful process by means of which a majority of citizens can induce the government to do what they most want it to do and to avoid doing what they most want it not to do."[28]

These debates mirror others within the field of comparative politics and international relations about democratic "performance" (see, for example, Bollen and Jackman 1985; Przeworski 2000; Russett 1993; Shin 1994) and "new institutionalism" (see, for example, Immergut 1998; Kaiser 1997; Przeworski 2004). This work is relevant because it argues that there is something about the particular configuration of democratic institutions that results in specific valued outcomes. Although most of this research is directed toward topics such as regime survival (see, for example, Alvarez et al. 1996) or economic growth (Alvarez et al. 1996; Barro and Lee 1993; Olson 1982; 1993), some attention has also been given to various democratic values that are prized by advocates of democracy such as political equality, electoral turnout, and the representation of women (Lijphart 1993) as well

---

[28] He continues immediately after this statement: "(n)ow it may well be that as a practical matter we cannot determine whether this justification is valid by rigorously comparing the performances of democratic and nondemocratic governments with evidence showing what citizens want their governments to do or not do. We might nevertheless be able to arrive at a reasonable judgement by comparing the opportunities that the democratic process (both in ideal form and in actuality) provides a majority of citizens for influencing the government to attempt to satisfy their urgent political concerns with the opportunities that a nondemocratic government, both in ideal form and in actuality, would provide. And on the basis of such a comparison, we would decide whether the claim is justified" (Dahl 1989, 95). I strongly believe that the evaluation of performance is exactly what we can and should do as well as what some investigations have already done. For example, research has already supported the argument that democracies employ less repression than autocracies – directly in line with theoretical expectations and assumed mass preferences. At the same time, we do not know if certain aspects of democracy are better than others at reducing human rights violations.

as to political stability and societal, nonstate violence (see, for example, Powell 1982). My work follows in this tradition.

While the literature agrees on the general point that coercive power must be rendered accountable to some political actor and that different configurations of political institutions are likely to yield distinct capabilities in this regard, debates have arisen about the specific nature of the accountability mechanism and the robustness of these relationships across different contexts. It is to these differences that I now turn.

The Mechanisms of Domestic Peace

Researchers, policymakers, NGOs, activists, and ordinary citizens have repeatedly asked the question: to whom, exactly, should political leaders be accountable in the matter of state repression? Opinions on this issue, drawn from a relatively large and historically contentious argument, diverge significantly.

Voice   *accountability to populace* There are those who suggest that, in an effort to decrease coercive behavior, government officials should be made accountable to those subject to their power – the citizens/constituents (see, for example, Dahl 1966; 1971; Lipset 1959; Locke 1963; Schumpeter 1962). This is most effectively accomplished by structuring the political system in such a way that authorities have to compete with one another in order to obtain and renew their positions, subjecting their rule to the observation, evaluation, and approval of the mass population. *competition for power in which standard in which winner for judging = public opinion*

There are two very different reasons for this. In one, citizens are deemed the best able to understand and protect their self-interest. It thus makes sense that authorities should be beholden to those most knowledgeable about what is taking place (Mill 1861). In another, it is believed that if the objectives of political leaders could be tied to electoral competition, then repressive behavior would be carefully regulated. Here, distinct political actors compete with one another in periodic contests for votes, and it is assumed that if citizens are dissatisfied with what was taking or what took place (for example, if they experienced repressive behavior), then they will vote out the individuals in power. This controls the activities of the rulers because if they are interested in retaining their positions, then they would adjust and/or avoid the production of diverse public goods and bads, with repression clearly being an example of the latter (see, for example, Ames 1987; Bueno de Mesquita 2003).

Introduction

Three points are worthy of attention. First,

democracy does not mean and cannot mean that the people actually rule in any obvious sense of the terms "people" and "rule." Democracy means only that the people have the opportunity of accepting or refusing the [people] who are to rule them.... No one aspect of this may be expressed by saying that democracy is the rule of the politician. (Schumpeter 1962, 284–5)[29]

Second, it is believed that the competitive process controls outcomes because those who are contending for power (rival political leaders) are expected to offer whatever is deemed insufficiently provided by the current leadership. This is another reason why existing government officials, who wish to retain power, will be on their best behavior; their potential replacements monitor them and offer whatever they have not provided. Finally, the representation of distinct political parties serves as another mechanism of accountability. Tied as these organizations are to specific constituents, it is expected that relevant organizations will do their best to defend the interests of their membership as well as those connected to them. The rationale is again punitive in nature and directed toward incentives: if those whom the party serves are not satisfied, then they will sanction their representatives, removing them from the position that they have held and presumably valued.

Of course, not all support such an argument. Challenging this position are those who do not believe in the pacifying capability of the masses. Commonly referred to as "elitist" theories of democracy, those who have disagreed with *Voice* maintain that average citizens are inherently incompetent and that "they are, at best, pliable, inert stuff or, at worst, aroused, unruly creatures possessing an insatiable proclivity to undermine both culture and liberty" (Bachrach 1967, 2). The suggestion is that because of how they are constituted, most citizens are actually dangerous to human freedom. Those who hold this view maintain that citizens should not be the caretakers of society but rather should be far removed from its management. Instead, such responsibility should be placed in the hands of those who are prepared for it – elites. A major part of the explanation for this is the fact that the elites are believed to be the individuals least likely to call for repressive action. Accordingly, Montesquieu (1989, 71) states quite clearly that there

---

[29] Schumpeter would definitely not be confused as someone who placed a great deal of faith in the incorporation of the masses because of their reasonableness and intelligence. Indeed, at one point he argues that "the electoral mass is incapable of action other than a stampede" (Schumpeter 1962, 283).

23

cf. Jefferson's "natural aristoi"

"are always persons distinguished by their birth, riches or honors" who are ready "to check the licentiousness of the people." These "persons" are elites.

Others criticize the argument from a different perspective, maintaining that elections are simply ineffective mechanisms of influence because while the occurrence of an election is infrequent and scheduled in advance, repression is nearly always possible. A reasonable response would be that political leaders understand that what they do will be evaluated at a latter date (that is, retrospectively) and that the result of this evaluation will either provide support for their continuation in power or their removal. There is some compelling evidence to suggest, however, that this is not the case: as elections approach, authorities adjust their repressive behavior then afterward revert back to the earlier activity (see, for example, Davenport 1997; 1998). Another argument against *Voice* concerns an old comment about the party system itself (see, for example, Michels 1962; Mosca 1980). Many suggest that party activists are connected to their constituents only in a very abstract fashion and they are less likely to feel the brunt of repression themselves. Here, citizens are not able to regulate authorities in the manner stipulated by *Voice* because "vertical" accountability is lacking (see, for example, Fox 2000). Considered from this viewpoint, parties, representatives, and the system of accountability will not be effective at regulating repressive behavior;[30] indeed, they may be the reason why it continues.

Veto   *Accountability to pol. figures.* There are those who suggest that political leaders should be held accountable to other political leaders (see, for example, Immergut 1998; Montesquieu 1989; Tsebelis 2002). Montesquieu (1989, 69), for example, argues that "constant experience shows us that every [individual] invested with power is apt to abuse it, and to carry [their] authority as far as it will go.... To prevent abuse [therefore], it is necessary from the very nature of things that power should be a check to power." Similarly, Madison remarked that ambitions needed to be made to counteract ambitions and that only in such circumstance will the abuse of government power be contained. Tsebelis (2002) is much less judgmental about the relative character or preparedness of the mass public to engage in pacifying government behavior

---

[30] Of course, Marxists and neo-Marxists would go further to argue that representatives merely represent elite interests and as larger numbers of individuals become enfranchised, this situation would not fundamentally change.

24

(a frequent occurrence within this situation), but his work is nevertheless consistent with this position.[31] I will discuss this briefly.

In his important study of veto players, Tsebelis maintains that political authorities engage in the creation, discussion, revision, and enactment of policy. Along the path of this potential legislation, there is a series of steps through which each proposal must pass, subject to the investigation, delay, or override of different political actors – *veto* players. Control is thus exerted over political outcomes because of how government is structured. This perspective would argue that if the repressive process were subject to *Veto*, then decision makers would hesitate to engage in the relevant behavior. First, in the language of political economists, as "transaction costs" are increased by discussion, negotiation, compromise, and side payments, authorities will come to view repression less favorably. To avoid these costs, they will avoid legislation relevant to coercion. Second, democratic political leaders will likely hesitate to push for repressive activity because in trying to implement such activity they could set in motion a process of negative repercussions. Specifically, efforts of politician or political group x to implement repression could lead to impediments from politician or political group y, followed by the denial or blockage of policies associated with y on x, and so on. To avoid these potential costs, legislation relevant to repressive action is avoided.[32]

Similar to the objections to *Voice*, there are those who do not believe in the pacifying capabilities of government officials (setting the fox against other foxes invariably still leaves one with animals). Many do not believe, for example, that political parties will diligently exercise their oversight and overruling capabilities, nor do they believe that government officials are truly representative of the citizens they represent, for they are tied to them only indirectly. Indeed, it is argued that political authorities/elites are more likely to side with other authorities/elites on most issues relevant to repressive behavior and thus will be unreliable protectors of citizen's rights – at least those rights of concern to most citizens.

Again, existing research is unable to inform us about the relative capability of *Voice* and *Veto* to decrease state repression. To date, researchers have either combined characteristics or have investigated each in isolation.

---

[31] He is quite aware of these similarities (Tsebelis 2002, 9–10)

[32] Of course, if authorities were predisposed to repressive behavior to begin with, then the influence of veto is somewhat unclear. Tsebelis's (2002, 165) argument is directed toward exploring policy stability (the impossibility of significantly changing the status quo), and thus policy adoption, while relevant, is less certain.

Two studies move in the general direction, but one focuses on an entirely different issue (Davenport and Armstrong 2004) and another suffers from extensive measurement problems (Bueno de Mesquita et al. 2005). There is one useful exception: James Gibson's (1988) "Political Intolerance and Political Repression During the McCarthy Red Scare." Within this study, Gibson investigates the adoption of anticommunist legislation in the United States in the late 1940s and the 1950s, to determine whether it was mass or elite preferences that influenced the repressive policy. Supporting the *Voice* argument, he finds that politicians were generally more likely than citizens to call for repression. This work is merely suggestive, however. As designed, it considers one country at only one point in time; it measures *Voice* and *Veto* indirectly; and it considers only one act as well as only one type of repressive behavior. Once again, we find that additional research is necessary.

Perhaps the biggest weakness with the existing research is that it ignores the question of how well democratic peace functions across diverse contexts. One such condition concerns political conflict (for example, violent dissent as well as civil and interstate war).

The Fragility of Peace

As conceived, the pacification argument is based on the premise that within democratic political systems citizens and their representatives are uniformly in opposition to state repression. To avoid removal from office and to facilitate remaining in office Authorities are therefore expected to limit their use of coercive activity. Such a position is acceptable when repression is uniformly viewed negatively – the implicit orientation within the literature on state terror and human rights violation. As there is no legitimate context within which authorities can apply repressive action, avoiding this behavior makes sense, especially within democratic governments. But the argument is not reasonable in all cases.

Extending back to Hobbes, researchers have maintained that political authorities bear a responsibility for protecting citizens as well as the personnel, policies, and institutions of the state from threatening behavior. Many see this type of action as defining "legitimate authority" itself (Weber 1946). If those in power could not and did not respond to threats, then citizens and leaders would be within their legitimate right in replacing the offending authorities and/or the political system. This is where things get tricky.

Introduction

The state's response to political conflict has always presented something of a loophole (see, for example, Agamben 2005; Davenport 1996a; Ferrara 2003). While most scholars, activists, and policymakers focus on the problem of "illegitimate" or "arbitrary" exercises of coercive power, they tend to ignore those applications that are deemed "legitimate" and "systematic." Additionally, most scholars fail to consider in any rigorous way exactly how much repression is or should be applied during episodes of threat. Some attention has been given the issue (see, for example), Linfield 1990; Rasler 1986; Stohl 1976), but it is largely ignored by most investigations of repression, and when it is considered, it provides only limited assistance because it rarely makes the link to noncrisis periods.

The influence of political conflict on the domestic democratic peace is important for two reasons: (1) it reveals that there are circumstances when repression can be supported by at least part of the citizenry and (2) it reveals circumstances under which the assumed uniformity underlying the domestic democratic peace will be weakened, if not significantly undermined. This is crucial for the current discussion because in times of political conflict, I expect an increase in repressive behavior even within a democracy. This was the case in both Rwanda (in confronting rebels in northern parts of the country as well as the Congo following the events of 1994) and in the United States (in confronting terrorism as well as terrorists domestically and abroad following 9/11).

The argument is similar to work that addresses problem of factionalization, coalition building, and political survival. In the area of domestic conflict, for example, numerous researchers have suggested that behavioral threats unify previously disparate actors within and outside government (see, for example, Coser 1956; Goldstein 1978; Stanley 1996). In turn, conflict behavior increases the willingness of individuals to support repressive behavior as well as the regime enacting it (see, for example, Davis and Silver 2004). Related to this, in the area of international conflict, Reiter and Stam (2002) note that democratic governments are generally less likely to engage in interstate conflict because they are more concerned with retaining power. The key to this retention resides in the leader's responsiveness to the perceived needs of constituents. As such, democratic political leaders will not engage in activity expected to generate resistance to the government, but it is possible that under specific circumstances (for example, conflicts that political authorities are likely to win), they will engage in activity that constituents view favorably, including coercive behavior.

Table I.1. *The Impact of Diverse Types of Conflict on Democratic Peace*

	Domestic Democratic Peace	Domestic Realism	Scale Conflict	Political Integrity
Violent dissent	Strengthen	Weaken	Strengthen	Strengthen
Civil war	Strengthen	Weaken	Weaken	Weaken
Interstate war	Strengthen	Weaken	Weaken	Strengthen

How then does political conflict influence the domestic democratic peace? Diverse hypotheses exist.

A strong version of the *peace proposition* suggests that regardless of the type of conflict, democracy always decreases repression. This suggests that democratic political characteristics always pacify respective of what the government is confronting. By contrast, an argument associated with what Stanley (1996) refers to as "Domestic Realism" suggests that conflict increases repression regardless of the type of regime in power. Thus, whatever the pacifying impulse within a democracy, it is overwhelmed when the political system is threatened by conflict (Blalock 1989; Hobbes 1950; Stanley 1996; Tilly et al. 1975). Related to this, an argument can also be made that democracies are less likely to repress when the nature of the threat is limited in *Scale* (for example, when confronting violent dissent such as riots, terrorism, and guerrilla warfare). When the threat is of lesser magnitude, there is likely to be greater variety in opinion about exactly how authorities should respond; some will invariably call for repressive action but others will not and instead will advocate tolerance, negotiation, and/or accommodation. Facing such a range of views, democratic authorities will be less inclined to use coercion. When threats exceed a minimum threshold, however, there is likely to be greater consensus about the appropriateness of repressive response and in such contexts the likelihood of coercion increases. Finally, there are situations where opinion is split in a different manner. For example, within what I label *Political Integrity*, democratic authorities limit repressive behavior during periods of violent dissent and international conflict because these forms of contention yield the greatest amount of dissension regarding the treatment of citizens but within periods of civil war, where the greatest amount of consensus exists, repressive behavior is likely increased. Table I.1 lists the different alternatives.

Introduction

Toward a Better Understanding of Democratic Pacification

In this book, I attempt to advance our understanding of both state repression and the influence of democracy on this behavior. I challenge existing literature by offering a statistical analysis of the relationship between diverse aspects of democracy and repression in the context of varying forms of political conflict, from 1976 to 1996. This historical period is particularly interesting because at the beginning of this time there was a clear increase in the number of democracies observed throughout the world, accompanied by a large degree of optimism regarding how things would change in its wake, not only with regard to state repression but with regard to other political, economic, and social phenomena as well. By the end of the period, however, the trend in democratization had leveled off (Karatnycky 1999, 114), there were discussions about reverse waves (Huntington 1991, 14–15), and new waves were under way (McFaul 2002).

Additionally, the general degree of optimism characterizing the earlier period had waned. Over this same period, there was wide variation in state repressive behavior reported by human rights groups, government reports, and the international media. Some noted improvements, but many others noted worsening conditions. Indeed, it is during this time that some of the most widely covered and egregious state activities in recent history have taken place in Cambodia, China, and Rwanda. As a result, the 1976–96 period presents us with a perfect opportunity to examine the domestic democratic peace and shed some much needed light on an important but not well understood period in world history.

To develop my argument, I begin Chapter 1 with a detailed discussion of what repression is and why democracy is expected to influence it. Here, I define relevant concepts, identify the theory underlying the application of repressive behavior, and review the quantitative literature about relevant causal effects.

In a move away from the coarse and highly aggregated concepts and measures that are currently applied, in Chapter 2 I discuss how best to disaggregate repression and democracy, continuing a theme developed in some of my earlier work (Davenport 1996a; 2004; Davenport and Armstrong 2004). This entails a consideration of state-sponsored violence and restriction to operationalize repression and a consideration of *Voice* (mass-based political factors) and *Veto* (elite-based political factors) to operationalize democracy. Chapter 2 also addresses the importance of political conflict as

29

a factor that can influence the pacifying influence of democracy on state repression.

In Chapter 3, I present the data and statistical methodology used to investigate causal relationships. Specifically, I identify the measurements of repression (a combination of violations of personal integrity and restrictions of civil liberties) and various contextual factors used in the analysis of 135 countries from 1976 to 1996.[33] Also within this chapter, I identify the methodological technique used to analyze relationships – ordered probit regression. This model is used to examine the influence of diverse political and economic variables on state repressive behavior (excluding democracy). This establishes the base model against which subsequent analyses are compared. The chapter concludes by identifying the measurements used to operationalize distinct aspects of political democracy.

Chapter 4 presents the findings of the statistical analysis where different indicators of *Voice* (suffrage and participation weighted by representation) and *Veto* (specific legislative veto players and general constraints wielded by political as well as societal actors) are used to account for variation in repression. This reexamines the standard version of the domestic democratic peace investigated in the literature but with attention to the relevant effectiveness of diverse aspects of democracy on distinct forms of repression. From this investigation, two striking results emerge.

First, in line with the peace proposition, I find that most aspects of democracy decrease the likelihood of repressive behavior but that not all characteristics are significant or identical in their influence across analyses. Investigating the different variables individually (within separate models), the largest influence is wielded by the degree of participation and competition within government (a measure of *Voice*) followed by general executive constraints (a measure of *Veto*), the number of official legislative veto players, and suffrage (another measure of *Voice*). This hierarchy of domestic democratic peace is found consistently across statistical examinations and is therefore deemed quite robust. Investigating the different variables competitively (against one another), only two democratic characteristics are statistically significant and again negative in their influence on repression: *Competition/Participation* (*Voice*) and *Executive Constraints* (*Veto*).

Second, I find that democracy is generally better at promoting applications at the lower end of a repression scale than at decreasing types of

[33] There are actually 135 countries from 1976 to 1990, but this number increases to 138 in 1991–2 and again increases to 139 from 1993 to 1996 as new countries emerge.

coercive behavior that are more lethal. Specifically, research discloses that when moved from its minimum to its maximum, *Competition/Participation* encourages (that is, increases the likelihood of adopting) lower-level repressive behavior and discourages (that is, decreases the likelihood of adopting) more lethal forms of repression. Additionally, research discloses that democracy is better at decreasing violence than at decreasing political restrictions.

Chapter 5 presents the results of the statistical analysis where diverse aspects of democracy are interacted with three types of conflict: violent dissent, civil war, and interstate war.[34] This approach allows me to gauge the robustness of the domestic democratic peace when political authorities are threatened. Similar to the findings of Chapter 4, the pacifying influence of democracy on repressive behavior is found to exist, but differing from the earlier analysis, the influence is generally found to be variable across analyses. In particular, three findings stand out.

First, when conflict exists, democracy is generally better at promoting lower-level applications of repression than at decreasing higher-level applications. This is consistent with another result, which reveals that democratic characteristics are better at pacifying when political authorities have previously employed moderate restrictions and violence as opposed to when they employed strategies that are more lethal.

Second, across types of conflict and repressive strategies, *Voice* (specifically *Competition/Participation*) is still the most powerful mechanism of pacification, outpacing the influence of *Veto* (specifically general *Executive Constraints*). This having been said, the simultaneously consideration of both *Voice* and *Veto* outweighs the pacifying influence wielded by either democratic characteristic viewed individually, but the margin of difference between *Voice* and *Veto* viewed individually versus *Voice* and *Veto* viewed together is variable.

Third, results disclose that the type of conflict alters the pacifying influence of democracy. For example, during violent dissent (riots and guerrilla warfare), *Competition/Participation* is more effective at reducing repression than *Executive Constraints*; in fact, the influence of the former is so powerful that there is very little explanatory power added when both aspects of democracy are considered together. By contrast, during civil war, *Competition/Participation* and *Executive Constraints* are about equal in their ability to

---

[34] Interstate war is less consistently examined across analyses because of the relatively small number of wars taking place between 1976 and 1996.

reduce repression when viewed individually, but both democratic character-istics taken together have a much greater impact than either viewed individually. Given these results, I conclude that, of the diverse arguments outlined previously, Political Intregrity is supported in *Competition/Participation*. And while Conflict Scale is partially supported in the context of Executive Constraints and Veto Players, the inconsistent findings across analyses lead me to be somewhat skeptical about drawing any conclusions.

In Chapter 6, I conclude with a brief summary of the book's objectives and major findings, discussing the relevance of this research for existing scholarship on and public policy concerned with state repression and political democracy. I then move to revisit the cases with which I began this research (Rwanda and the United States). Finally, I identify several questions that should be the subject of additional investigation in the future.

1

Repression and the Search for Peace

Repression is one of those concepts that everyone believes he or she understands – not particularly well but well enough. People want to venture only so far into the dark side of human behavior. For instance, if asked to define repression, most would respond by identifying some high-profile campaign(s) such as the purges in Russia during the 1930s, the European Holocaust during the 1940s, the political harassment of communists throughout the United States in the 1950s, or the mass killings that took place in Cambodia during the 1970s and Rwanda in the 1990s. Alternatively, individuals would identify some high-profile event(s) such as the beatings that occurred at the Democratic National Convention in Chicago in 1968 or the massacre of protestors that took place at Tiananmen Square in 1989. Of course, the list could be extended (both spatially and temporally), but the basic point would not change: repression consistently evokes images of specific instances of state coercive action directed against those within the government's territorial jurisdiction. As for why authorities use this behavior, most would point to specific objectives (influencing the target's thought and/or action or fulfilling certain needs within the state), particularly ruthless government officials (Stalin, Hitler, Pol Pot, Hoover, Stroessner, and Bagosora), or specific political systems (for example, totalitarianism or autocracy). Again, the list here is not exhaustive. There are a great many motivations, leaders, and types of government that could be included, but the basic point is again simple: political authorities frequently use repression against those under their care and particular structural as well as behavioral factors are consistently associated with this behavior.

By the late twentieth and twenty-first centuries, the world's citizens were not unaware or indifferent to such activity. Indeed, as people have generally accepted the norms of the human rights movement, codified in

33

national constitutions as well as in regional and international legal documents, repressive behavior has come to be considered morally as well as legally reprehensible throughout the world – something to be monitored, identified, discussed, and punished.

The preceding characterization is sufficient for most individuals because it appears to capture the essence of the thing under discussion. At the same time, however, for those who spend the majority of their time investigating repressive behavior, it is unsatisfactory because it does not include a broader conception of what is involved or a general understanding of the complexity behind exactly why/when such behavior is likely to be used. In this chapter, I review the relevant quantitative literature on state repression and seek to provide some understanding of what is included when we discuss this behavior. Additionally, I address why repressive action is used, as well as why democracy, in particular, is expected to decrease it. This discussion guides the criticism and suggestions presented in the next chapter. These, in turn, guide the statistical investigations of Chapters 4 and 5.

(Almost) Everything You Wanted to Know About State Repression

The key to understanding the difference between what a general observer of politics who is thinking about repressive behavior would highlight and a scholar specifically focused on this activity is revealed by considering alternative perceptions of what took place in Bisesero, Rwanda, during 1994. At the start of the genocide in the first week of April, some thirty thousand to fifty thousand people from all over the country fled to Bisesero, the Kibuye province at the edges of the Rwandan state near Lake Kivu. There an effort was made to fend off the advance of a diverse and growing coalition of military personnel, militias, and everyday citizens who had come to eliminate those who resisted the government. While this persisted for months, by June only one thousand remained. During the three-month period, individuals were not only killed, but, they were also beaten, humiliated, raped, and tortured.

Upon considering this case, the casual observer would highlight the particulars of the event: for example, the perpetrators (Hutu extremists and their supporters), the victims (political leaders and everyday citizens who opposed the government), the actions (abductions, rape, torture, and killing), the place (Bisesero and Kibuye), and the duration of time that it took before the activities were completed (over the course of several months). By contrast, scholars focused on repression would highlight these factors

draw comparisons

but would then[put them into a broader context of Rwandan history]iden-tifying the spatial and temporal differences of the violence that preceded the Kibuye massacre as well as previous repressive activity since independence, the socioeconomic context of poverty and subsistence agriculture, the objectives and techniques of diverse state agents (politicians, the military, gendarme, militia as well as farmers, students, and so on), and the general structure of the Rwandan government.

The difference here is not simply one of greater or lesser attention to detail. Rather, it reflects a fundamental difference in orientation. For example, to the general observer, repression is rare, inherently illegitimate (not accepted in law or custom), and secondary to, and potentially irrelevant for, the state's existence. When this behavior occurs, the various components of the event are important, but they are viewed as essentially isolated from the general workings of the society and political system. To the specialist, however, repression can be rare or frequent, it can be legitimate or illegitimate, but it is always essential to the very definition of the state – one of the most basic functions of the institution. Adopting the latter view, state repression is a mechanism of force wielded by the government – an overtly manifest device, always available to political authorities – that restricts the freedom and/or inflicts bodily pain/injury on citizens up to and including the destruction of human life itself (Wrong 1988, 24). The type, scope, and frequency of this activity varies across time and space, but it is generally present in some form.[1]

---

[1] The differences between orientations are well captured by Eckstein (1980) in his discussion of alternative approaches to the study of conflict, which he referred to as "inherency" and "contingency". According to Eckstein (1980, 142–3), the former, which I associate with the specialized viewer, leads one to develop the following "sketch": "1. [t]he fundamental disposition of individuals [groups] in politics is to maximize influence, or power, over decisions. . . . 2. Since there are alternative channels for seeking power, the choice of [repression] must be activated, but activation readily occurs – though, of course, not as readily at the extreme. . . . 3. The critical problem for inherency theory, given the normality of [repression], is why [this behavior] does not occur more often than it does. 4. The activation of the choice [to use repression] is a matter of tactical consideration [not arousal of virulent affect]" (p. 143). The latter [contingency], which I associate with the casual viewer, alters this description in almost every way. For example, in this case, 1. "[t]he fundamental disposition of individuals [or groups] in politics is toward 'peace': the resolution or avoidance of . . . conflicts. . . . Satisfaction of political values is normally sought through pacific competition (electoral, through interest groups, by petitions, etcetera). [Repression] is not in the normal 'repertoire' of political competition. 2. The disposition toward pacific politics may be blocked and diverted under specifiable and special [aberrant] conditions. . . . 3. The critical problem in studying [repression] thus is why it occurs as often as it does. 4. Choices of collective political violence are highly 'affective' rather than coolly calculated" (p. 143).

While frequently viewed as comparable to various concepts in the social science literature, there are some distinctions between the concept that I am discussing and other areas of research. For instance, my conception differs from typical definitions of "power" and "influence" because the application of the relevant behavior is exclusively overt and physical in nature; it is not left to perception or to one's imagination.[2] Additionally, in my conception, the actual attainment of a particular outcome is irrelevant to the designation of relevant behavior. As conceived, much of the debate and research on power and influence hinges upon the attainment of specific objectives following discrete applications (for example, "intended" as opposed to "unintended" consequences). I maintain that such a distinction is essentially unimportant for repression; for example, the torture at Abu Ghraib prison is no less "repressive" because it failed to yield desired information. Rather, it is "repressive" because of who uses it and the influence that relevant behavior has on the human body as well as mind. Indeed, perhaps the best way to conceive of repression is simply to think of it as a "power attempt" (an effort exerted by political authorities toward a specific end that relies upon physical force). Now, of course, the ends pursued by state repression are important: survival, tenure in office, behavioral acquiescence, political legitimacy, fear reduction, and resource extraction. The effectiveness of this behavior is simply a separate area of interest from that which I discuss. Finally, repression is similar in nature to the concept of "social control," which focuses on coercive as well as noncoercive efforts of societal actors to control others. Whereas repression concentrates on the coercive behavior of the state, research on social control highlights nonstate actors and so is deemed quite different.

The focus on the means/process of repression is important because it unifies the literature. Without this orientation, it would be difficult to imagine bringing together research on arrests, imprisonment, surveillance,

---

As Eckstein notes, "It should . . . be evident that what is primary, important, necessary in one case is secondary, minor, chancy in the other. Most important, the sketches lead in quite different directions in research: most patently, toward conditions that arouse exceptional types and degrees of affect [especially anger] versus conditions that influence calculations of cost-benefit ratios in choosing modes of political goal-seeking. Most fundamental, as in all political theorizing since ancient times, are two antithetical conceptions of political [beings]: as a creature in search of either peace or power" (pp. 143–4).

[2] Repression may have these influences but this is not central to the definition or most descriptions. Similarly, what I mean by repression is also different from the various "faces" of power because the latter work tends to highlight nonphysical and more subtle factors. Repression is nothing if not blunt and direct in its meaning, identification, and practice.

disappearance, political bans, pepper-spraying, the closing of a newspaper, and mass killing. At the same time, the normative position regarding the means/process of repression divides the work in this area. For example, drawing upon some of the oldest notions of the subject (Hobbes 1950; Machiavelli 1980), there are those for whom repressive behavior serves a useful purpose. Here, the coercive actions of the state are believed to assist in creating a political system and keeping it together as well as sustaining morale in times of resistance and challenges.[3] Differing from this view, there are those who consider repression to be an indication of systemic malfunction, deficiency, and/or pathology – a mechanism of rule unlike any other, whose very use signifies the abdication of that which is right, just, and appropriate (for example, Arendt 1951; O'Kane 1996). In this case, state coercive action is nothing less than a violation of humanity. Finally, there are those who consider repression as a generally "neutral" mechanism of influence, simply one strategy among many employed by political authorities against those within their territorial jurisdiction (Dallin and Breslauer 1970; Weber 1946). My take on the subject is clearly associated with this view.

Each of these positions represents a unique community within which researchers create knowledge, discuss findings, and generate recommendations for policy/action. Unfortunately, however, these communities are largely insulated from one another, and thus there is little exchange of ideas between them. Consequently, those who suggest that repression can be or is "good" (that is, where it is accepted in law and custom) have essentially nothing to say to those who advocate the position that repression is or could be "bad" (that is, where it is never accepted). These distinctions preclude consideration of how repression varies – how it is supported in certain circumstances but not supported in others. Obviously, the neutral position comes closest to facilitating a comprehensive analysis, but it tends to downplay the extremist tendencies of particular explanatory factors that are prominent in the other two perspectives.

The implications of these differences are significant. First, they influence how we talk (or do not talk) about state coercive action (see, for example, McCammant 1984; Rejali 1994). In everyday language, for example, the word "repression" is a pejorative, so the behavior of interest is deemed inherently unacceptable. This eliminates discussion entirely for some; those

---

[3] Inherent within the position is the view that state coercive power could not be overused. It is an interesting point that this assumption was never examined in detail.

who believe repressive behavior serves a useful purpose or those who view repression more neutrally are placed in a largely indefensible position by definition. Ironically, then, the near universal acceptance of human rights hinders the discussion of the topic and development of the literature dedicated to investigating relevant behavior.

The divisions identified previously influence how we measure relevant state action. In the favorable and neutral perspectives, authorities subject citizens to arrest, they impose bans, and/or they declare martial law. The techniques highlighted by this work generally involve restrictions placed on the human body. In the negative perspective, authorities employ techniques against citizens that cause injury as well as pain to the body and/or mind. Clearly, the distinctions between the two are not always obvious. Authorities engage in actions like imprisonment, which restrict the body but also subjects it to some form of psychological duress. Additionally, while the target is not aware of the use of physical and electronic surveillance, these activities can place psychological stress on the victim and are also commonly used to facilitate more overt types of repressive behavior. There are thus many gray areas within the relevant body of work.

Finally, the differences within the literature are also important because they influence how we explain repression. There is some complexity here because although all employ a similar theoretical approach, each emphasizes distinct components of the model. At present most researchers employ some version of a rationalist-structuralist hybrid whereby the authorities engage in some decision calculus about whether or not they can/should apply repression. It is influenced by four factors: (1) benefits (quiescence), (2) costs (resources, removal from office), (3) the likelihood of success (concentration of the population, past effectiveness), and (4) available alternatives (normative power). When benefits are high, costs are low, the likelihood of success is high, and no alternatives exist, repressive behavior will be applied. When benefits are low, costs are high, the likelihood of success is low, and alternatives exist, however, repression will not be applied.

The differences across the distinct communities are clear. Those who view coercive behavior favorably (as a mechanism of order) tend to focus on the pursuit of benefits such as political quiescence (decreasing dissent). Here, repression is applied in an effort to achieve specific ends that are crucial to the state and its repressive agents. Those who view repressive action less favorably (as a pathological process) tend to focus on the inability of costs to function (that is, as a mechanism that will reduce coercive behavior).

Here, these studies highlight the point that factors generally able to hinder repressive action (such as democracy) are limited in their capacity to wield an impact, and those that compel relevant behavior (such as military and leftist governments or lagged repression) are much more influential. Finally, those who view repression neutrally tend to examine all factors together, seeing the use of repression as increasing or decreasing according to the particular context that confronts authorities.

Despite the existence of distinct orientations that largely reflect deference to earlier research in this area, the statistical models employed by different researchers include similar variables.[4] Although dozens of explanatory factors have been examined over time, after thirty-five years of quantitative investigation, three have consistently received support across time, space, context, and methodological technique.[5] Each is discussed here.

Dissent Provokes   The first explanatory factor consistently identified in the literature concerns political dissent – sit-ins, strikes, demonstrations, guerrilla warfare, domestic terrorism, and civil war. Research has been very clear about the influence of this variable: in every statistical examination of the subject, dissent increases repressive behavior. The theoretical model identified earlier is relevant for understanding this finding because authorities benefit from efforts to reduce domestic threat. Activities extended in this direction fulfill one of the state's primary objectives (political control) and thus they serve as a major source of legitimacy for the authorities.[6] Related to this, protest decreases the costs of repression by providing political leaders with a legitimate mandate to coerce. Within such contexts, states are able to frame their activity as a "law and order" measure,

---

[4] The "allure of unparsimonious combination" within conflict studies discussed by Eckstein (1980, 143) was seemingly just too great.

[5] Numerous other factors have been identified as relevant but are generally considered less significant: trade dependence (Aflatooni and Allen 1991; Timberlake and Williams 1984), economic development (see, for example, Davenport 1995b; Hibbs 1973; Poe and Tate 1994; Ziegenhagen 1986), military influence (see, for example, Davenport 1995a, ideological orientation (see, for example, Pion-Berlin 1989), and population (see, for example, Henderson 1991; 1993).

[6] This consistency is quite different from that revealed when the casual arrow is reversed, that is, when repression is used to account for variation in political dissent. In this case, every possible relationship has been identified including no relationship (Lichbach 1987; Moore 1998; Zimmermann 1983).

which is less likely to be viewed unfavorably. For example, as Stanley (1996, 17) identifies:

> [f]or a state to use deadly force against its own citizens raises certain normative and political problems, subjecting state elites to international criticism and even potential domestic criminal prosecution should a change of government take place. For state elites inclined to use violence [however], the blurring of international and domestic concepts inherent in "domestic realist" thought provides a convenient rhetorical cover. [For example, it] enables them to justify their actions by redefining [any] domestic opposition threat as an international one, justifying the use of military force against citizens as if they were external enemies of the nation state.

Of course, the challenge need not be linked to international factors. It is sufficient that a state (its personnel, policies, and institutions) and/or its citizens be threatened in some manner.

Repression Persists   The second explanatory factor consistently identified in the literature concerns prior repressive activity (see, for example, Dallin and Breslauer 1970; Davenport 1995a; 1995b; Davenport and Armstrong 2004; De Swann 1977; Goldstein 1978; Poe and Tate 1994; Walter 1969). In this case, research discloses that previous mass arrests, political bans, and mass killing influence the subsequent application of these activities. Again, the dominant theoretical model is useful for explaining why. As conceived, previous repression decreases the costs of engaging in this behavior later because it familiarizes political leaders with what is involved when they employ such behavior, thereby reducing uncertainty. At the same time, using repressive behavior creates and reinforces an ethos within the relevant state organizations responsible for this activity. As these actors – like all bureaucracies – exist to fulfill a particular objective (in this case, the application of coercion and pursuit of political order), each act serves as an opportunity to move in this direction.[7]

Democracies Pacify   The third (and last) explanatory factor consistently identified in the literature – political democracy – is the one most relevant to the present study. As noted earlier, the negative influence of this variable of

---

[7] One could argue that each act also provides an opportunity for moving away from this direction (for example, with chronic failure). It is my belief, however, that relevant political actors would highlight positive outcomes and discount unfavorable ones; this would further influence the likelihood that the decision to employ repression would be undertaken in the future.

repression has been supported in every statistical investigation that has been undertaken (see, for example, Davenport 1995a; 1995b; 1996a; 1996b; 1997; Davenport and Armstrong 2004; Hibbs 1973; Keith 2002; King 2000; Krain 1997; Richards 1999; Zanger 2000; Ziegenhagen 1986). Three findings from this literature are particularly noteworthy.

First, the level of democracy in a given nation-year decreases repression in the same period; in short, *democracy pacifies contemporaneously*. This influence is identified whether one considers the "rate" (the number of events taking place over a specific amount of time)[8] or the "level" of repressive behavior (some cumulative assessment of scope and magnitude).[9] One finds the same negative influence even when nonlinear effects are considered. In fact, the only difference in results within the research concerns the exact point at which democracy matters. For example, one recent article reveals that "there is a threshold of democratic domestic peace ... [between 1976 and 1996]. Below certain values, democracy has no discernible impact on human rights violations, but after a threshold has been passed ... the level of democracy decreases state repression" (Davenport and Armstrong 2004, 32) Second, the research tells us that instances of regime change toward democracy at time $t - 1$ decrease the rate of some repressive behavior observed in the next year (see, for example, Davenport 1999; Zanger 2000); some forms are not influenced. In short, *democratization pacifies*, and movement along a political continuum toward democracy tends to reduce state coercion. Third, research discloses that levels of democracy and movement toward democracy have negative influences on repression that persist for several years after the year in question, that is, from time to time $t + n$ (see, for example, Davenport 1996b). In short, *democracy and democratization pacify and for quite some time*.

As for the explanation of why democracies are less likely to use state repression, again the existing theoretical framework proves useful. For instance, democracy increases the costs of repressive behavior by increasing the possibility that sanctions are levied against authorities for undesired behavior. This emphasis is by no means new. Indeed, it draws upon a rather long tradition, which is discussed next.

---

[8] See, for example, Davenport 1995a; 1995b; 1996a; 1996b; 1999; Hibbs 1973; King 1998; Krain 1997; Ziegenhagen 1986.

[9] See, for example, Cingranelli and Richards 1999; Davenport 2004; Keith 2002; Mitchell and McCormick 1988; Poe and Tate 1994; Poe, Tate, and Keith 1999; Richards 1999.

The Fundamentals of Democratic Pacification

Our understanding of the impact of democracy on state repression follows quite logically from an older literature in political science that focused on nondemocratic rule (Arendt 1951; Dallin and Breslauer 1970; Friedrich and Brzezinski 1962; Walter 1969). Within these political systems, repression was a constant feature. As noted by Linz (2000, 102), coercion in nondemocratic societies is noteworthy because of

(1) its unprecedented scale, (2) its use against social categories without consideration of guilt for specific acts, (3) the disregard for even the appearance of legal procedures, the formalities of the trial, and the opportunity for some kind of defense, in imposing penalties, (4) the moral self-righteousness and often publicity surrounding it, (5) the extension of the terror to members of the elite, (6) the extension to members of the family of the accused not involved in the crime, (7) the emphasis on the intent and social characteristics of the accused rather than on his actions, (8) the use of organizations of the state and/or the party rather than of so-called uncontrolled elements, and the size and complexity of those organizations, (9) the continuing and sometimes growing terror after the consolidation of the regime in power, and (10) the nonexclusion of the leadership of the armed forces from the repressive policy.

The reasons for repression followed quite directly from this discussion.

First, researchers believe that nondemocratic political leaders *preferred* repression to other mechanisms of influence, even if alternatives were available. Generally closed off from the rest of society and insulated from other political actors, nondemocratic authorities would rather run their societies via directives and force than in other ways. There are numerous reasons for this approach to governance: for example, political leaders in nondemocratic governments believe that most individuals should follow their leader's directions; authorities in nondemocratic governments are often actively engaged in building social, political, and economic systems within traditional societies that are somewhat resistant to change; and/or authorities in nondemocratic governments cannot withstand a direct challenge from citizens because the foundation upon which their governments stand is limited in the degree to which it is supported by the populace. Directing citizens is easier than negotiating with them or convincing them, so such a position makes sense. Of course, one may look at this command issue in another way as well. Within autocratic political systems, repression appears to be inextricably bound up with the identity of the authorities, who have frequently emerged from the military or some equally strict background. The use of coercive action thus draws upon the leaders' earlier training and

Repression and the Search for Peace

belief system (or worldview) – that is, they are merely employing what they had learned earlier in their careers as appropriate ways to communicate with/influence others.[10]

· Second, it was believed that nondemocratic political leaders had the *capability* of using repressive behavior (see, for example, Dallin and Breslauer 1970; Duvall and Stohl 1988; Linz 2000; Walter 1969). Within these political systems, the role and influence of the coercive apparatus is prominently featured. Realizing that nondemocratic governance (with little input from society) is difficult to sustain, it is generally believed that authoritarian leaders rely heavily upon coercive agents, channeling resources, status, and access to them.

Third, it was believed that autocratic political leaders _needed_ to use repression. Within nondemocratic contexts, there are essentially no alternatives for controlling the population – all they have is this behavior (see, for example, Dallin and Breslauer 1970). There may be some normative influence, based principally upon some form of paternalism, but little material influence can generally be employed.[11] Additionally, many individuals make the argument that nondemocratic political systems are inherently unstable, seething with resistance and the potential for rebellion (Kelley 1994; Scott 1985; Walter 1969; Wedeen 1999; Wintrobe 1998).[12] As a result, leaders are in constant fear of removal from office by those who want to gain entry to the political system or to overthrow it entirely.

Out of this research, democracy – representing the opposite of autocracy – became the primary means for resolving the problem of repressive

---

[10] Why focus on nondemocratic political systems as the base from which all discussion about repression takes place? The majority of political systems began as nondemocracies, and it is from there most of their political understandings and aspirations evolved. In typical development fashion, nondemocratic governments serve as the foil against which one can understand the opposite end of the spectrum, which is general democracy. As a result, nondemocracy becomes the backdrop against which the field of study of domestic democratic peace was born. To move away from repression (and by definition from nondemocratic government), one must therefore move toward democracy.

[11] We do not accept that economic development and system type are completely collinear but rather we seek to accurately portray what is conveyed in this literature. As Linz (2000, 57) suggests, "[in] spite of the significant relationship discovered between the stability of democracy in economically developed countries and the higher probability that those having reached a certain level of economic and social development would be democracies, there is a sufficient number of deviant cases to warrant a separate analysis of types of political systems, social systems and economic systems."

[12] Geddes (1999) finds that this is not true. Some (for example, single-party governments) are quite stable.

43

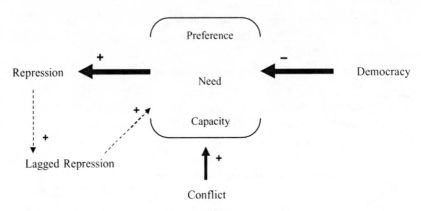

Figure 1.1 The Basic Repression Model

behavior. Indeed, it was thought that the more democratic the political system, the lower the preference, capacity, and need to apply repression. This view was not limited to the academy. Quite to the contrary, it influenced the behavior of policymakers, activists, funding organizations and everyday citizens throughout the world (see, for example, Diamond 1995). The basic model that emerges from this perspective is illustrated in Figure 1.1.

While the argument outlined here has been extremely influential in focusing existing research, advocacy, activism, and public policy, the question remains: is this approach to the study of repression valid? In the next chapter, I argue that this model is flawed in that it homogenizes and simplifies what is in reality a much more complex process. For example, neither repression, nor democracy, nor the context within which decisions about repression are made is as uniform as research suggests. Indeed, important differences within each category compel us to rethink the logic and validity of the domestic democratic peace.

Categories ≠ uniform

44

2

Disaggregation and Contextualization

This chapter challenges many of the assumptions characterizing the extant and relevant literature on state repression. Specifically, I argue for a more disaggregated and nuanced conception of the repressive process than is normally adopted. I use this approach to develop hypotheses that guide the statistical analyses in Chapters 4 and 5.

Disaggregating Repression

All of the quantitative research on state coercion[1] differentiates political authorities only by the extent to which they restrict and/or kill their citizens.[2] The former includes behavior such as the outlawing of the African

---

[1] State coercive behavior has been the subject of countless historical analyses undertaken by Western scholars, essentially covering all parts of the globe across time, space, and political-economic context (see, for example, Dallin and Breslauer 1970; Della Porta 1995; Franks 1989; Goldstein 1978; 1983; Mason and Krane 1989; Monshipouri 1995; Moore 1954; Van den Berghe 1990; Walter 1969). This work has addressed some of the most famous/infamous moments in modern history: the Holocaust in Nazi Germany, the McCarthy Red Scare and Cointelpro in the United States, "Bloody Sunday" in Ireland, the "Killing Fields" of Cambodia, the events in Tiananmen Square of 1989 in China, and the Rwandan genocide of 1994. One can only expect that as the efforts to counter terrorism around the globe continue, research on the current period will grow as well. State repression has also been the subject of hundreds of statistical investigations (see, for example, Bueno de Mesquita 2003; Cingranelli and Richards 1999; Davenport 1995a; 1995b; 1996a; 1996b; 1999; 2004; Fein 1995; Franklin 1997; Hafner-Burton 2005a; 2005b; Henderson 1991; 1993; Hibbs 1973; Keith 2002; King 1998; Krain 1997; Markus and Nesvold 1972; Poe and Tate 1994; Poe, Tate, and Keith 1999; Richards, Gelleny and Sacko 2001; Rummel 1997; Zanger 2000; Ziegenhagen 1986). Again, this covers diverse parts of the globe and a wide variety of times, places, and contexts.

[2] Violations of political and civil liberties and personal integrity have been the most consistently identified strategies of state repression, but other techniques (ignoring/tolerating or

45

National Congress in South Africa under Apartheid (1960); the latter includes behavior such as the killing of students at the University of San Carlos by the Guatemalan military during the mid-1970s and 1980s. Interestingly, these two repressive strategies (imposing restrictions and enacting violence) are normally treated interchangeably within the literature.[3] For example, individuals investigating each of these activities employ similar theoretical frameworks, explanatory variables, and statistical models, and they frequently cite one another, suggesting that they are addressing different types of the same phenomenon [for example, considering negative sanctions, see Davenport (1995b); considering political violence, see Poe and Tate (1994)].[4]

However, are state-sponsored restriction and violence equivalent? Do these two repressive strategies and/or distinct combinations between them respond to the same causal forces, or are their determinants distinct? Ignored within prior research, these are addressed here.

Restrictions or Violence

The key to understanding state repression lies in considering the similarities between the two basic forms of state coercive power identified earlier while ✗ acknowledging the differences and the significance of diverse combinations. Two factors are worthy of consideration: objectives and the relevant costs as well as benefits.

Objectives As conceived, there are a great many ways that repressive behavior can serve the interests of the state, and a great deal of effort has been expended toward understanding what these different interests might

accommodating) are generally ignored. For good discussion of alternatives, see Goldstein (1978) and Earl (2003).

[3] For exceptions, see McCormick and Mitchell (1997) and Cingranelli and Richards (1999). These two studies investigate the degree to which violations of personal integrity existed on one dimension. The former discovered that there were basically two dimensions of repressive behavior, while the latter discovered that different violations fell along one dimension but in different historical sequences. This research compels one to think about the degree to which one can accept killing as a general approach to coercive governance. Neither of these studies considered political and civil liberties, nor did they investigate causal determinants of different repressive strategies. Consequently, they are of limited utility for the current study.

[4] Some even combine the two strategies, drawing no distinctions at all (see, for example, Karatnycky 1999).

be (Bay 1958; Hobbes 1950; Machiavelli 1980; Pion-Berlin 1989; Stanley 1996; Walter 1969; Wantchekon and Healy 1999). Regardless of this diversity, however, the main reason for state repression is the pursuit of political order. According to Hobbes and Weber, this stands as perhaps the most important role of the state. Exactly how governments pursue this objective, however varies.

For example, when states restrict citizens, their goal is less to remove individuals/groups from society than it is to mold them within it, demarcating where members can and cannot go and defining who they can and cannot be. In other words, they are aiming first at capacity and then will.[5] Relevant to this point, the establishment of martial law in Poland on December 13, 1981 (commonly referred to as *stan wojenny*), was not about removing individuals/groups from Poland but hindering the ability of specific individuals/groups to mobilize against the government (Solidarity in this case) by increasing the difficulty of engaging in speech, association, and assembly.[6] Restrictions thus establish parameters within which individuals (victims as well as bystanders) modify their behavior in an attempt to avoid sanctions in the present and future.

In contrast, killing citizens eliminates a part of society deemed unacceptable while compelling acquiescence or guided change within others. This act thus aims at eliminating the will of those previously challenging authority, as well as breaking the will of those who remain – reducing capacity as an afterthought.[7] In this context, the 1969 killing of Black Panther Party (BPP) leader Fred Hampton by Cook County state's attorney's office in Chicago was partially aimed at removing a critical speaker, organizer, and inspiration to advocates of black power in the relevant geographic locale, but it was also undertaken in an effort to stifle subsequent organizational efforts of the Panthers in Chicago and nationally – weakening their ability to recruit, ally themselves with other social movement organizations, and generally engage in contentious behavior.

---

[5] Clearly there is some variance. The licensing of associations would likely be viewed differently from the banning of a political organization. My classification system places these two together without highlighting any differences.

[6] Obviously, this concerns a time before cell phones, pagers, and two-ways were inoperative. We are only left to speculate about how long particular repressive regimes could have lasted with the presence of these electronic devices.

[7] On this point, many suggest that the Stalinist purges of the 1930s and the Guatemalan terror of the 1980s were applied in order to facilitate the development of a new society by "clearing away" remnants of the old (kulaks and indigenous people, respectively).

Costs and Benefits   Differences in tactics also highlight distinct elements of the calculation undertaken by political leaders who consider repressive behavior. For example, with the imposition of restrictions, authorities benefit from the diminished capacity of challengers who have to navigate their way around/through diverse curfews, bans, and so forth. Authorities may further benefit from the acquiescence created by the mass fear inspired by the sanctions. It is also clear, however, that political authorities have to pay for the management of the restrictions they impose (for example, salaries for coercive agents to enact and monitor curfews, bans, and other activities).[8] These costs are most likely not marginal, although we do not know very much about them.[9] Additionally, repressive authorities may suffer from political illegitimacy when restrictions are employed (see, for example, Franks 1989), and the organizational capacity of challengers may later be reestablished in an effort to counter the earlier coercive action – referred to as "backlash" (Francisco 2004).

With regard to political killing, the situation is similarly mixed. On the one hand, authorities benefit from the elimination of challengers and from the fear that such elimination might provoke within citizens. On the other hand, authorities have to pay the cost of imposition, and they may have to pay the cost of diminished political legitimacy and increased challenge being waged against them that may arise at home as well as abroad. In this light, although the killing of BPP leader Hampton diminished specific Panther activity (for example, the promotion and further ascendance of Hampton to the position of chief of staff in the dissident organization, which would have increased the visibility, and behavioral, and recruitment capabilities of the Chicago chapter), it enhanced other behavior – galvanizing diverse African American and other communities to action, including a commission of inquiry (which investigated, chastised, and sued the relevant police organizations for their behavior) and numerous demonstrations. Such behavior would have been unheard of before the police action against Hampton.

---

[8] This is not to say that those who kill citizens do not have to be paid, but rather to suggest that those who engage in sustained and labor-intensive repressive activities (like the imposition of martial law) are likely to be paid more frequently over time.

[9] It is estimated that in South Africa under Apartheid, for instance, the rising cost of maintaining the relevant system of repression was the principle reason this type of government was eliminated (see, for example, Denmark 1984); the costs of repression were simply too much to bear in the context of a largely insulated economic market created by international boycotts as well as by reduced investment and credit.

Restrictions and Violence

It is useful to consider distinct repressive strategies individually, but it is also useful to think of them in tandem, for this is generally how they are employed. For example, when distinct techniques are used simultaneously (that is, when particular restrictions are used with particular forms of violence), this is done in an effort to take advantage of what distinct methods of repression have to offer and to communicate different messages to targets/victims and audiences. Essentially, there are four basic combinations. First, there are those governments that use neither restrictions nor violence. Here, governments try to facilitate popular involvement in political and social life, staying out of the way as much as possible. Second, there are governments that use restrictions at significant levels but that use only limited amounts of violence. This entails an attempt to limit the parameters of sociopolitical engagement – reducing the ease with which alternative ideas and behaviors can be expressed – while avoiding the most lethal and objectionable forms of state repression. Third, there are situations where limited restrictions are imposed on citizens but where the use of violence is common. Here, there is simply an assault on those within the nation-state in an effort to remove the most threatening elements, but there are no efforts made to mold individuals within it. Fourth and finally, there is a situation where both restrictions and violence are significant. In this case, authorities have essentially declared war on the citizenry while simultaneously attempting to constrain the parameters of sociopolitical life. Such an approach eliminates those deemed unlikely to play by the rules and significantly influences the behavior of those who do decide to play.

The identification of these diverse combinations is important because they each provide distinct costs and benefits. For example, complete disengagement from repressive behavior allows authorities to establish a perception of tolerance within the society, which simultaneously reduces the costs associated with these activities. Restrictions without violence allow government officials to regulate behavior without provoking the negative ramifications associated with state-sponsored violent action. Violence without restriction allows authorities to eliminate challengers but avoids the administration, monitoring, and pretense of legality commonly affiliated with civil liberties restrictions. Restrictions with violence provide the best and worst of both worlds. In this context, authorities are able to eliminate particularly threatening individuals/groups as well as attempt to hinder general levels of mobilization and communication.

49

It is clear that the combinations identified earlier in this text merely approximate what is most likely a more complex reality: authorities, human rights organizations, and social movements generally make greater distinctions than the gross characterization provided here. Even within my earlier work (2004) and later in this text, I consider a greater number of combinations. The introductory discussion here is informative because it allows us to understand the basic parameters of what is involved.

Of course, I do not simply believe that we must disaggregate repression to understand the domestic democratic peace. I also believe that we must consider alternative aspects of democracy as well. I now turn to this issue.

Disaggregating Democracy

Even though there are many aspects of democratic government relevant to the peace proposition, none is more important than the accountability of political leaders – especially the executive branch (see, for example, Rosato 2003). This system characteristic is worthy of attention because it increases the likelihood that costs would be imposed on those in power when they impose restrictions on rights or violate personal integrity; that is, when repression is applied, it is expected that the most influential government officials in a democracy (those responsible for the general safety of the citizenry and the specific application of coercive behavior enacted by state agents) would be held accountable and sanctioned in some manner. In an effort to avoid these costs, it is assumed that under democratic contexts authorities would refrain from coercive action.[10]

Are different aspects of democracy equally capable of diminishing repressive behavior? Current research generally ignores this question, combining

---

[10] As Powell (1982) observes, "[d]eadly violence is not, systematically and cross-nationally, a product of patterns of citizen involvement and support, but of the strategic efforts of small groups of political elites." Although Powell is explicitly discussing riots and political deaths, violence attributed to societal members, it is clear that the point is relevant to state repression, for deaths from violence are largely attributed to government activity. Explicitly considering repressive behavior, Goldstein (1978, xxvii) is even more direct on this point, when he states that "(t)he most important, and the *only* variable which *must* change for levels of political repression to change, is the attitude of policy-making authorities. . . . In order for political repression to increase, political authorities must decide to take actions that will increase it; in order for political repression to decrease, political authorities must decide to take actions that will decrease it. These actions manifest a shift in attitude on the part of political authorities, and this shift is the only variable which, by itself, can change the level of political repression."

various elements together when democracy is measured (for exceptions, see Bueno de Mesquita Przeworski, Stokes, and Manin 2005; Davenport 1996b; Keith 2002; Richards 1999). This practice is inappropriate. Indeed, drawing on a long tradition in democratic thought, there are two distinct reasons why political authorities would avoid repression related to distinct aspects of democratic institutions: (1) they fear the action of the masses – referred to as *Voice*, and (2) they fear the action of other elites – referred to as *Veto*. After discussing each of these alternatives individually, I address the issue of relative capability.

Voice

Within democracies, it is clear that political leaders fear being removed from office by citizens for engaging in activities that are deemed antithetical to the popular interest (see, for example, Lipset 1959; Mill 1861; Powell 1982; Przeworski, Stokes, and Manin 1999).[11] The logic of this position is straightforward. Citizens do not like being restricted or violated, and they will do whatever they can to avoid such behavior. The awareness of such a response is not lost on those in power. As Rummel (1997, 78) suggests, "(w)here there is a government by elected representatives who can be run out of office if they oppose the will of the people, it will be most reluctant to start costly and lethal (repressive campaigns), or to bear the continuing costs of such (activities)." Shifting the state's preferences away from repression, the cost of accountability is central to the domestic democratic peace.

Exactly how does this influence manifest itself? There are several possibilities.

First, there is the concern with electoral contests. For example, when authorities contemplate repressive behavior they naturally think about the possible aftereffects of this behavior on their tenure in office. It is believed that behavior that has a deleterious impact on citizens (for example, torture or mass arrests) would result in unfavorable evaluations and those that have a positive impact on citizens (for example, withholding from torture and mass arrests) would result in favorable ones. This situation compels those responsible for the imposition of repression to think about when

[11] In line with Hirschman (1970), I use the word *Voice* in an effort to convey that citizens engage in some activity to communicate their desires to those in authority so that they may be heard. This is achieved through the diverse mechanisms available in a democracy. While elections are critical for this, they are not the only way that citizens communicate.

they are most vulnerable to the actions of those subject to coercive state power such as when they are up for popular election (Sartori 1987, 127–9). Simultaneously, it prompts them to engage in behavior that would be positively evaluated.

The potential effectiveness of elections in this regard is widely understood. Comparatively, although other techniques such as public opinion polls represent a cost for leaders who engage in undesirable behavior, they are not as costly to political authorities; indeed, while presidential approval in public opinion polls may be important, low ratings do not automatically result in the official's removal from office. After a politician loses an election, however, there is no other recourse but acceptance of the outcome unless they wish to resist the outcome, which imposes yet further costs on the political leader and those affiliated with them. As a consequence, it is expected that democratic political leaders avoid repressive action because they know that they may be made to suffer for this behavior later at the ballot box.[12]

The second aspect of *Voice* concerns the outcome of the vote itself in the form of political representation. As designed, elections compel authorities to concern themselves with constituents but only indirectly and infrequently. The presence of political actors whose job it is to act on behalf of (that is, give *Voice* to) constituents directly as well as consistently is the role played by the politician. In standard pluralist fashion, it is not simply the existence of representatives that has an influence but the scope of this representation in terms of how many distinct interests are accounted for. Within contexts in which a wide range of parties and interests receive representation, the matrix of constituents whose interests require protection increases, and it is difficult to separate targets from ordinary citizens who could later sanction authorities for inappropriate behavior. In this situation, I expect that specific forms of state activity that involve negative aftereffects for those targeted such as repression would be reduced. By contrast, when fewer parties and interests are represented, then there is less of a possibility that diverse actors and interests overlap. Here, targets can be easily separated from constituents, and repressive behavior would be more likely.

---

[12] Of course, some argue that democratic leaders care less about being in office. If they lose one election, it is possible for them to win again at a later date. Additionally, unlike autocratic governments, just because democratic leaders lose power does not mean that they lose all of their private wealth and privilege. Indeed, considering the employment and investment opportunities that await former U.S. presidents, the prospect might not be problematic at all. This makes me wonder if there are other elements to *Voice*.

Disaggregation and Contextualization

Invoking the same logic, one could conceive of electoral outcomes in a different way. For example, in plurality democratic systems, the victors assume office, and the losers are subject to the activities of the victors without direct participation in the decisions that might affect their lives. By contrast, in proportional democratic systems, there are essentially no losers: all are able to have some representation (i.e., *Voice*) within the system. In the former situation, repressive action is expected because there are few connections between perpetrators and targets, thus diminishing the accountability and responsibility of the authorities. In the latter situation, however, there are a larger number of connections between perpetrators and targets.

From this, I derive my first hypothesis:

Hypothesis 1: The greater the amount of *Voice* (mass participation and the repre- sentation of diverse interests), the lower the likelihood of state repression.[13]

↑ VOICE →
↓ REPRESSION

Before moving to a discussion of another aspect of political democracy, it is useful to consider an example of how *Voice* actually functions in the real world. For this, I consider Apartheid South Africa.

Voice *in South Africa*

By most accounts, black South Africans had suffered immensely under Apartheid (between 1948 and 1990). During this time, blacks had no national political representation, and three of their most important political parties were banned – the African National Congress (ANC), the Pan Africanist Congress (PAC) and the South African Communist Party. In addition, much of their politically oriented literature was officially restricted;[14] key political leaders were harassed, censored, imprisoned, exiled, or killed; and several million were forcibly evicted from land that they rightfully owned – leaving them homeless and destitute. As an outgrowth of the latter process, blacks were herded into geographically and

---

[13] As conceived, the preceding argument is consistent with others found within the literature. For example, Bueno de Mesquita (2003, 180–1, 346) maintain that political authorities will be less inclined to harm citizens when the number of individuals that assisted them with their political victory is large (what they call the "minimum winning coalition") and when they are beholden to a large section of the population for political power (what they call the "selectorate").

[14] A good list is kept at the Beacon for Freedom of Expression: www.beaconforfreedom. org.

economically isolated as well as politically insulated Bantustans, or they were living in the shantytowns and slums around white cities.[15]

Within this context, perhaps no group of individuals understood the logic underlying *Voice* better than white South Africans. Given the demographic imbalance of the diverse ethnic groups and white repressive activity, it was obvious that if suffrage were extended to the blacks (approximately 72 percent of the population during the Apartheid era), then it would be difficult for any government wishing to stay in power to repress those falling into the demographically superior position. Repressive behavior would have been equivalent to political suicide. Although, the right to vote was extended to the majority of blacks as early as 1987, it applied only to specific, nonpolitical matters concerning the Bantustans; there was effectively no impact on the central government. Moreover, as large numbers lived outside Bantustans, the reality of the situation was that they did not officially engage at all in politics on the national level.

As such, the pre-enfranchisement discussion about the incorporation of the black majority was extremely delicate, with whites wishing to protect their rights, their property, their ethnicity, and their very lives. The election that would sweep the National Party into power in 1948, likely the period in which the orientation of the government was most explicitly articulated and before the worst repressive activities occurred, depicted the options quite starkly:

[o]n the one hand there is the policy of equalization which propagates equal rights for all civilized and developed people, regardless of race or colour within the same structures and the gradual granting of the vote to non-whites in proportion to their capacity to avail themselves of democratic rights. On the other hand we have the policy of apartheid which has grown out of the experience of the settled white population and is based on the principles of justice and fairness. Its object is the maintenance and protection of the white population as a pure white race. (*Die Transvaler* [1948] cited in Giliomee 1987, 364)

Essentially all political concerns were acted upon with the awareness that if blacks had had the right to vote and the ability to remove political leaders who treated them badly, then it was highly probable that many (if not most) of the authorities in office during the relevant period would be voted

---

[15] In contrast, Indians had the South African Indian Council established in 1964 and coloureds had limited representation as early as 1969 within representative councils. Most within the respective communities viewed these as ineffectual at best and offensive at worst – frequently leading to boycotts and protests when they were active. A tricameral parliament was not created for coloureds and Indians until 1983.

out and would never again be reelected. The issue of what could/should be done with those involved in the repression of the nonwhites led to intense debates over the next forty years – about amnesty, the protection of minority rights (those of whites in particular), the potential retribution of the blacks if they were to assume power,[16] the composition of the security forces, the establishment of separate geographic domains within South Africa, the protection of the newly vulnerable minority, and the growth of white extremism in the period leading up to the regime change.

After the incorporation of the black majority in the 1990s, many white perceptions were realized. Blacks did address the repressive activities of those in the Apartheid government (and the violent activities of others) but not with electoral sanctions because whites essentially left public life and thus were not subject to the mechanisms identified previously – revealing a weakness highlighted by Powell (2000). Rather, blacks addressed these issues in the Truth and Reconciliation Process (e.g., Gibson 2004). Clearly, however, the threat of *Voice* hampered the post-Apartheid government in ways that did not impact previous South African regimes – revealing the strength of *Voice*. Like the sword of Damocles, the black voter lurked above all state activities, and, in order to maintain power and legitimacy, post-Apartheid governments had to avoid any hint of repressive legislation, at least officially. Aware of this situation, one scholar of the area noted that "(i)n the post-apartheid era significant attempts were made to transform both the police and forces into more accountable entities so that they would be geared towards public service rather than repression" (Lamb 2002, 42). Unfortunately, these efforts saw mixed results. Lamb continues: in the final analysis, "(l)imited transformation successes were achieved, including the disbanding of controversial units such as the Internal Stability Unit" (Lamb 2002, 42). Indeed, the researcher identifies that several years after the transition "certain reactionary and racist elements still remained within the security forces" (Lamb 2002, 42). Politically excluded, blacks could be repressed. However, once included (making them the majority within the political system), the South African government could not support any coercive behavior at all. In fact, given its history, the government had to go out of its way to avoid appearing repressive, even when it might be necessary to engage in coercive state activity.[17]

---

[16] Some predicted genocide in South Africa (Mamdani 2001).

[17] Although drawn from an earlier time, a similar argument is made by Dahl (1971) regarding the repression of blacks in the American South. As he states, "in order for the white people

Of course, these are not the only components of the domestic democratic peace worthy of discussion. While *Voice* works through and for the masses, another mechanism, *Veto*, is concerned with and determined by others within the political system and society. Specifically, it involves those who can more directly influence the repressive decision-making process.[18] This idea is addressed next.

Veto

Drawing upon a distinct literature from that highlighted in the case of *Voice*, the advocates of *Veto* ignore the masses, and they focus on the role played by politicians and political-economic elites – not as representatives of mass interests but as rival political actors whose job it is to "watch and control the government," shedding light on abuses and throwing offending parties out of office when the abuses are deemed considerable as well as out of fear of what inaction would mean for the government itself (Mill 1861, 229). The existence of countervailing political actors is important because, within democratic political systems, authorities are constrained in their ability to use repression only to the extent that they have to deal with and/or override other power holders. Accordingly, government officials (that is to say, executives) who are isolated as well as insulated from actors who can wield political influence over them are better able to push forward policies because the isolation and insulation of these regimes facilitates discretion, and discretion facilitates repressive behavior. If, however, political authorities are countered by others, then they are then less able to do what they wish.

Exactly how does this influence manifest itself? The mechanism is straightforward. When authorities contemplate repressive action, they do

to develop a dual system, a kind of polyarchy for whites and hegemony for blacks. It is important to keep the distinction in mind, not for the sake of logic chopping, definitional purity, or "saving" polyarchy at all costs, but precisely because of the empirical generalization that it reinforces: if freed Negroes had been allowed to participate in the system of public contestation in the South, they could not have been subjected to systematic repression by coercion and terror, I believe, for they were much too large a minority. It was only by excluding them forcibly from the polyarchy that the system of coercion and terror could be maintained in the South" (Dahl 1971, 28–9).

[18] In line with the arguments of Tsebelis and Keefer, I use the word *Veto* because this clearly conveys the fact that particular actors can interfere with others and which influence the political process. The distinction here is crucial for although in the case of parties, the same acts are involved; in one case (*Voice*) they are representatives of the citizenry (completely beholden to them), and they act as indirect influences, and in the other (*Veto*), they are self-serving political actors who act relatively independently as well as more directly.

not concern themselves with future electoral defeat or with the matrix of interest that may be deleteriously influence. Rather, they concern themselves with the process of governance itself as conducted on a daily basis in an interconnected chain of relationships. Some of the costs here are comparable to *Voice* (removal from office and the loss of political legitimacy). Others, however, are distinct (for example, oversight and investigation, current and future resistance to coercive and other policies). As a consequence, the larger the number of points at which authorities can be evaluated/contested (that is, overseen, investigated, vetoed) and the larger the number of organizations that have this capability (that is, veto "players"), the higher the likelihood that authorities would perceive costs and refrain from repressive behavior. By contrast, if there were fewer points of evaluation/contestation and/or organizations (players), then there would be fewer perceived costs, and the likelihood of repression would increase.

This leads to the following hypothesis:

Hypothesis 2: The greater the amount of *Veto* (either points or players), the lower the likelihood of state repression.

[handwritten margin note: ↑ Veto → ↓ Repression]

In an effort to illustrate how *Veto* works, I again return to the South African example, this time focusing on the late 1980s.

Veto *in South Africa*

With suffrage restricted to the minority white population, parliamentary democracy appeared to function quite well with regard to this group (see, for example, Freedom House 1986–7, 345). From 1948 to approximately the mid-1980s,[19] one party dominated the political process – the National Party. This organization consistently garnered the most votes, and public opinion polls generally identified a unified white community across diverse dimensions.[20] Accordingly, it was during this time that the largest number and most prominent repressive actions were enacted (for example, the Suppression of Communism and Group Areas Acts [1950], the Sharpeville

---

[19] There were small challenges during this time, as defections occurred (for example, to the Cape National Party in the 1970s), and there was the constant (largely symbolic) pressure of MP Helen Suzman of the Progressive Party, but the National Party was still able to maintain its preeminent position. Indeed, even as late as 1983 they had withstood the mobilizing efforts of the Progressive Federation Party.

[20] Against this, Giliomee (1987) offers a fascinating account of the varying tensions that existed within white opinion regarding Apartheid. He does not, however, provide any assessment of exactly why the National Party was able to hold on to political power as long as it did.

massacre and the Unlawful Organizations Act [1960], the Terrorism Acts [1967], as well as the millions of prosecutions of pass law violations and related offenses [Denemark 1984: 145–6]).

During the relevant period, small challenges were made against the National Party (for example, defections to the Cape National Party in the 1970s, the constant pressure of MP Helen Suzman of the Progressive Party, and as late as 1983 the mobilizing efforts of the Progressive Federation Party). Perhaps the most severe challenge occurred, however, after the Conservative Party was created in 1982. Regardless of these efforts, however, at every turn the National Party was able to maintain its preeminent position as well as the repressive policies of the Apartheid regime.

Following P. W. Botha's ascent to the leadership of the National Party (in 1978) and the increased calls for moderation from diverse political actors, there was a reduction in the most obvious forms of political repression (the so-called petty Apartheid violations such as pass laws), and in 1983 the one parliamentary chamber that had been open exclusively to whites increased to three chambers: one house for whites, one for coloureds, and one for Indians. For several years in the mid-1980s, Botha and the party were able to insulate themselves from the influence of rival political actors by imposing security legislation – an action that further increased arrests without warrants, indefinite detention, and acts of censorship that simultaneously limits the influence of political veto players. The act was short-lived, however, and in 1989 the position of the National Party was undermined by the formation of the Democratic Party. This organization was "committed to nonracial democracy, civil liberties, and private enterprise" (Wood 2000, 179) and represented an increasingly large number of white South Africans. The implications of this shift were profound. As whites and their political representatives became polarized, the National Party was confronted with a weakened position regarding its ability to enact repressive policies without suffering political repercussions imposed by other political actors. In this context, coercive behavior decreased, and the host of abuses associated with Apartheid came to an end.

Of course, focus on "official" political organizations represents only one aspect of *Veto*. The South African case considerably reveals the importance of nonstate actors. Repeatedly throughout the latter years of the Apartheid regime, business, labor, and religious organizations interacted with government more or less regularly in an effort to modify the restrictions placed on the black population. Some issued manifestos, some sponsored conferences, and some held unofficial as well as unsanctioned political meetings with black leaders/organizations (for example, with the ANC in Dakar during the 1980s). Regardless of the actor and/or specific locale of action, all attempted to provide information to authorities about what was taking place, and all attempted to influence the government process through discussion and distribution of information.

The outcome of these governmental and nongovernmental efforts was significant and clearly consistent with *Veto*. As stated by Southall (2001, 16), post-Apartheid,

South Africa now proudly proclaims itself as a constitutional state and its government as bound by the rule of law. Indeed, under the final constitution of 1996, democracy is presented as being promoted not only by the popularly elected National Assembly's ultimate ability to dismiss the executive. It also refers to the government's freedom to act being constrained by a Bill of Rights, an independent judiciary and by a set of institutions ... whose particular status is meant to provide for the functioning of key bodies independently from government and for the exercise of external review of major areas of official performance.

Adding this to the multitude of civil society and private corporations inside South Africa that arose after Apartheid, this creates a strong counter balance to central government. In fact, faced with a multitude of *Veto* players (inside as well as outside of government), the provisions directed to protect citizens rights actually exceed those of most international human rights institutions (Penna 1998, 111). South Africa, at one extreme of repression during Apartheid, has moved to the opposite end of the spectrum.

The Critiques and Relative Capabilities of Voice *and* Veto

Although both characteristics of democracy previously identified are expected to reduce repressive behavior, there are important differences between them that directly address their relative effectiveness as instruments of democratic peace. I will identify arguments for both sides and then present my own perspective.

In the existing literature, critics of *Voice* consistently discuss the uncertainty and volatility of the masses. Essentially, this argument is "founded on two basic assumptions: first, that the masses are inherently incompetent, and, second, that they are, at best, pliable, inert stuff or, at worst, aroused, unruly creatures possessing an insatiable proclivity to undermine both culture and liberty" (Bachrach 1967, 2). Such a position is problematic because one would generally expect that "outbreaks of political repression – when they do occur – are attributable to the mass public" (Gibson 1988, 512). In this scenario, ordinary citizens perceive a need for repressive behavior (for example, they perceive a threat to entrenched interests), and they lobby for coercion. Being responsive to their citizens, governments apply relevant behavior. Here, *Voice* is an unstable mechanism of peace, and it would be less important than *Veto*, which relies upon the relatively well-educated, even-tempered, and generally tolerant impulses of political elites. Indeed, according to this work, it is these actors and only these actors that can bring peaceful relations within nations; they are generally not pliable, inert, aroused, or unruly, thus serving as ideal protectors of liberty.

One could criticize *Voice* from another perspective as well. For instance, some argue that authorities do not fear sanctions from citizens because of the complexity of the representative system. As Powell (2000, 51) argues,

[in a democracy] citizens are allowed to throw somebody out, but they do not really know who is responsible for the policies. If citizens in a democracy cannot identify responsibility for policy, they cannot use elections precisely to hold policymakers retrospectively accountable for their actions. When policy responsibility is unclear, the incentive for policymakers to anticipate what citizens want and work to achieve it is also lessened. Clarity of responsibility, then, is an important condition if elections are to serve as instruments for citizen control in a democracy.[21]

By comparison, *Veto* does not suffer from a lack of clarity and thus the pacific influence on repression is more robust. Political elites know exactly with whom they are dealing and who is responsible for what type of action. In fact, this is part of the justification for checks and balances – the belief

---

[21] Powell (2000, 50–1) also remarks that "[d]emocratic theorists have diverse expectations about what elections can accomplish. For proportional theorists elections are primarily an occasion to reconsider and rebalance the opportunities for influence; accountability does not loom so large in this vision. For some majoritarians an occasional all-or-nothing rejection of the incumbents, perhaps based on citizens' contradictory evaluations and concerns, is all one can expect of democratic elections.... They have little hope of seeing substantive connections between citizens' preferences and government policies. For other, perhaps most, majoritarians the possibility of throwing the rascals out is essential in order to retain policymakers who do what the citizens want and evict those who stray from citizens' preferred policies. Perhaps more than the occasional evictions themselves, the threat of eviction should encourage responsible behavior." Unfortunately, Powell (2000, 51) continues, retrospective control assumes that citizens know who is responsible for the relevant policy (repression in this case), and they have an opportunity to influence the outcome of the electoral contest against the offending policymaker. Without these two conditions, however, the principle of retrospective control is unable to function. This is an important critique of the pacifying argument identified earlier, but it has been unexamined.

Disaggregation and Contextualization

that only those who understand and operate within the political system can effectively counter others within it.

These differences are important for state repression and the domestic democratic peace because this leads us to believe that

Hypothesis 3: *Veto* generally exceeds *Voice* in its ability to diminish repressive behavior.

[handwritten margin note: Veto more effective than voice]

Just as there are those who champion political leaders as the advocates and guarantors of noncoercive governance, however, there are others who favor the mass population and *Voice*, identifying political and socioeconomic elites as the major reason for why state repression is applied in the first place. Here, it is mentioned that the most likely recipient of repression action, the ordinary citizen, is the most concerned, vigilant, and capable actor in monitoring as well as reducing the amount of repression applied against citizens. By contrast, politicians are indirect representatives concerned not only with the lives of their constituents but also with their lives as politicians – securing benefits and status for themselves as well as continuing in their positions as long as possible. This view is problematic because the effectiveness of *Veto* depends on the degree to which politicians see themselves as representatives serving some mass interest or as a member of a distinct class of individuals that could collude with one another to serve their own needs. Viewed in the latter perspective, power holders would not be inclined to counter other power holders in the manner previously identified – functioning in a manner consistent with "checks and balances." Quite the contrary, they would act in a manner that largely reinforces their position as elites. They would be functioning in a manner that would make repressive policy more likely and so would result in greater sociopolitical control. Following this, the previous proposition is inverted:

Hypothesis 4: *Voice* generally exceeds *Veto* in diminishing state repression. *[handwritten margin note: H3 inverted]*

Comparing the two mechanisms of pacification and thinking about their relative degrees of effectiveness, I argue that *Voice* is more powerful than *Veto*. There are two reasons for this.

First, enfranchisement and the popular vote[22] actually institutionalize the principles of inclusion and acceptance. This is important because when

---

[22] Here, I am not referring to those "sham" elections where a large percentage of the population votes, but the result has already been decided (for example, Rwanda in 2004).

citizens are incorporated into the political system, leaders have acknowledged that citizens have a place within the government and nation-state as well as a right to influence the outcomes emerging within these locales – to some degree at least (see, for example, Dahl 1989; Lane and Ersson 2000). Specifically, democratic citizens have the right to evaluate as well as change leaders when given the opportunity, and they have the right to provide their opinion through diverse avenues, including the vote but also via the media, petitions, and lobbying. Incorporation thus signals a completely different model of sociopolitical control.[23]

Accordingly, I believe that *Voice* exceeds the influence of *Veto* because the former diminishes the perceived need for repression far more than the latter. After citizens are incorporated into the political system, they are in the domain of elections, representation, debate, lobbying, and referenda – all activities that offer citizens at least the perception of participation and influence. These are completely different mechanisms of influence and control, believed by some to be far more effective in controlling the population than other strategies available to political authorities. In contrast, if *Veto* instead of *Voice* is developed, then this clearly institutionalizes a potential cost for those contemplating and implementing repressive action, but it does not effectively eliminate the need for applying this behavior or its feasibility; indeed, given some of the negative attributes of the mass population often associated with this argument (highlighted earlier), it is clear that the inherent elitism within this perspective would be consistent with a view that significant differences between authorities/elites and others exist, thereby facilitating (and potentially prompting) state repression.

My second point is less about the strength of *Voice* as a mechanism of tolerance than it is about the weakness of *Veto*. As discussed earlier, according to most theories of the domestic democratic peace, authorities fear

---

[23] By this logic, repression is likely used against those who have no place or status within a political community. At the extreme, this is why scholars of genocide focus on the process of dehumanization – the establishment of "otherness" itself, which facilitates the application of repressive behavior. Implicit within this work is the idea that perpetrators do not direct coercion against those similar to themselves. On the contrary, targets of repressive government behavior must be portrayed as something else, something different from oneself. Much less extreme, one can observe a similar process in the area of criminal deviance as this relates to the authority's portrayal of criminals in crime control efforts (arrest, policing, and so forth).

the potential costs that may be exacted by citizens (votes) and/or by other political authorities (vetoes). This assumes however that there is no agreement/collusion between government actors to avoid any backlash from constituents who might deem the behavior offensive. On this point, I find the arguments of elite power theorists such as Mosca, Pareto, and Michels convincing, if centralization of power among elites is the most likely occurrence within political life, then the possibility of elite fractionalization and the counterbalancing of power holders discussed by *Veto* is less likely than imagined. Given the high degree of similarity expected among members of the sociopolitical elite, it makes sense that they would tend to align more with each other than join with members of the citizenry against other power holders. This accounts for the large amount of stability we see in most political systems throughout the world.

Bringing Repression Back In

Of course, not all forms of repressive behavior are equally likely to be influenced by the different aspects of political democracy discussed here. Concerning exactly how *Voice* and *Veto* influence repressive behavior, I again expect to find differences.

For example, earlier I suggested that when states restrict citizens, they are less interested in removing individuals within society than shaping their attitudes and behavior within it for the purpose of demarcating where members can and cannot go (physically as well as politically) and defining who they can and cannot be (socially as well as politically). I would take this a step further arguing that restrictions are extremely important for democracy. As Whyte and MacDonald (1989, 23–4) note,

[t]here can be little doubt that [the political and constitutional arrangement within democratic countries] recognizes that liberty as a political value . . . when undervalued erodes the basic structures relating to both public and private ordering. It is for these reasons that at the level of constitutional ideology [those in democracies] have a high degree of tolerance for private choice and unrestricted private action.

It is also for this reason that restrictions are intimately connected to democratic rule. As new, unforeseen issues threaten the democratic citizenry, it is the restrictions applied by the state that facilitate the protection of the populace – at least in principle.

One can see this very clearly in the research of (McPhail, Schweingruber, and McCarthy 1998, 57), which focuses on what they label "public forum and protest law" – diverse political restrictions that relate directly to expression and association. Responding to the force used by political authorities in their efforts to control mass demonstrations witnessed in the United States during the 1960s and 1970s at Kent State and outside the Democratic National Convention in 1968, numerous laws were enacted to afford individuals a space and time within which they could simultaneously protest and be protected by the police while engaging in relevant behavior.[24] Public forum law thus created and drew important distinctions between "the traditional public forum" (commons, public streets, parks, and sidewalks), "limited or designated public forum" (airports, university meeting places, and municipal theaters), "nonpublic forum" (post offices and jails), and private property. While providing a space within which democratic participation could take place, however, this body of law also increased the number of restrictions on participation, thereby revealing an important connection and compatibility between certain forms of repression and political democracy.

Although democratic beings endowed with political existence are guided through constraints, in contrast, no such connection exists between democracy and state-sponsored violence. With regard to this form of repression, beings are not endowed with any place within the political system and their removal is complete. Indeed, in this case, it is clear that violence represents "a sharp discontinuity in behavior that has profound meaning and value" (Rummel 1997, 154–5, emphasis in original) – something antithetical to democracy and its method of governance.

---

[24] For example, "[b]etween 1960 and 1995, [U.S.] federal courts handed down a large number of decisions bearing on the content, time, place, and manner of protest in the public forum. First and foremost among these decisions bearing on the sanctity of protest content, including *Brandenburg v. Ohio* (1969) and *Watts v. United States* (1969), which protect even the right to advocate violence if there is no call for immediate violent action. Furthermore, *Chicago v. Mosely* (1972) was but the first of several decisions to reiterate that the "First Amendment means that government has no right to restrict expression because of its message, its ideas, its subject matter, or its content," regardless of how provocative and offensive those may be. These ranged from the protection of civil rights marchers from hostile onlookers (*King Movement Coalition v. Chicago*, 1976) to the protection of Nazis from counterdemonstrators (*Skokie v. National Socialist Party*, 1978) to the protection of the right to burn the U.S. flag (*United States v. Eichman*, 1990)" (McPhail, Schweingruber, and McCarthy 1998, 58).

Disaggregation and Contextualization

This suggests that

Hypothesis 5: *Voice* and *Veto* decrease state violence more than political restrictions.

[handwritten margin note: Are Voice & Veto more effective than pol. restrictions]

Again, the South African case provides an ideal example of the relative importance of these two aspects of democracy.

Voice and Veto in South Africa

In 1989, F. W. de Klerk was voted into office with what appeared to be a clear mandate for ending Apartheid-related repression. After three successive losses in by-elections to the increasingly competitive Conservative Party, however, it appeared that the mandate was lost. Whereas two of these losses were generally expected, one had taken place in a locale where National Party support was believed to be steadfast. The electoral shift is important for this discussion because the Conservative Party was against dismantling Apartheid and scaling back repressive activity, something that it could effectively delay and potentially overturn in its role as the "legal opposition" – a prime example of *Veto*.[25]

Faced with what appeared to be a consistent stream of defections from the National Party and increased resistance from the Conservative Party, de Klerk went "public" with white South Africans for an up or down referendum on whether he should proceed with the dismantling and a clear indication of *Voice*. The result of this effort was astounding: 85 percent of whites participated (the highest turnout in South African history), and 60 percent said that, yes, the dismantling should continue.

Clearly, this was not as big a gamble as it seems. Leading up to the referendum, public opinion had consistently indicated that (1) the National Party was losing support while Conservatives were increasing, (2) whites felt scared about what might happen if things continued unchanged, and (3) the ANC was increasingly viewed as a major political force to be reckoned with. In this context, whites opted for negotiation, political inclusion, and reduced repression. Consequently, *Voice* reduced the coercion associated with Apartheid.

---

[25] This represents merely one *Veto* player among many that existed at the time. Most would suggest that with regard to South Africa in 1989, it is necessary to look beyond the official *Veto* players and consider the nonofficial actors to get a better understanding of the situation.

Regime change notwithstanding, the problem of state repression did not completely end with the dismantling of Apartheid. Rather, it was transformed. Thus, as one scholar noted, after Apartheid

[t]here can be no serious debate about whether or not South Africa now has a government that is more accountable to society than its National Party predecessor, that was elected on a racially restricted franchise and, latterly at least, worked in very close, yet almost wholly opaque collaboration with unaccountable security services. That is now not the issue. Much more important is the question whether the constitutional provisions designed to render government accountable under the new constitution are working adequately. (Southall 2001, 16)

The answer to this question was not positive. As this researcher continued, "[u]nfortunately, there are already more than sufficient indications that they are not" (Southall 2001, 16).

Although democratization (*Voice* in this case) moved repression down the scale of lethality, repressive behavior still persisted in some form, and it remains to be seen how (and if) democracy (especially *Veto*) will be capable of reducing this behavior further.

Thus far, I have focused on two factors: state repression and political democracy. My examination now moves to a third factor essential for properly evaluating the domestic democratic peace: domestic and international behavior that threatens authorities.

Disaggregating Conflict

Conventional wisdom maintains that democracy decreases repression while political conflict increases state coercive behavior. These relationships are generally evaluated independently of one another, but this is unrealistic (Gartner and Regan 1996). Indeed, I argue that it is imperative that the two be considered at the same time. In the following sections, several arguments are identified concerning the relative importance of democracy and conflict in influencing repression. The first and second arguments concern situations where political authorities are affected by one factor or the other. The third and fourth identify situations where the influence of democracy is conditioned by the type of conflict involved.

Democratic Peace (Democracy Trumps Conflict)   In considering the factors that might alter the influence of democracy on repression, it is clear that situations of conflict are commonly viewed as the ultimate test of the peace proposition. The logic here is straightforward. Dahl (1966, xvi), for example, argues that

> [o]nce a system that permits peaceful party opposition is highly institutionalized and surrounded with legal protections, the costs of destroying it are likely to be extremely high. For a government [in this context] can destroy the opposition only by wrecking the constitutional system. At this stage of [political] evolution, to destroy the opposition requires a revolution. And the costs of revolution often run high.

Although Dahl stresses that the opposition needs to be "peaceful" (that is, nonviolent) in order to be "permitted"[26] (that is, not repressed), it seems plausible that such toleration could also be extended to those forms of conflict that are violent in nature.[27] That dissidents engage in extremely challenging behavior should not, by definition, override the highly institutionalized system of political and legal protections for citizen's rights existing within a democracy.[28] Indeed, this accounts for the rather complex debate about the ability of democratic states to confront political conflict like domestic terrorism. On this point, some support a relatively coercive response but a great many argue that repressive behavior undermines the very structure and integrity of the political system under attack, therefore requiring a different kind of response.

This argument is not simply applied to domestic political conflict. Essentially, the same logic could apply to international threats as well. For example, even though it is possible that national crises (like war) compel political authorities to seek out and eliminate domestic challengers who support the foreign actor (lending moral and financial support as well as undermining the capability of the state to fight the enemy), in a democratic government international crises would be less likely to increase repressive behavior because of the belief in the right to communicate opinions even when they challenge existing authorities, institutions, and/or policies. Indeed, democracy is configured in a way that such behavior is actively facilitated.

How might political conflict modify the domestic democratic peace proposition? There are several possibilities.

---

[26] This is generally similar to Lipset's (1959) argument about "moderate" societal tension.

[27] I disagree with McLennan (1973), for there is nothing in Dahl's research that suggests that his argument could not be extended to other political contexts.

[28] This discussion is currently being undertaken with regard to the domestic activities of governments throughout the world post-9/11.

First, some argue that

Despite dem peace, voice & veto → ↓ repression [handwritten margin note]

Hypothesis 6: Despite the presence of conflict, *Voice* and *Veto* are still able to decrease state repression.

There are weak and strong versions of this argument; the former stipulates that when conflict exists, the negative influence of democracy is as great as when conflict is not present (Hypothesis 6a), and the latter stipulates that when conflict exists, the negative influence of democracy or repression is even greater (Hypothesis 6b).

Revisiting the previous discussion about the relative effectiveness of *Voice* relative to *Veto*, it is important to acknowledge potential differences between the two forms of democracy. For example, in line with elitist democratic theory, I anticipate that

Conflict: Veto more effective than Voice [handwritten margin note]

Hypothesis 7: When conflict is present, *Veto* is more effective than *Voice* at decreasing repression.

Here, in the face of political conflict, the masses would be irrational, guided by emotions, and therefore more apt to call for and reward activities like repressive behavior. By contrast, despite the threat to domestic order, elites would be more likely to uphold the principles of tolerance and democracy, thereby decreasing the use of coercion.[29]

In line with more mass-oriented democratic theory, however, it is expected that

H7 inverted [handwritten margin note]

Hypothesis 8: When conflict is present, *Voice* is more effective than *Veto* at decreasing repression.

Here, citizens would be more interested in and capable of protecting their freedoms by communicating their interests to relevant authorities, leveling threats against political leaders, and even trying to sanction those who apply coercive behavior.

Finally, I consider differences between forms of repression. For example, in line with each discussion about the influence of democracy, it seems reasonable to argue that even though conflict might compel democratic authorities to use repressive behavior, it does not necessarily compel them to

[29] In this context, the state is a repository for public power [a "distinterested instrumentality ready to execute public will" (Matua 2001, 220)] that would yield to the presence of the excited constituency and apply coercive action when requested, if not for the presence of reasonable and essentially more enlightened political actors – elites.

use the most violent forms of coercive power. Indeed, if state use of violence is such a dramatic shift in government behavior, then even when confronted with violent challenges, democratic authorities should be unwilling or less willing to engage in the most extreme forms of coercion. Accordingly, I anticipate that

Hypothesis 9: When conflict is present, state violence is decreased by democracy, but state restrictions are not.

[handwritten marginal note: Conflict. Dem → ↓ violence, but not restrictions]

In the diverse hypotheses just listed, the influence of democracy out-weighs political conflict. It is also important to consider situations where conflict overwhelms democratic peace.

Domestic Realism (Conflict Trumps Democracy) At present, much social science research (see, for example, Della Porta and Reiter 1998; Franks 1989; Rapoport and Weinberg 2001; Sherr 1989), including some of my own work (Davenport 1995a; 1995b; Davenport and Eads 2001), main-tains that violent conflict increases repressive behavior, even within a rel-atively open political system.[30] Exactly when, however, is such a response "warranted"? I would argue that repression is anticipated when the param-eters of threat exceed the parameters of what is deemed "legitimate" (accepted by social practice) and "legal" (accepted by law). For example, even though democracies generally accept a wide variety of behavior that can be viewed legitimate and legal, it is clear that leaders do not permit all forms and/or levels of challenge. As long as behavior stays within desi-gnated parameters (that is, when dissent is nonviolent and/or challenges do not attempt to displace leaders), repression is not expected. Once the parameters of legitimate and legal activity exceed realms of acceptability (for example, when dissent is violent and/or challengers call for the displace-ment of existing authorities), state repression is anticipated.[31] In short, the

---

[30] I do not address the objectives of specific dissidents or the state. For example, Stam (1996, 65–70) discusses the use of repression of violent as well as nonviolent dissent in an effort to facilitate the war effort.

[31] Such a position appears to be in line with existing research. For example, as noted by Whyte and MacDonald (1989, 25), "the rule of law requires the creation and maintenance of an actual order of positive laws which preserves and embodies the more general principle of normative order.... The Rule of Law in this sense implies ... simply the existence of public order." Dahl (1966) also makes this connection. In listing goals pursued by democracy, he states that "[t]he first criterion ... emphasizes opportunities for dissent; and it is no doubt their concern for this goal that explains, in the main, why liberals and radicals have usually

challenge[32] of political conflict undermines the otherwise pacifying influence of democratic government (Powell 1982, 161, 168).[33]

This thinking modifies the domestic democratic peace proposition in an important way for we would anticipate that

[handwritten margin note: Conflict: voice & veto NOT → ↓ repression]

Hypothesis 10: When conflict is present, *Voice* and *Veto* are unable to decrease state repression.

There are again two versions of this argument. The weak version stipulates that conflict simply dampens the pacifying influence of democracy on repression (Hypothesis 10a); the strong version stipulates that conflict eliminates the pacifying influence entirely (Hypothesis 10b).

Even though the two hypotheses just identified reflect existing literature well, I also advance arguments that different forms of conflict influence the domestic democratic peace in distinct ways.

---

been keenly sensitive to problems of political opposition. For to look at any political system from the point of view of an opposition inclines one to stress the virtues of dissent, of opposing. Yet, the last criterion in our list emphasizes the virtues of stability; and the penultimate criterion, the importance of resolution and dispatch, avoiding deadlock, paralysis, impotence in government. Sensitivity to these criteria leads one to be concerned with the high costs of unlimited dissent and to stress the importance of consensus, particularly if governments willing to protect dissent are to survive" (p. 388, emphasis in original). It follows that in order to fulfill the objectives of democracy, authorities must allow for political challenges but at the same time must limit them when they are violent and/or when they call for displacing the existing authority.

[32] Again, I do not differentiate between forms of conflict here. For example, concerning domestic conflict, Rummel (1997, 133) suggests that if democratic representatives failed to respond with force to domestic violence, they might be "turned out of office for not maintaining order, or for cravenly submitting to violent demands." This is especially the case with violent forms of conflict that are believed to violate "the rules of the game" (O'Kane 1996). As O'Kane puts it, "[i]n democracies, state coercion is used against those who perform illegal acts. The punishment of those found guilty serves to warn of the consequences of future actions for both present and future culprits" (p. 19). Concerning international threats, Stohl (1976) and Rasler (1986, 924) suggest that when a state's position in the international system is threatened, it is more opt to coerce its populations.

[33] It could also be argued that democratic authorities, normally hindered from eliminating challengers, use moments when they are challenged significantly to eliminate rivals who are deemed especially threatening. There are clearly different takes on this theme. Using a psychological approach, Levin (1971, 4) argues that democratic states use political "hysteria" (a passionate crusade to eliminate an imaginary threat) over a relatively concentrated period of time to purge all that is feared within society. Such behavior "exorcises," "cleanses," "renews," and "(re)unifies" a democracy, by design, normally left without a clearly identifiable center or core. This is similar to the psychological and structural argument of Coser (1956).

Conflict Scale   One argument maintains that in situations of conflict the influence of democracy on repression varies according to the magnitude of conflict involved. Here,

Hypothesis 11: When low-level domestic conflict is present, *Voice* and *Veto* are able to decrease state repression but at relatively high levels they are unable to function.

[handwritten margin note: High-level conflict neder voice & veto Ineffectual]

This difference is explained by the fact that within situations of low-level threat, opinion about the government's behavior is more likely fractured/diverse. Fearing a split within the population and the possibility of enacting a policy that is offensive to part of the population, democratic authorities withdraw from repressive activity. By contrast, higher-level conflict is less likely to create divisions in the population. In this context, there is near-unanimous support for those in government to take whatever steps are necessary to reduce the threat, and democratic authorities are more likely to use coercive action.

Political Integrity   Another hypothesis concerns other situations in which opinions could be split and democratic authorities could modify repressive behavior. For example, when democratic states are at war, repressive behavior is likely to decrease because the restrictions and violations of citizens during these moments are highly controversial policies and authorities, preferring to avoid these situations because of the potential costs involved, reduce coercive action. The reasons here vary. First, although some desire to provide an environment in which criticism of foreign policy can be made, others also desire to eliminate all criticism compelling citizens to uniformly support the war effort (rallying around the flag). Second, there is concern for the problem of the "fifth column" such as the American fear during the Cold War that Soviet agents inside the United States would assist the Soviet Union in undermining the domestic political situation. Because many fear that internal collusion with an external enemy can undermine a country's war effort, this generates concern about and support for increasing repression. At the same time, it is clear that the threat of a fifth column could be (and has been) exploited by authorities to eliminate domestic challengers who are not connected with an external enemy but who were otherwise deemed a threat to existing authorities. In short, war can provide cover for a domestic purge. The plausibility of these different arguments and the complexity contained therein lead me to believe that in the context of international conflict repressive behavior would be diminished.

Similarly, when democratic states experience violent dissent such as guerrilla warfare or terrorism (lower-level domestic threats), repression is likely to diminish because the authority's behavior interferes with the freedom of citizens. Clearly opinions on this matter are varied. Some view dissent that is violent as a betrayal of the contract maintained between democratic governments and its citizens; in this situation, "all bets are off," and repression is not only allowed but favored. For others, even violent dissent does not alleviate from democratic authorities the necessity for refraining from repressive action. Again, the plausibility of the different positions and the complexity involved result in state pacification as political leaders attempt to navigate around different positions, avoiding the negative after-effects of harming citizens interests and/or offending their opinions.

By contrast, in times of civil war (an instance of high-level domestic conflict), it is less likely that there will be any disagreement regarding the state's repressive response. For one, those in favor of the challengers can move to reside under the opponent's jurisdiction, and those remaining are likely to be so scared about revealing any sympathy for the enemies of the existing government that they will not speak out. Furthermore, among those remaining within the territory of the established authority, there is likely to be an increased willingness to repress challengers because the safety of the nation is at stake (in a less abstract manner than civil war) and one would wish to signal (in obvious fashion) one's allegiance to the government.[34] In this context,

Hypothesis 12: When low-level domestic conflict and interstate conflict exists, *Voice* and *Veto* are still able to decrease state repression but in the context of high-level domestic conflict they are not.

Hil + inil conflict

---

[34] At first blush, it would appear that interstate and civil war would be similar: both threats are great. What is important for this discussion is the fact that in one situation – interstate war – the enemy is external to the state, and one is discussing the repressive behavior directed against those who may or may not be linked with the enemy but are somewhat sympathetic to the cause. In the other – civil war – the enemy is internal to the state, and one is discussing the repression of those who may or may not be linked with the enemy; nevertheless the possibility of the connection given the way in which these confrontations are fought is much more threatening to the political system of interest. Obviously there are situations where the two overlap. For example, during the interstate/civil war in 1990–3 between the Rwandan Patriotic Front and the Rwandan government, there were references to both dynamics.

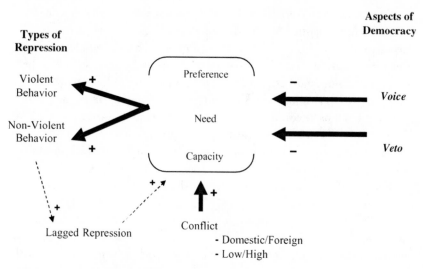

Figure 2.1 Revised Repression Model

Summary

Within this chapter, I outlined a new approach for understanding how democracy might influence state repression and under what circumstances one would likely see a relationship. My perspective is unique in that it leads to a view that is at once more comprehensive and somewhat more complex than that traditionally considered. Figure 2.1 depicts the revised repression model.

As designed, there are three main differences from what I presented in this chapter and the approach generally found within the existing literature.

First, I argued that different types of repression are used by political authorities: restrictions of civil liberty (for example, political bans, curfews, and limitations on association) and violations of personal integrity (for example, torture, disappearances and mass killing): each is employed toward distinct ends, and each is subject to different costs and benefits. As a consequence, in order to understand when repressive behavior will be employed, it is essential to incorporate this more comprehensive view of available tactics into our investigations. This is especially the case because of the two forms of state coercion; it is violent activity that is most likely to be influenced by democratic institutions.

Second, I identified that there are essentially two different aspects of political democracy that influence repressive behavior: *Voice* – a mass-oriented characteristic such as the popular vote – and *Veto* – an elite-oriented characteristic such as the number of restrictions placed on the executive. Both will theoretically have an impact on state repression; however, after a careful evaluation, I suggested that the former would be better at decreasing state coercive activity. Essentially, this is explained by three factors: (1) although elites have an interest in protecting constituents, there are circumstances under which these interests could be diminished; (2) ordinary citizens have more at stake in regulating state repressive behavior because they are likely the ones targeted by such activity; and (3) the political inclusiveness associated with *Voice* offers authorities an alternative mechanism of sociopolitical control that the elite competitiveness associated with *Veto* does not.

Finally, I argued that the peace proposition is most likely context-specific. For example, when faced with political conflict such as violent dissent or civil and interstate war, it is expected that the pacification associated with democracy is overwhelmed as authorities respond to behavioral challenges. In these contexts, the peace brought by democratic institutions is weakened and/or completely removed. When there are no threats to the political system and/or its members, however, democracy is able to reduce repressive action and serve as a mechanism of peace. Without considering the confounding influence of conflict, one is apt to misunderstand what takes place.

Within the next chapter, I outline my research design and discuss the data as well as the methodological technique used for the statistical analysis. The results from these investigations are provided in Chapters 4 and 5.

3

Data and Methodology

In this chapter, I discuss the measures used to operationalize political repression. Additionally, I discuss the diverse explanatory factors employed in the statistical analyses to test the hypotheses developed in the previous chapter: lagged repression, the difference from regional repressive behavior, diverse forms of political conflict (violent dissent as well as civil and interstate war), and development/modernization (GNP per capita and population size). These variables are used to establish the basic repression model, which is examined with ordered probit, the methodological technique used throughout the book. Following this, the different measures employed to operationalize political democracy (*Voice* and *Veto*) are reviewed. Chapter 4 continues the statistical analysis by investigating the direct influence of democracy on repression. In Chapter 5, I assess interactive relationships between democracy and political conflict as they influence repressive behavior.

Measurement

The measurement strategy that one adopts is intricately connected with the research question that one is interested in. As my concern is with the general influence of specific democratic political institutions on state repression, I am interested in what is commonly referred to as a large-*N*, cross-national examination. Now, it is clear, operationalization across time and space is always a precarious enterprise. Inherently, some do not believe that it is possible to derive valid measures across large numbers of countries because all are unique. Others appear to accept the approach, maintaining that as long as one is careful about what as well as how they measure relevant variables and how they conduct examinations, useful analyses are possible.

When attempting to measure social, economic, and political phenomena, it is important to be as precise as possible about the concept one is measuring. Additionally, it is important to be as clear as possible about exactly how the underlying concept is connected to the specific values of the relevant indicator (Adcock and Collier 2001). Toward this end, I sought measurements that (1) provided global coverage over a relatively large amount of time (from 1976 to 1996) and most countries of the world (137 countries); (2) are generally considered reliable as well as valid by researchers who specialize in the phenomena of interest; and (3) captured the distinct aspects of the particular variables of interest. Next I discuss the different measures beginning with the dependent variable.

State Repression

With regard to operationalizing this variable, two measures proved to be ideal: restriction on civil liberties provided by Freedom House and personal integrity violations provided by Gibney as well as by Poe and Tate.[1] I use a combination of these data in order to create my dependent variable – the lethality of repressive behavior. Each component is discussed individually and then in combination.[2]

---

[1] Both of the measures identified here have been discussed numerous times with regard to their validity and reliability, and thus I will not go into too much detail. For Freedom House, see Bollen 1986, 85–6; Goldstein 1986, 620; McCamant 1981, 32; Munck and Verkulien 2002, 24; Stohl et al. 1986, 599; for the Political Terror Scale measure from Poe and Tate (1994) see, Poe et al. 1999.

[2] To be clear, there are diverse ways to assess the quality of repression data. Because the data in this area of research are not as well known as other conflict data, despite thirty-five years of history, it is worthwhile to discuss briefly. First, diverse measures can be compared against each other. Second, diverse measures can be compared against some other source of information (for example, narrative/eyewitness accounts, topical expert). Third, the influence of diverse explanatory factors can be compared across distinct measures. The first has been conducted but only in a few cases and with only a few repression variables. This research discloses a high-degree of similarity across data, suggesting that the measures are generally tapping the same phenomenon. The second has rarely been attempted in repression research – especially in a rigorous manner (see Davenport and Ball 2002, for an important exception). Research here discloses that diverse sources generally point in the same direction but there are important differences. For example, differences are less likely when behavior exceeds particular thresholds (for example, size and scope) and when the behavior is undertaken in public. The third has not been examined, explicitly, but one can draw upon existing research to address this issue. Across measures, historical periods, places, and methodologies, similar explanatory variables yield comparable influences on the respective categories of restrictions and personal integrity violations. This allows us to have a significant amount of confidence that the available measurements, for each type of repression, are both valid and reliable.

Data and Methodology

Restrictions As discussed in the last chapter, one repressive strategy consistently used by governments against those within their territorial jurisdiction involves constraints on political behavior. Authorities, that is, employ a wide range of techniques aimed at inhibiting and/or interferring with the ability of citizens to enjoy specific rights and/or to mobilize in a collective manner. These include a wide range of activities such as imposing political bans and curfews, censoring speech, and engaging in mass arrests.

To measure this activity, I use the "civil liberties" indicator developed by Freedom House (Karatnycky 1999), by far the most widely utilized measure for relevant behavior in the literature.[3] As designed, "[t]he checklist for civil liberties begins with a requirement for free and independent media, literature and other cultural expression" Freedom House (1991–2, 86–7). "The checklist also includes the rights to have open public discussion and free private discussion, and freedom of assembly and demonstration," as well as "whether citizens are equal under the law, have access to an independent, nondiscriminatory judiciary, and are respected by (protected from) the security forces" (Freedom House 1991–2, 87). The importance of political authorities is crucial for this determination. As stated by Freedom House, "Civil liberties are the freedoms to develop views, institutions and personal autonomy apart from the state" (Freedom House 1991– 2, 66).

Specifically, the Freedom House civil liberties measure has seven values. These are provided in Table 3.1, along with a discussion of the particular level (that is, how one would know it when they saw it) as well as a few illustrative examples. The information used to create this indicator is derived from a thirteen-question survey[4] given to "a broad range of international sources . . . including both foreign and domestic news reports, NGO

---

[3] The Freedom House measure has recently been used as an indicator of political democracy, but it was initially used and essentially created to measure state repression and human rights (Goldstein 1986; McCammant 1981; Stohl et al. 1986). Indeed, the U.S. State Department used it to develop its own human rights status reports (Scoble and Weisberg 1981, 152); and Gastil (the creator of the measure) identifies that what they do at the organization is comparable to the work of other human rights organizations such as Amnesty International (Gastil cited in Scoble and Weisberg 1981, 162). According to Gastil, "Civil rights are the rights of the individual against the state, rights to free expression, to a fair trial; they are what most of us mean by freedom" (Gastil 1973, 5). The measure thus captures an outcome of a political process and allows one to evaluate whether or not a particular nation-state is "free" (that is, not repressed in a negative rights manner). This does not capture the process by which one could achieve freedom (that is, political democracy as conceived by Dahl, Schumpeter, and others).

[4] These questions are provided within the Freedom House yearly review (for example, Karatnycky 1999, 548–9):

Table 3.1. *Measuring Civil Liberties Restrictions*

Value	Description	Examples
1	Those countries that "come closest to the ideals expressed in the civil liberties checklist,[a] including freedom of expression, assembly, association, and religion" (Karatnycky 1999, 551)	Countries within this category include the United States, Trinidad between 1987 and 1993, and Japan from 1976 to 1990
2	A situation in which the country has "deficiencies in three of four aspects of civil liberties,[b] but are still relatively free" (Karatnycky 1999, 551)	Examples here include Costa Rica 1993–6, Gambia 1976–80, and Poland 1990–6
3, 4, 5	Range from those that are in at least partial compliance with virtually all checklist standards to those with a combination of high or medium scores for some questions and low or very low scores on other questions" (Karatnycky 1999, 551)	Respectively, examples include Nigeria 1978–83, Guatemala 1977–8, and Hungary 1977–86
6, 7	The score of 6 denotes a situation where there are few rights, and a score of 7 denotes a situation where there is "virtually no freedom" (Karatnycky 1999, 552)	Respectively, examples include Haiti 1976–85 and Congo (Kinshasa) 1982–8

[a] The information used to create this measure is derived from a survey in which of "a broad range of international sources of information [are consulted], including both foreign and domestic news reports, NGO publications, think tank and academic analyses, and individual professional contacts" (Karatnycky 1999, 546).
[b] For example, if a country experiences a deterioration in the freedom of expression, association, and assembly, then this score would be moved to this category.

Freedom of Expression and Belief –

1. Are there free and independent media and other forms of cultural expression?
2. Are there free religious institutions and is there free private and public religious expression?

Association and Organizational Rights –

3. Is there freedom of assembly, demonstration, and open public discussion?
4. Is there freedom of political or quasi-political organization?
5. Are there free trade organizations and peasant organizations or equivalents, and is there effective collective bargaining? Are there free professional and other private organizations?

Rule of Law and Human Rights –

6. Is there an independent judiciary?
7. Does the rule of law prevail in civil and criminal matters, is the population treated equally under the law, are police under direct civilian control?
8. Is there protection from political terror, unjustified imprisonment, exile, or torture, whether by groups that support or oppose the system, is there freedom from war and insurgencies?

publications, think tank and academic analyses, and individual professional contacts" (Karatnycky 1999, 546). The responses from this survey are then codified according to the decision rules outlined earlier.[5]

In addition to this form of repression, I also consider another type of behavior as well.

Violence Perhaps the most feared repressive strategy used by authorities involves political imprisonment, physical torture, disappearance, and mass killing.[6] In measuring of this concept, I use an indicator that is generally considered to be the most valid and the one that is the most widely employed in the literature. Specifically, I use the "personal integrity violation" measure [known as the Political Terror Scale (PTS)] conceived and initially coded by a number of scholars (e.g., Carleton and Stohl 1985; Gibney and Dalton 1996) but popularized by Steve Poe and C. Neal Tate (1994) as well as others affiliated with this research program (see, for example Keith 1999; 2002; Poe, Tate, and Keith 1999; Zanger 2000).[7]

Personal Autonomy and Economic Rights –

9. Is there open and free private discussion?
10. Is there personal autonomy? Does the state control travel, choice of residence, or choice of employment? Is there freedom from indoctrination and excessive dependency on the state?
11. Are property rights secure? Do citizens have the right to establish private businesses? Is private business activity unduly influenced by government officials, the security forces, or organized crime?
12. Are there personal social freedoms, including gender equality, choice of marriage partners, and size of family?
13. Is there equality of opportunity, including freedom from exploitation by or dependency on landlords, employers, union leaders, bureaucrats, or other types of obstacles to a share of legitimate economic gains?

[5] In contrast to the civil liberties indicator, the measure for political liberties has been severely criticized for its lack of clarity and inadequate coding rules. See, for example, Bollen 1986, 85–6; Cingranelli and Richards 1999; Goldstein 1986, 620; McCamant 1981; Munck and Verkuilen 2001, 24; Poe and Tate 1994; Scoble and Wiseberg 1981. It was also argued that there was a strong political bias within the political liberties measure toward the United States, their allies, and those with which it had some form of connection (monetary or otherwise). It is generally believed that after the removal of Gastil from the organization (in the mid-1980s), the quality of the data was significantly improved, but this issue has not been discussed explicitly.

[6] I do not consider the "outsourcing" of personal integrity violations (i.e., when one country sends individuals to another country to be tortured).

[7] These data went to 1993 but through personal correspondence with the creators I was able to obtain data through 1996. Following standard procedure, I employ the State Department data using the Amnesty International data to fill missing values.

The PTS measure is derived from a systematic coding of Amnesty International and State Department country reports for which the research team reads the various documents and affixes numerical codes to diverse aspects of repression (for example, the type of activities that are generally used, as well as the frequency and scope with which these activities are undertaken). Specifically, the measure has five values.[8] The coding categories and their criteria are provided in Table 3.2.

Repressive Lethality   To construct my dependent variable, I overlay the violence and restriction measures presented above.[9] Specifically, I use the information provided by the two data projects in order to classify low, medium, and high values. In the case of Freedom House, the categories include 1 and 2 for the lowest levels of restriction, 3, 4, and 5 for the moderate/middle-range applications, and 6 and 7 for the highest levels. Across the same categories, the values for the PTS include 1 and 2 for the lowest levels of violation, 3 for the moderate application, and 4 and 5 for the highest levels. This yields nine types of repressive behavior. Table 3.3 provides the different combinations as well as a few illustrative examples.

Even though there are diverse ways to arrange the different combinations (Davenport 2004), I have ranked the nine categories by the degree of lethality involved (the magnitude of violence); the value assigned to each combination is identified in the upper-left corner of the cell. As a result, the least repressive category (where both restrictions and violence were low or nonexistent) was labeled 1, the second least repressive strategy (where violence was low but restrictions were at moderate levels) was labeled 2, and so on until category 9 (where both restrictions and violence were high).

---

[8] This indicator found that State Department and Amnesty International country reports were initially biased toward the right and left, respectively, in their evaluations of different countries around the globe. This converges over time as the evaluations of the two organizations have moved closer to one another. Changing the source of the data does not alter the results of the analyses reported here.

[9] One could argue that the two indicators overlap in certain respects. For example, Poe and Tate pay attention to political imprisonment and trial activity while Freedom House pays attention to similar items. Additionally, the authors of the Freedom House measure do consider political violence at extremely high levels, albeit inconsistently. Despite potential similarities, the two indicators correlate at .54, and conceptually these areas of interest are distinct enough to draw meaningful distinctions. In contrast, Keith (1999) maintains that they do represent distinct dimensions but does not consider their combinations (preferring to examine them individually).

Data and Methodology

Table 3.2. *Measuring Personal Integrity Violations*

Value	Description	Example
1	Within this category, countries are under a secure rule of law, people are not imprisoned for their views, torture is rare or exceptional . . . , [and] political murders are extremely infrequent (Poe, Tate, and Keith 1999, 297)	The United States, Venezuela 1977 and 1981, and Senegal 1976–81
2	There is a limited amount of imprisonment for nonviolent political activity. However, few persons are affected, torture and beating are exceptional . . . political murder is rare (Poe, Tate, and Keith 1999, 297)	Mexico 1976 and 1983 as well as Gambia 1982
3	There is extensive political imprisonment or a recent history of such imprisonment. Execution or other political murders and brutality may be common. Unlimited detention, with or without trial, for political views is accepted[a]	Cuba 1976, Cameroon 1979, and Poland 1976–7
4	The practices of [Level 3] are expanded to larger numbers. Murders and disappearances are a common part of life. . . . In spite of its generality, on this level terror affects primarily those who interest themselves in politics or ideas	El Salvador 1978–92 and Rwanda 1990–1
5	The terrors of [Level 4] have been expanded to the whole population. . . . The leaders of these societies place no limits on the means or thoroughness with which they pursue personal or ideological goals.	Haiti 1991, Sudan 1988, Rwanda 1994–6 and China 1989

[a] The Current situation in Guantanamo would not be placed in this category because the sheer scope of the activity is not extensive.

I chose this approach because I believe that the combinations identified in the table are distinct from one another and that the explanations underlying their use are unique. This schema captures my assumption that authorities prefer to increase political restrictions before escalating violence because they perceive the latter to be politically more costly, provoking domestic and international pressure to change the practice, as well as reducing legitimacy across the same audiences. The alternatives identified in the table clearly reflect what is deemed important to various parties: those subject to these

81

Table 3.3. *Alternative Strategies of State Repression*

	Political Terror Scale Dimension		
	No/Low Violence	Medium Levels of Violence	High Levels of Violence
No/Low Restrictions	(1) Examples: Argentina 1984 and 1986–9, India 1977–9, France 1976–96 ($N = 659; 23\%$)	(4) Examples: Angola 1976, Chile 1990–92 ($N = 19; < 1\%$)	(7) Examples: Philippines 1986, South Africa 1995–6 ($N = 45; 1\%$)
Medium Levels of Restriction	(2) Examples: Bulgaria 1990–2, Mexico 1976 and 1983 ($N = 603; 21\%$)	(5) Examples: Haiti 1979, South Korea 1977, Sudan 1979 ($N = 398; 13\%$)	(8) Examples: India 1985, Nicaragua 1979 ($N = 235; 8\%$)
High Levels of Restriction	(3) Examples: Bulgaria 1979–80, Ghana 1984–8, Qatar 1992–6 ($N = 312; 10\%$)	(6) Examples: Burundi 1986, Cambodia 1978–81, Cuba 1976 ($N = 284; 9\%$)	(9) Examples: China 1989, Guatemala 1980–4, Rwanda 1994–6 ($N = 302; 10\%$)

Legend: $N =$ number of cases; due to rounding the total does not sum to 100%.

activities (citizens), those who seek to protect individuals from such activity (human rights NGOs), and those drafting documents to guide state behavior toward more pacific treatment of citizens (international law). Essentially, all of these actors are interested in reducing the "repressiveness" of political authorities within a country, privileging the existence of life relative to the constraints on life.

It is readily apparent that during the period under investigation (1976 to 1996) most authorities were pacific in nature and fell into the lowest category (1). Consideration of the two lowest categories (1 and 2) accounts for 44 percent of the cases, whereas consideration of the three lowest categories (1–3) accounts for 54 percent of the cases. By contrast, states rarely used low levels of restriction in combination with either moderate (category 4) or higher degrees of violence (category 7). Indeed, the low number of cases in these combinations frequently prevents me from rigorously investigating these repressive techniques. Comparatively fewer governments apply moderate levels of violence with either moderate or high levels of restriction (categories 5 and 6, which account for approximately 13 and 9 percent of the cases, respectively). Even fewer governments can be found at the highest levels of violence with either moderate or high levels of restriction (categories 8 and 9, which account for approximately 8 and 10 percent of the cases, respectively). All told, the four strategies just identified account for approximately 40 percent of the cases in the dataset.

Interestingly, when one considers change over time, the general trend does not conform with popular opinion. Considering the mean, although decreasing for a year in 1978 and increasing for four years (between 1991 and 1994), the lethality of state repressive behavior was almost constant over the relevant period at value 3 (low violence but high restriction).

In the next section, I identify the independent variables employed within the statistical analysis.

Identifying, Measuring, and Assessing the Base Model

Political conflict and socioeconomic development/modernization are inextricably bound up with the assessment of democracy on repression. Indeed, in order to understand how democratic institutions influence repressive behavior, one must first understand how these variables influence state coercion.

Political Conflict

Although the problem of order is an ancient concern (Blalock 1989; Eisenstadt 1971; Hobbes 1950; Liska 1992; Tilly 1978; Tilly et al. 1975; Wrong 1994), it is only in the last thirty-five years that scholars have systematically focused on it – on how behavioral challenges (protest, strikes, civil war, and interstate war) and previous repression prompt political authorities to respond with state repression (see, for example, Cingranelli and Richards 1999; Davenport 1995a;1995b; Goldstein 1978; Harff 2003; Hibbs 1973; Krain 1997; Markus and Nesvold 1972).

The basic logic here is simple. Authorities are assumed to prefer political order (quiescence, obedience, and active political support) to disorder (mass unrest) because it influences the perception of government legitimacy and performance. When the status quo is challenged,[10] those in government

---

[10] These empirical findings were viewed distinctly in the introduction and Chapter 1, for the discussion there was concerned with the impact of specific explanatory variables, not distinct explanations of general categories used in the examination of state repression. It should be clear: to my knowledge, I am the only one in this literature who has placed commonly

may expand efforts to stabilize the situation by applying coercion. Repression serves two objectives. First, authorities believe it to be an effective means of maintaining social control over a wide variety of contexts, times, and places. Second, the state is prepared and, indeed, designed for the application of coercive action, as it holds the monopoly on the legitimate use of force. As a result, some satisfaction is derived from fulfilling one of the primary objectives of the organization.

In line with this argument, every investigation of the topic finds that behavioral challenge increases repression. Measures for political (dis)order have taken two forms: (1) the number of times that challenges occur (see, for example, Davenport 1995b; Hibbs 1973; King 1998) or (2) the type of events such as violent dissent (see, for example, Davenport 1995; Ziegenhagen 1986). Although variables generally concern lower level conflict behavior within the country of interest, some attention has also been given to civil and interstate war (Poe and Tate 1994).[11] These variables have consistently influenced repression in a manner consistent with the political disorder argument.

The influence of another variable – lagged repression – has also largely been supportive of the political order argument. The explanation for this is clear. For example, as Gurr (1986, 160) tells us,

[o]nce [specialized agencies of state coercion and terror] are in operation (i.e., repression has been used), elites are likely to calculate that the relative costs of relying on coercion are lower.... [As he continues these] strategic considerations tend to be reinforced by habituation; in other words, the development of elite norms that coercive control is not only necessary but desirable. Moreover, a bureaucratic "law of the instrument" may prevail: The professional ethos of agencies of control centers on the use of coercion to restrain challenges to state authority. [The] directors [of these organizations] may therefore recommend violent "solutions" to suspected opposition, or use their position to initiate them, as a means of justifying the agencies' continued existence.

employed variables into distinct theoretical traditions. Most view the independent variables in the unparsimonious manner criticized by Eckstein (1980). It is reasonable though that the seemingly eclectic combination of variables employed within these analyses emerges from well-known traditions within the fields of comparative politics and international relations even though many working in the subfield do so without acknowledging it.

[11] Although seemingly quite different, interstate war has been seen as a source of political repression as political leaders under international threats have to concern themselves with those who would challenge the war effort as well as those who would side with the external enemies (see, for example, Goldstein 1978; Stam 1996; Stohl 1976).

Data and Methodology

Again, the results in support of this argument have been stable across analyses. In every investigation of the topic, prior repressive behavior increases subsequent repressive activity.

Following from this discussion and following the standard practice within the repression literature, I employ the following variables to operationalize political disorder:

1. Violent dissent conflict including guerrilla warfare ("any armed activity, sabotage, or bombings carried on by independent bands of citizens or irregular forces and aimed at the overthrow of the present regime") and riots ("any violent demonstration or clash of more than 100 citizens involving the use of force")[12] as measured by Banks (2001) – these are scored as 1 when either is present and 0 when they are not.

2. Civil war (large-scale internal violent behavior with clearly defined combatants, one of which involves the state, that yields one thousand battle-deaths per event)[13] and interstate war (large-scale external violent behavior with clearly defined combatants, both of which involve internationally acknowledged states, that yield one thousand battle-deaths per event) as measured by the Correlates of War project (Singer and Small 1994) – these are scored as a 1 when either is present and 0 when they are not.

In addition to these variables, I consider measures of lagged repression and regional repressive activity as they represent a different form of conflict. These require a bit more explanation, however, than the measurements just identified.

Lagged Repression In an effort to operationalize this variable, the uncritical researcher could simply lag the ordinal variable and include the new variable as an independent variable within estimated equations. However, if the dependent variable is "ordinal enough" that one cannot assume its

---

[12] These definitions were provided by the *Cross-National Time-Series Data Archive* (www.databanks.sitehosting.net/).

[13] For detailed discussion of the problems with this conceptualization, see Sambanis (2004). Because the sheer number of civil wars during the 1976–96 period is relatively low, the varying coding rules observed the diverse civil war projects do not yield much of an influence on my results. Future investigations of my statistical analyses shall consider different measures of civil war and armed conflict.

categories are evenly spaced (thereby legitimizing the use of ordinary least squares regression), then they cannot justify making that assumption about the same measure when using it as an independent variable. Another reasonable way to deal with this problem is to lag the repression measure by creating dummy variables for each of the k categories, and include $k - 1$ of them as independent variables. I conducted a test of these two different alternatives to ascertain which operationalization of the lagged indicator was most appropriate.[14] Appendix 1 contained on the webpage affiliated with this project presents the coefficients and measures of fit for both models (Tables 1 in Appendix 1).[15] When examined, the difference in the likelihood ratios[16] suggests that the model with the dummy variables is better.[17] This is corroborated by the difference in the Bayesian Information Criterion (hereafter BIC) between the two models.[18]

I now move to consider a different aspect of coercive action.

Deviation from Regional Repression To measure this behavior I simply identified the mean level of repression within the relevant geographic region and gauged the difference between this value and the country of interest (identified in Table 2 of Appendix 1). This scheme seems appropriate because it appears as if the most important element about the coercive activity of surrounding countries was not simply whether neighbors used a

---

[14] Assume for the time being that regional repression can accurately be captured by the regional mean (an assumption that will be addressed below).

[15] Provide URL@cambridge.org

[16] With seven degrees of freedom, $p < .000$, this yields a score of approximately 424.

[17] When the models are compared, the results suggest "very strong" support for the model with the lagged dummy variables compared to the model with the lagged continuous dependent variable. I follow the suggestion of these tests and use the lagged dummy measure for my investigation.

[18] The BIC, occasionally referred to as the Schwarz Criterion, is used to assess model fit among nonnested models (Congdon 2003; Gill 2001; Long 1997; Long and Freese 2001; Raftery 1995). The BIC is defined as $BIC = D + p \log e(n)$, where D refers to the deviance of the model, p is the number of estimated parameters, including the constant, and n is the sample size. This measure of fit imposes a penalty for increasing the number of variables in the model, which makes it superior to using only the likelihood or some function thereof. BIC statistics, similar to log-likelihoods, are not meaningful in and of themselves. They acquire meaning only when compared BICs from other models. One of the advantages to the use of this measure is the relatively straightforward guidelines used to interpret differences in BIC statistics. Given to models 1 and 2, if $BIC1 - BIC2 < 0$, then model 1 is preferred. If $BIC1 - BIC2 > 0$ then model 2 is preferred. The magnitude of this difference can be interpreted as follows. Subtracting $BIC1 - BIC2$: if the difference is 0–2, then support is "Weak"; 2–6 equals "Positive"; 6–10 equals "Strong"; and, > 10 equals "Very Strong" (Raftery 1995, 139).

great deal or very little state repression. Rather, it seemed most important to identify where a specific country existed relative to that mean.

Here, I envision that repressive behavior does not simply signal and prompt domestic actors about relative power capabilities but that it also signals international actors as well. Consequently, actors would generally like to use repressive behavior about the same as those around them, lest they trigger some form of response in the form of a boycott, denouncement, or militarization of the border. Thus, for example, if a government applied repression far above the mean, then they would be influenced by neighbors in one way (pulling it down), but if a government applied repression far below the mean, then they would be influenced by neighbors in a different way (pulling it up). To gauge this, I created a measure of regional repression and subtracted the mean from the level of repression in a given year.

A second explanation for state repression used consistently within the literature comes from development/modernization theory (Apter 1965; Burkhart and Lewisbeck 1994; Coleman 1960; Cutright 1963; Huber, Rueschemeyer, and Stephens 1993; Lipset 1959). This is addressed below.

Socioeconomic Development/Modernization According to existing research, states apply repressive behavior because they possess no viable alternatives for control and there are good reasons to expect political instability. By this logic, when societies are poor and populations are large (that is, when they are less "developed" or "modern"), fewer resources are available for influence such as bribery, higher wages, and welfare payments (see, for example, Dallin and Breslauer 1970). Lacking these strategies, political authorities are compelled to rely upon state repression. Additionally, when societies are poor and populations are large, it is likely that citizens would be dissatisfied with this situation and predisposed toward joining movements seeking to challenge or transform the political-economic situation. As a preventive measure, therefore, authorities use repressive behavior in these situations as well (see, for example, Henderson 1991; Mitchell and McCormick 1988, 478).

Largely following other research in comparative politics and international relations, measures for economic development/modernization have been relatively consistent over time and across studies. Most researchers use per capita gross national product (GNP) (see, for example, Poe and Tate 1994), energy consumption (see, for example, Davenport 1995b), or population (see, for example, Henderson 1991) in an effort to proxy the economic and demographic conditions. Support for the development/modernization argument in quantitative investigations is generally mixed. Population increases repression in every single case, but economic development/modernization is less consistent. Indeed, with reference to the latter system characteristic, some find positive influences, some find negative influences, and some find no influence at all (see, for example, Harrelson-Stephens and Callaway 2003).[19]

[19] Other economic characteristics reveal similar variability. Within the literature, several authors have found a positive effect of trade on state repression, supporting the dependency argument (Carleton 1989; Davenport 1995b; 1996a; Pion-Berlin 1989; Ziegenhagen 1986). Others have found a positive relationship (again supporting dependency theory), but only within particular contexts (Alfatooni and Allen 1991). Mitchell and McCormick (1988) find that extensive trade and investment are associated with increasing some forms of human rights abuse, but that the relationship between these variables and state repression disappears when they control for population size. Still others have found no effect at all (see, for example, Rothgeb 1989; Timberlake and Williams 1984). Two recent studies have expanded the domain of inquiry into the economic ties – human rights question beyond previous analysis (Apodaca 2001; Richards, Gelleny, and Sacko 2001). Differing from the works identified previously, these studies both lend support to the Liberal position, deviating from most other research. Apodaca (2001, 292) looks at the impact of both trade and investment on human rights for a broad group of developing nations and transitional economies of Eastern Europe during the period 1990–6.

Unfortunately, the limited nature of her spatial and temporal domain makes it difficult for us to generalize to a broader set of cases. Richards, Gelleny, and Sacko (2001), who find that investment improves human rights (that is, it decreases repression), also focus exclusively on developing states, again limiting our ability to generalize their results. Additionally, this work is limited temporally (they include only the years 1981, 1984, 1987, 1990, 1993, and 1995 in their analysis of the 1981–95 period) as well as conceptually (trade dependence is not considered in this analysis).

Other scholars have investigated the subject in yet another manner by focusing on the role of multinational corporations (MNCs) and foreign direct investment (FDI) in influencing state repression. For example, Meyer (1996) focuses on whether MNC presence decreases human rights violations. He examines two disparate views about the presence of MNCs: (1) what he terms "the engines of development thesis" (where MNCs stimulate economic growth and development, which are conductive to human rights) largely in line with the Liberal argument, and (2) "the Hymer thesis" (where the negative consequences of an extensive MNC presence), which is similar in many respects to the dependency position (Meyer 1996, 378). In examining these competing propositions, Meyer concludes that the evidence supports the Liberal view that foreign direct investment improves human rights. Unfortunately (again), his research is based on a limited analysis. This study includes a cross-sectional analysis for only two points in time – the years 1985 and 1990. In addition, Meyer focuses his attention exclusively on developing nations and considers only the impact of U.S. FDI.

While modifying Meyer's measures, but still analyzing a similar set of cases, Smith, Bolyard, and Ippolito (1999) also investigate the impact of MNCs, but their research departs significantly from the Liberal vision identified by Meyer. Smith et al. remind us that MNCs have frequently "provided economic and military assistance to antidemocratic

Data and Methodology

To operationalize the relevant variables, I follow the dominant approach in the literature and employ the following measure:

The log of total population size and per capita GNP provided by the database compiled by Poe, Tate, and Keith (1999).

Having discussed the variables used within the statistical analysis, I now discuss the method employed for examining the data.

Methodological Techniques

Ordered Probit

Within the existing repression literature, ordinary least squares (OLS) regression is commonly used to assess causal relationships (Davenport 1995a; 1995b; 1999; Henderson 1991; Hibbs 1973; Mitchell and McCormick 1988; Poe and Tate 1994; Poe, Tate, and Keith 1999; Zanger 2000; Ziegenhagen 1986) – this mirrors the dominant tradition applied within most quantitative social science research. In the area of repressive behavior, many suggest that this might not be appropriate when an ordinal dependent variable such as the one discussed in this study is employed (e.g., Richards 1999). In these contexts, ordered probit is more appropriate (see, for example, Long 1997).[20]

Ordered probit models are relevant here because they permit estimation of the probability that nation-years will fall within a particular category of repressive behavior. Specifically, the analysis estimates the coefficients corresponding to each of my independent variables and the threshold parameters separating adjacent categories of repressive combinations. Estimates thus provide the underlying probability that states fall within a particular category (1–9), based in part on the explanatory factors included in the

governments" and when they have supported repressive labor practices (Smith, Bolyard, and Ippolito 1999, 208). Moreover, these scholars point to the questionable empirical basis for the Liberal assumption that FDI is always an engine of development or that development necessarily means better human rights standards. Using different measures for the central variables of interest, this study finds "that the logic of capitalism produces investment decisions indifferent, or possibly antithetical, to human rights" (Smith, Bolyard, and Ippolito 1999, 219).

[20] For discussions of ordered analysis, see Greene (2000). Within the analysis, I acknowledge that this represents merely one way that repressive categories could be examined and I also have left them unranked, investigating them with a multinomial logit. The findings are comparable and thus I am confident that the selected categories are not problematic.

model and in part on the unobserved factors influencing the distribution of states on the repression measure discussed previously.

There is an added benefit to using this methodological technique. Observing "cut points" for each model, one can assess the threshold parameters between categories of the ordinal variable (Long 1997, 118–19). The cut points provide us with information about the continuous nature of the dependent variable and additionally about the appropriateness of other methodological techniques (in this case OLS regression). As designed, if thresholds are about the same distance apart, then it is reasonable to assume that the measure was continuous and that OLS regression would be appropriate. If thresholds are not evenly spaced, however (as was consistently identified in this study), then it is not reasonable to use other techniques.

An important difference between ordered probit and others (such as OLS) concerns the interpretation of the results. As frequently noted within statistical textbooks, because the effects of the independent variable are assumed to be nonlinear, we cannot interpret the parameter estimates directly. This is important because influence might vary across values of repression. For instance, we would not expect democracy to influence all categories of the dependent variable employed within this study in a negative manner. Instead, we would expect lower values of repression to be influenced positively, with democracy increasing the likelihood that the least repressive categories would be used. At the same time, we would expect higher values of repression to be influenced negatively, with democracy decreasing the likelihood of the most repressive categories. This is consistent with the argument that democracy generally reduces repression, but it also acknowledges that when distinct categories ranging from low to high lethality are considered, the direction of the causal influences will vary.[21]

There are essentially two possibilities for how democracy could function in this framework. On the one hand, a strong version of the argument would be that democracy positively influences category 1 repression (where both restriction and violence are low) while negatively influencing the other categories. Here, democratic governments promote the least restrictive and violent state policies adopted while discouraging all others.

---

[21] This is not the case with all variables. For instance, we would expect that lower values of repression would be influenced negatively by dissent and higher values would be influenced positively.

Data and Methodology

On the other hand, a somewhat weaker version stipulates that democracies increase the likelihood of achieving the lowest categories (e.g., 1 and 2) while decreasing the likelihood that higher categories will occur. Here, democratic government promotes two distinct repressive strategies that are relatively less restrictive and violent but again reduces all other approaches to state repression.

The technique of estimation identified previously is not only appropriate given the research question of interest and structure of the dependent variable but also especially useful when one anticipates that nonlinear relationships exist between repression and democracy. For example, Davenport and Armstrong (2004) find that democracy influences repression in a nonlinear fashion, specifically, that at lower levels of democracy (measured by a cumulative polity index created by Polity as well as the modified version of Vanhanen's Competition/Participation indicator, which is discussed later) there was substantively no influence on repressive behavior. Relatively high values of democracy, however, diminished repression and the highest value of democracy reduced this behavior even further. Even though the approach adopted in this book does not allow me to assess the varied influence of democracy across its full range (at each value of the democracy measure), it does allow me to assess the varied influence of democracy on diverse forms of state repression.

The implications for established models are fairly straightforward. If relationships were linear, the causal influence would move from positive to negative across the nine values of the dependent variable.[22] If nonlinearities existed, however, we would observe greater instability in causal influence as we moved across the nine values of the dependent variable (for example, when the relevant democratic characteristic is changed from its minimum to its maximum, 1, 2, and 3 are negatively influenced; 4 and 5 are positively influenced; and 6 through 9 are negatively influenced).

When utilizing ordered probit, one must be aware of the specific problems that plague the type of data employed in this study (for example, data on diverse countries viewed over time). Thus, for example, to address the fact that observations are likely independent across countries (between South Africa and Rwanda) but not within them (Rwanda in 1993 and 1994), I use the Huber/White/Sandwich estimator of variance when estimating models. This allows me to obtain robust standard errors. Additionally, the use of a lagged dependent variable not only permits me to assess the

---

[22] This assumes that the distance between values was even.

importance of political order for subsequent state repressive activity but also assists me in addressing any temporal dependencies that exist within the data.[23]

Seeking to understand and communicate how different explanatory factors influence the diverse categories of repression (across equations), I calculate the predicted probabilities of achieving a particular combination of restrictive and violent repressive behavior, given a movement of a specific independent variable from its minimum to maximum value (holding other variables at a specific value, normally the median). Predicted probabilities are useful because standard statistical results merely provide statistical significance but do not help with understanding substantive influence. Probabilities, by contrast, help us assess the substantive impact of an independent variable on state repression such that we can understand the magnitude of relevant influences. This is the technique applied throughout the remainder of the book.

Results are also communicated in another way. As discussed earlier, I assess the influence of some aspect of democracy on repressive lethality as the former is increased from its minimum to its maximum. While influential in getting a general understanding of relationships, this does not consider the fact that governments do not start at the same level of repression. Some governments might have previously been using coercive behavior that was low in political violence but moderate in restrictions (at level 2) – Turkey between 1976 and 1979, Haiti in 1986, or Ecuador between 1994 and 1996 – whereas others might be high in violence but moderate in restrictions (at level 8) – Iran between 1977 and 1978, Brazil between 1990 and 1996, Haiti in 1994, South Africa between 1989 and 1994, and Rwanda in 1993. These are very different contexts and represent extremely different scenarios within which democracy is expected to have an impact. To address this issue of diverse starting points, I consider the most likely value of current repression (that is, at time t), given a specific value of previous repression (that is, at time $t - 1$).

Understanding the Base Model

With an ordered probit model, the relative importance of political order and development/modernization for state repression is provided below.

---

[23] At present, there are no simply ways to estimate ordered probit models with a more rigorous estimation and correction for time-serial problems.

Data and Methodology

Although both explanations find support across types of repressive behavior, the political order argument is generally more robust.

In Table 3 of Appendix 1, I incorporate all relevant independent variables discussed earlier in an attempt to understand variation in repressive behavior. From the analysis, one can identify several things. First, all variables increase the lethality of coercive action except economic development/modernization and the difference from regional repression, which have negative influences. Second, diverse aspects of political order reveal the same empirical finding: threats to government increase the lethality of repressive behavior and prior coercion increases the likelihood of subsequent applications.

For a clear understanding of exactly how these explanatory factors influence diverse strategies of repression, I present predicted changes in probabilities (that is, the likelihood that each repressive category will be achieved given a shift in the variable of interest from its minimum to its maximum). To simplify the discussion of these results, I have estimated the effects of lagged repression, setting the value of this variable to 5.[24]

To read Figure 3.1, one simply looks at a specific category of repression (that is, 1–9, along the x- axis) with reference to the independent variable of interest (identified on the legend along the top or at the right side of the figure). One then identifies the corresponding change in the probability of achieving this category derived from moving the relevant explanatory variable from its minimum to its maximum.[25] If the value for the specific category is positive, then, given an increase in the independent variable, the likelihood of a particular combination of repressive behavior is increased. Correspondingly, if the value is negative, then, given an increase in the independent variable, the likelihood of a government using a particular strategy of repression is reduced.

Almost immediately, one can see from Figure 3.1 that there are important differences between the explanatory variables associated with political order and those associated with development/modernization in terms of

---

[24] Recall that the foregoing analysis suggested that dummying out the different values of the lagged dependent variable was the most appropriate strategy for measuring this variable. In order to calculate the result for the statistical procedure employed here, however (in a relatively straightforward manner), I decided to select a value of repression near to the mean.

[25] Within the previous model, each of the values was investigated individually, but in order to acquire a simple and straightforward understanding of the general impact of these variables, I employed this somewhat coarse methodological technique.

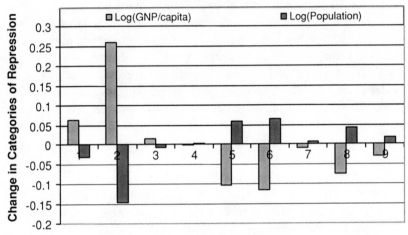

Figure 3.1 (a) Changes in Probability for Maximal Changes in Base Model Variables

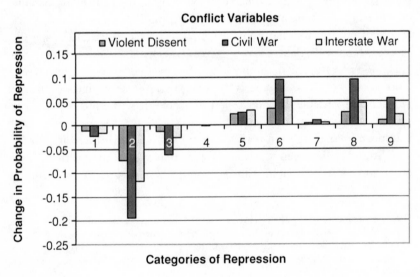

Figure 3.1 (b)

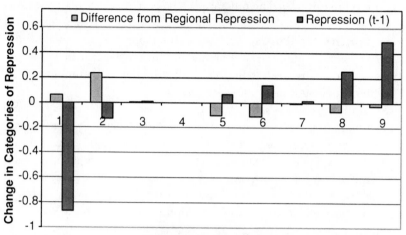

Figure 3.1 (c)

how they influence state repression. Overall, except for GNP per capita and divergence from regional repression (whose influence on repression across categories is reversed), the basic finding is that development/modernization and conflict decrease the likelihood that low-level repressive activity will be observed, but as one considers more lethal forms of repression, the influence becomes positive, increasing the likelihood that these strategies will be observed. These latter effects are generally weaker, however. Results also disclose that no factor is more important in terms of the magnitude of influence than previous repression – at least at the extremes of the measure (category 1 where both violence and restrictions are low as well as categories 8 and 9 where violence is high and restrictions are respectively moderate and high). By contrast, the other variables in the model almost never wield an influence greater than 20 percent, a value achieved only in category 2.

In order to familiarize the reader with how to read Figure 3.1 and understand how repressive behavior is influenced by the basic model, each category of the dependent variable (i.e., each combination of violence and restriction) is discussed individually.

Low Violence, Low Restriction (Category 1) With regard to this form of coercive strategy, results disclose that one aspect of socioeconomic development/modernization and one aspect of political order (divergence from

95

regional mean) function in a pacific manner (increasing the probability of lower level repression). The other aspects of development/modernization, as well as all other variables concerning conflict, reduce the probability that this approach to repressive governance will be adopted. None of these influences wield much influence on attaining this value of the dependent variable except for lagged repression, however, which significantly diminishes the likelihood of being in the least repressive category.

Specifically, results disclose that when per capita GNP increases from its minimum to its maximum, the likelihood of achieving the least repressive strategy of repression increases to approximately .06 (which means that there is a 6 percent chance of achieving this category under this circumstance). In short, wealth promotes domestic democratic peace but only marginally. Also in line with existing research, population size tends to diminish the likelihood of authorities adopting this technique of repression by about 3 percent. Overpopulation, that is, diminishes domestic democratic peace when moved from its minimum to its maximum but again the influence is only marginal.[26]

The statistical findings disclose that four out of five conflict variables decrease the likelihood of achieving the least repressive category, at varying levels of magnitude. For example, when lagged repression is increased,[27] it wields the greatest influence of all conflict variables, at approximately −0.80 or 80 percent (decreasing the likelihood of achieving this category by a large margin). By contrast, violent dissent, civil war, and interstate war also wield negative influences but at levels that are extremely small.

The first variable is especially intriguing because it appears to deviate from previous literature where lagged repression increases the likelihood of subsequent coercive activity. The comparison with the earlier literature is limited however because of how the dependent and independent variables are coded. For example, with regard to the specific category of repression being discussed (category 1, where restrictions as well as personal integrity violations are low), I consider the influence of previous repression that had been more lethal than the category being considered (category 9 where both violence and restriction are at high levels). This would be analogous to considering a situation where there were few arrests and political executions

---

[26] Note that despite the fact that both of these variables emerge from the same theory, the way in which the two variables were coded results in the opposite causal influence. Poverty and overpopulation thus represent opposite sides of the scales with which the data were compiled.

[27] Lagged repression is held at level five except for this calculation.

after a situation where arrests and executions had been much more frequent. Previous quantitative literature has not addressed such an influence although such scenarios are common in more qualitative work. For example, repressive behavior directed against the Republic of New Africa – a black power social movement in the United States during the 1960s and 1970s – was significantly decreased after the New Bethel incident, which resulted in the largest single arrest of members. After this time, physical and electronic surveillance, arrests, raids, and grand jury investigations all declined. Comparatively, the impact of the three variables, violent dissent, civil war, and interstate war, is weak (at approximately 2 percent). Here, we find that diverse forms of political conflict decrease the likelihood of lower level repression. Repressive tolerance is thus undermined by diverse threats to political order but once more only at marginal levels.

Low Violence, Moderate Restriction (Category 2)   Suggesting that relatively low applications of repression are comparable to one another, the findings for this category are generally consistent with those from the previous level. There are two noticeable differences between these two coercive techniques. First, as gauged by the predicted probabilities, the influence of all variables increases in their impact except for lagged repression, which diminishes fourfold. Second, again, as gauged by the predicted probabilities, the divergence from regional repression and GNP per capita increases the likelihood of this form of state repression at relatively comparable amounts (approximately 25 percent). Deviation from regional coercive practices and wealth tends to increase the likelihood that lower level repressive behavior is employed. At the same time, the likelihood of achieving this category is diminished by all three indicators of nonstate violence and lagged repression at varying levels of influence (between 8 and 19 percent). Once more, passivity is undermined by threats to political order but at slightly larger magnitudes of influence.

Low Violence, High Restriction (Category 3)   Somewhat surprisingly, the third category of repression is again generally comparable to the first two. This was unanticipated, for I had suggested that when either technique of repression (restrictions or violence) reached a high level of application, the explanatory factors would be unique. This was not the case, however. Two differences between this category and the last two are worth considering.

First, as gauged by the predicted probabilities, all causal influences are smaller than the first two repressive strategies. Second, the influence of lagged repression is now positive. When moved from its minimum to maximum, the likelihood of being in category 3 is increased marginally. Past applications of lethal repression that were somewhat significant tend to increase the likelihood that repressive strategies outside of the lowest level combinations will be used; this supports the bureaucratic inertia argument put forward in the literature.

Moderate Violence, Low Restriction (Category 4)   When I attempted to estimate causal relationships for this repressive strategy, it was clear that there were not enough observations to make a reliable estimation. It is rarely the case that authorities employed moderate levels of violence and low levels of restrictions. Consequently, there were no results to report.

Moderate Violence, Moderate Restriction (Category 5)   When considering the fifth repressive category, we find numerous relevant variables statistically significant, and, as expected, the nature of their influences are very different from what they were in the categories already examined. In line with expectations, for example, the influence of the development/modernization variables is reversed. Here, as population increases, the likelihood of moderate violence and restriction is increased, albeit modestly. By contrast, as GNP increases, the likelihood of being in category 5 diminishes.

With regard to the political order variables, we again see important differences from the earlier categories of state repression. For example, when increased from the minimum to the maximum, almost all conflict variables wield positive influences (increasing the likelihood that moderate restriction and violence would be applied). These influences tend to be rather small (below 5 percent). The lone exception, divergence from regional repression, diminishes the likelihood of being in this category: when previous repressive activity exceeds that of neighbors, the probability of moderate violence and moderate restriction is enhanced. This moves against my argument highlighting that political authorities are quite independent in their uses of repressive behavior. Similar to category 3, the likelihood of attaining category 5 coercion is increased by lagged repression so that after governments have prior experience with repressive action, they are more inclined to use it later. That the level of coercive behavior employed for the lag is high comports well existing literature, albeit marginally in terms of the substantive influence, which significantly differs from existing research.

Data and Methodology

Moderate Violence, High Restriction (Category 6)   In many respects, the findings for this category and the next three are comparable to the last, although with minor differences. First, as gauged by the predicted probabilities, GNP per capita, and divergence from regional repression wield comparable [negative] influences of approximately 1 percent, whereas population and the influence of violent dissent, civil war, interstate war, and lagged repression increase the probability of achieving this category. Second, there is a change in the order in which diverse forms of conflict influence repressive behavior. Again, lagged repression wields the largest influence (increasing the probability of attaining this value of repression at 14 percent). This is followed by civil war (9 percent), interstate war (5 percent), and violent dissent (3 percent). Similar to earlier results, the least contentious activity wields the smallest influence on repressive behavior, whereas the most contentious in terms of the sheer magnitude of violence wields the largest.

High Violence, Low Restriction (Category 7)   According to the results and similar to category 4, no variables in this model do very well in changing the probability of observing this form of repressive behavior. Again, this is attributed to the small number of cases ($N = 45$); rarely do authorities employ personal integrity violations without restrictions.

High Violence, Moderate Restriction (Category 8)   Consistent with categories 5 and 6, most variables in the model wield the same influence on achieving this combination of repressive strategies. Again, some differences merit attention.

First, the negative influence of GNP per capita and the positive influence of population decrease in magnitude (below 8 percent in the former and below 5 percent in the latter). Deviating from existing scholarship, this suggests that development matters less with more lethal forms of state repression. My research suggests that prior research was misspecified because prior research did not consider the possibility that development/modernization could influence different repressive strategies in a unique manner. Second, the influence of violent dissent, civil war, and interstate war are almost identical to category 6 in terms of magnitude and the order of influence. Third, the positive influence of lagged repression has once again grown to approximately 25 percent, continuing a trend from category 5; this is the only variable to increase in its significance as the value of repressive lethality increases.

High Violence, High Restriction (Category 9) In this category, the trends identified in categories 5, 6 and 8 continue, leaving previous repression (at approximately 50 percent) as essentially the only variable worthy of attention. While diverse variables have statistically significant effects, these are all marginal in terms of their impact; the story of high-level restriction and violence is one of repressive behavior persisting. Development/modernization and nonstate contentious behavior play no prominent role in this scenario.

Up to this point, we have considered only the influence of political (dis)order as well as development/modernization. I now turn to the primary focus of the book: the two different aspects of democracy as already discussed – *Voice* and *Veto*. In the next section, I identify the indicators for these concepts. Within the next chapter, I add these variables to the basic model and investigate their influence on repressive lethality.

Measuring Diverse Aspects of Democracy

In measuring democratic characteristics, most authors take their cue from the extensive work of Robert Dahl (Dahl 1966, 1971; 1989) – for discussion, see Munck and Verkuilen (2002) or Beetham (1994). In his earlier work, Dahl (1971, 3) defined democracy (labeled "Polyarchy") as a political system with two characteristics: participation (for example, voting) and competition (for example, the right of diverse leaders/beliefs to compete for support and the representativeness of available leaders/beliefs). These categories are not without their problems for a study of state repression.

For example, Dahl's (1971, 20) initial conception seemingly conflates the two dimensions identified with what I consider coercive activity (that is, freedom of expression, association, and assembly). Consequently, freedom to form and join organizations was viewed as "required" institutional guarantees that permit democracy to exist.[28] In the same work, however, Dahl (1971, 27) appears to separate the two. For example, he argues that

[t]he lower the barriers to public contestation and the greater the proportion of the population included in the political system, the more difficult it is for the government of a country to adopt and enforce policies that require the application of extreme sanctions against more than a small percentage of the population; the less likely, too, that the government will attempt to do so.

Here, the level of democracy is as a factor that hinders repressive behavior; it is not part of the definition.

---

[28] Huntington (1991), among others, continues in this practice albeit not consistently.

Data and Methodology

In his later research, Dahl (1998, 37–8) appears to change his position. At this juncture, he is more interested in differentiating between those elements of repression that are necessary to the definition of democracy and those that democracy is likely to influence once it has been established. Regarding the first point, he asks,

[i]s it not self-evident that in order to satisfy [the requirements for democracy] a political system would necessarily have to insure its citizens certain rights? Take effective participation: to meet that standard, would not its citizens necessarily possess a right to participate and a right to express their views on political matters, to hear what other citizens have to say, to discuss political matters with other citizens? (Dahl 1998, 48–9)

He continues: "(i)n addition to all rights, freedoms, and opportunities that are strictly necessary in order for a government to be democratic, citizens in a democracy are certain to enjoy an even more extensive array of freedoms" (1998, 49). This is clearly a much stronger position than he had previously taken regarding both the separability of democracy from repression and the substantive influence of democracy on specific government outputs/policies. The argument is consistent with others concerned with empirical democratic theory (e.g., Cnudde and Neubauer 1969; Powell 1982; Russett 1993).

In line with my view, most efforts to operationalize Dahl's concept tend to separate out state repression from the two highlighted dimensions, providing what Collier and Levitsky (1997) refer to as a "minimalist" conception of the term.[29] Additionally, most efforts at measurement tend to ignore one dimension while highlighting others. For example, when one considers the distribution of characteristics identified by a recent review of democracy indicators (Munck and Verkuilen 2002), it is clear that most measurements ignore at least some part of Dahl's conception. These are shown in Table 3.4.

In the table, it is shown that Gurr, Bollen, Coppedge, and Reinicke, as well as Alvarez et al. (1996) ignore mass participation in the political process, whereas Hadenius ignores competition/contestation. Directly relevant to my *Voice–Veto* distinction, there is also significant variation here. For example, some databases highlight the behavior of authorities (see, for example, Alvarez et al. 1996; Coppedge and Reinicke 1991; Gurr 1974),

---

[29] Perhaps the most important exception here is offered by Bollen, who combines measures of repression (political liberties) with measures of participation (fairness of voting).

Table 3.4. *Alternative Measurements of Democracy*

Authors of Index	Attributes
Alvarez et al. (1996)	Dahl: Contestation Other: Offices
Arat (1991)	Dahl: Participation, Contestation ("Competitiveness, Inclusiveness)
Bollen (1980)	Dahl: Participation ("Popular Sovereignty")
Coppedge and Reinicke (1991)	Dahl: Contestation
Gasiorowski (1996)	Dahl: Contestation (Competitiveness, Inclusiveness)
Gurr (1974)	Dahl: Contestation (e.g., Competitiveness of Participation and Regulation of Participation)
Hadenius (1992)	Dahl: Participation (Elections)
Vanhanen (2000)	Dahl: Contestation, Participation

Note: Content of this table derived from Munck and Verkuilen (2002).

whereas others ignore them completely (see, for example, Arat 1991; Vanhanen 2000).

In attempting to address all aspects of democracy relevant to the theoretical debates concerning state repression, I consider a range of democratic features. This avoids the highly aggregated measuring normally found in the literature (e.g., Gurr's Polity measure, which is likely the most frequently employed in the literature). Specifically, I use four measures to capture distinct aspects of democracy. Two address different components of mass-oriented democratic behavior – *Voice*: (1) the legal right to participate (Suffrage) and (2) actual participation weighted by the degree of competitiveness in the electoral system. Another two address different components of elite-oriented democratic behavior – *Veto*: (3) a strict conception of *Veto* Players (official government actors who have investigation, oversight, and override capability) and (4) general constraints on the executive exercised by different social, economic, and political actors within the relevant territorial domain.

According to existing research, both aspects of democracy should influence state repression negatively. In the case of *Voice*, it is expected that when citizens participate in the political system in a meaningful way (for example, when they have the right to vote, when they vote in large numbers, and when diverse interests receive representation), authorities would be less inclined to use repressive behavior because they are monitored by citizens and/or by political representatives whom they do not wish to disappoint, for those people could remove them from office for engaging in offensive behavior. In the case of *Veto*, it is believed that when the actions of political authorities can be blocked or countered in some way (for example, when specific limitations exist within very precise domains such as the legislature and when diverse restrictions can be placed on authorities from a variety of political actors), they will be less likely to engage in repression because this could have a deleterious impact on a constituency with *Veto* power or connection to it. In trying to protect the interests of those they represent as well as their own position, the relevant authorities would interfere with the policy in question as much as needed.

The consideration of these two dimensions and four indicators makes sense because they are commonly applied within democratization efforts. When policymakers and NGOs (U.S. AID, the National Endowment of Democracy, the German Marshall Fund) consider creating democratic governments, their efforts involve creating and strengthening the characteristics discussed here (see, for example, Goldman and Douglas 1988). For example, this was readily observable when U.S. AID

established the promotion of democracy as one of the agency's central aims and involved it extensively in assistance programs for free and fair elections, constitutional drafting, legislatures, judicial systems, local government, anticorruption efforts, regulatory reform, civic education, and independent organizations and media in civil society (including human rights, legal aid, women's, professional, and church groups). (Diamond 1995, 13)

In the next section, we consider each measure in detail.

Voice

Suffrage   Provided by Bollen (1998) and Paxton et al. (2003), this measure identifies the percentage of the population enfranchised or, more specifically, "the proportion of the adult population that has the right to vote in national elections" (Paxton et al. 2003, 94–5). As they state, "[this] Suffrage score . . . measures the percentage of the adult population [twenty or older] who are eligible to vote in a given year and ranges from 0 percent [zero franchise] to 100 percent [universal suffrage]. Franchise age below twenty years does not lead to higher percentages." The primary source of data for this project is the *Chronicle of Parliamentary Elections* (or *Chronicle*). "The *Chronicle* is an annual report that provides general information on the constitution and its amendments, parliament, the electoral system, and the background and outcomes of parliamentary and presidential elections of countries that have held an election during the year under review" (Paxton et al. 2003, 94). The derivation of the yearly scores is straightforward: "[the researchers] begin with a base score of 100 for each country and then [they] subtract percentages for every restriction listed in the *Chronicle's* voting requirements. For restrictions based on ascribed characteristics such as race and sex, the size of the percentage deducted was determined from population proportions" (Paxton et al. 2003, 95).

The creators of this data were very careful about how they collected their material. Seeking to guard against false political participation, for example, the project closely monitored the actual behavior of citizens.[30] As such, "the formal or constitutional statement of franchise is not taken as meaningful unless the population actually has the opportunity to vote" (Paxton et al. 2003, 95). This consideration is informal, however, and they direct the bulk of their attention at identifying exactly who may and who may not cast a ballot.[31]

To investigate the impact of electoral behavior on repression (another objective measure of democracy), I use the data collected by Vanhanen (2000).[32]

Competition and Participation   To date, researchers of repressive behavior have used this variable occasionally but not extensively (Davenport and Armstrong 2004; Poe and Tate 1994). The Vanhanen data are unique in that they identify democracy as "a political system in which ideologically and socially different groups are legally entitled to compete for political power, and in which institutional power-holders are elected by the people and are responsible to the people" (Vanhanen 2000, 252). Additionally, this effort has been unique because it is interested not only in what citizens can do but also in what they actually do (how many citizens participate) and what emerges from these efforts (how many different perspectives in the society achieve political representation).

---

[30] For additional concerns regarding the creation of this measure (for example, what to do when zero franchise exists, how to deal with the issue of changes taking place during a year, and the complete listing of restrictions/exclusions that were used by the study), I refer individuals to the literature concerning this research effort and/or the project Web page.

[31] The Web page for this project can be found at the following locations: www.soc.sbs.ohio-state.edu/pmp/ or www.unc.edu/~bollen/. This type of indicator has never been used within a study of state repression.

[32] Clearly, use of this data should not in any way be interpreted as supporting the recent remarks made by Vanhanen considering race.

Data and Methodology

Explicitly drawing upon Dahl, Vanhanen was interested in two dimensions of democratization: the degree of competition and the degree of participation. To measure the former he drew upon extensive historical materials and identified "the smaller parties' share of all votes cast in parliamentary or presidential elections, or both" (Vanhanen 2000, 253). To measure the latter he identified "the percentage of the population who actually voted in these elections" (Vanhanen 2000, 253). As he states, "[t]he two basic indicators of democratization can be used separately to measure the level of democracy. However, because they are assumed to indicate two different dimensions of democratization, it is reasonable to argue that a combination of them would be a more realistic indicator of democracy than either of them alone" (Vanhanen 2000, 255). He continues:

My argument is that participation is as important a dimension of democracy as competition. If only a small minority of the adult population takes part in elections, then the electoral struggle for power is restricted to the dominant stratum of the population, and the bulk of the population remains outside national politics. Power-sharing is certainly more superficial in such countries compared to societies where the majority of the adult population takes part in elections (presupposing, of course, that elections are competitive). Because I see both dimensions of democratization as necessary for democracy, I have weighted them equally in my Index of Democratization (ID). However, users of the dataset can weigh the two dimensions in other ways and experiment with different combinations. (Vanhanen 2000, 255–6)[33]

In line with an earlier study (Davenport and Armstrong 2004), I chose the construction of the Vanhanen measure suggested by Gates et al. (2003), based mostly on the participation measure.

[As designed w]hen competition is greater or equal to 30 percent, then the participation measure is left alone. When competition is less than 30 percent participation is multiplied by Competition/30 percent, thus "down-weighting" participation in low-competition environments. Gates et al. then add one (1) to the measure

---

[33] Interestingly, Vanhanen (2000, 256) comments on the connection between democracy and repression members, advocating a position with which I disagree. He says: "Other possible dimensions of democracy have been omitted here. For example, my index does not attempt to measure the level of civil and political liberties, which Diamond, Linz, and Lipset (1995) regard as the third important dimension of democracy.... My argument is that there are hardly any countries in which legal competition for power through elections takes place without the existence of civil and political liberties. It is equally difficult to imagine a country where individuals and groups enjoy civil and political liberties but political power is concentrated in the hands of one group. I fully agree that civil and political liberties are important characteristics of democracy, but it does not seem necessary to estimate their existence by a separate indicator, since my variables indicate their existence or non-existence indirectly."

to remove all zeros (changing the range of the available to [1,101] and take the natural logarithm of this variable, divided by the natural logarithm of 101. This generates a variable that has a theoretical range from zero (China 1977–1996) to one (Italy 1992–1995 with a maximum value of .916). (Davenport and Armstrong 2004, 546)

This measure thus privileges the competition component of electoral participation but hedges it by the proportion of the population enfranchised.

Having now discussed my measures of *Voice*, I now proceed to my measures of *Veto*.

Veto

The other application of democratic governance believed to be important for repressive behavior concerns situations in which government action or proposed action can be monitored, modified, or halted by diverse sociopolitical actors. Which actors wield such power? Two distinct perspectives are considered.

Veto *Players* Despite the relevance of the role of these political actors to the domestic democratic peace and its connection to earlier arguments[34] of "checks and balances" as well as to the separation of powers (see, for example, Kaiser 1997; Tsebelis 2002), no studies to date have considered their role as an influence on state repression. In part this is because the body of work relevant to veto, although drawing upon older traditions, is relatively recent. For example, as stated in a review of literature relevant to this aspect of democracy, Roller (2003, 5) argues that "[w]hile the distribution of power has always been an essential item in institutional theory, it is not until the development of the *Veto*-player approach in the nineties that it became an analytically precise and measurable concept." The relevance to state repression is immediately apparent. As conceived, the basic logic revolves around that idea that "[i]n order to change policies...a certain number of individual or collective actors [specified within a country's constitution and/or political system] have to agree to the proposed change" (Tsebelis 2002, 2).[35] As such,

---

[34] Those associated with veto player theory are well aware of its historical antecedents. For example, Tsebelis (2002, 9) points directly to individuals such as Madison and Montesquieu.

[35] This is consistent with other views on the topic. As Kaiser (1997) maintains: "[v]eto points are neither physical entities, as Tsebelis' notion of 'institutional *Veto Players*' seems to imply,

Data and Methodology

[v]eto-player theory conceptualizes the institutional configurations of political decision-making structures from the perspective of actors, naturally from the perspective of government and its ability to pass laws...or to produce policy change.... This ability is dependent upon whether, or how many, *Veto* points or *Veto* Players the institutional configuration provides, that is, at which points or by whom a governmental proposal must be ratified or can be rejected. (Roller 2003, 5)

Essentially, this body of work "conceptualizes and renders more precisely a specific type of rule, namely those rules that determine the degree of autonomy or power of the government. [In sum] the dispersion of power is [simply] conceptualized as the number of *Veto* Players" (Roller 2003, 6). For my purposes, a measure of *veto* points/Players is ideal. Within situations where these exist, political authorities will be more hesitant to engage in activity that has potential to be resisted during the decision-making process. The higher the number of veto players or places where important decisions can be delayed/interrupted (*Veto* "points"), the harder it would be to implement and/or change policy; the smaller the number of players and points, the easier it is to implement and/or change. Repression clearly falls within these parameters.

Following this logic, I employ a measure called "Checks" within the database developed by Keefer (2002). Viewed as the best measure of its kind, for both OECD and developing countries (Keefer and Stasavage 2003), this 0–16 measure[36]

has the advantage of being based on objective criteria and of capturing the existence of coalition governments or divided control of two chambers in a bicameral system...More generally, the measure is based on a formula that first counts the number of *Veto* Players, based on whether the executive and legislative chamber(s)

---

nor a mere metaphor. They are 'points of strategic uncertainty where decisions may be overturned'...or at least modified. Therefore actors who want to ensure that they can influence decisions in a political arena (i.e., limit, change or eliminate them when deemed necessary) will strive to establish *Veto* points" (p. 437).

[36] This measure does not allow us to address the variety of *Veto* points discussed by Kaiser (1997, 436) (for example, consociational, delegatory, expert and legislatory) because it does not address the intended effects on the decision-making process of the measure provided. Instead, it focuses on the structure of the government similar to the Suffrage variable discussed earlier. Additionally, I have not logged the variable in line with Keefer and Stasavage (2003) because existing theory does not suggest that unequal weight should be given to the one unit change from 1 to 2 as opposed to 3 to 4 or 5 to 6. In line with my earlier research with Armstrong (2004), some of these differences are examined, but the conclusions of such an investigation are speculative.

are controlled by different parties in presidential systems and on the number of parties in the government coalition for parliamentary system. . . . The index is then modified to take account of the fact that certain electoral rules (closed list vs. open list) affect the cohesiveness of governing coalitions. (p. 415)[37]

The index is then modified yet further according to the degree of ideological distance between the opposition and executive party (Keefer 2002; Keefer and Stasavage 2003).

As designed, the Keefer measure is specifically tied to officially recognized actors within the political system (that is, those explicitly identified in political/legal documents). It is possible, however, that actors within the society and with no official role in the government wield influence over political authorities as well. I consider this next.

Executive Constraints   In an effort to identify a less strict conception of *Veto*, I employ the subjective measure of Executive Constraints developed

---

[37] The specific coding rules for the variable (Checks) follow (Keefer 2002, 21–2):

1. The measure equals one if the legislative or executive index of competition (respectively the Legislative Index of Electoral Competitiveness, or LIEC, and the Executive Index of Electoral Competitiveness, or EIEC) is less than 5 – countries where legislatures are not competitively elected are considered countries where only the executive wields a check.
2. In countries where LIEC and EIEC are greater than or equal to 5: Checks is incremented by one (a) if there is a chief executive (it is blank or NA if not); (b) if the chief executive is competitively elected (EIEC greater than 6 – this is the main difference from the deleted CHECKS2a, which increased by one when EIEC was greater than 4); (c) if the opposition controls the legislature.

   In presidential systems, Checks is incremented by one (a) for each chamber of the legislature *unless* the president's party has a majority in the lower house *and* a closed list system is in effect (implying stronger presidential control of his/her party, and therefore of the legislature); (b) for each party coded as allied with the president's party and which has an ideological (left-right-center) orientation closer to that of the main opposition party than to that of the president's party.

   In parliamentary systems, Checks is incremented by one (a) for every party in the government coalition as long as the parties are needed to maintain a majority (the previous version of Checks – Checks3 in DPI3 – incremented by one for each of the three largest parties in the government coalition, regardless of whether they were needed for a legislative majority); (b) for every party in the government coalition that has a position on economic issues (right-left-center) closer to the largest opposition party than to the party of the executive.

   In parliamentary systems, the prime minister's party is *not* counted as a check if there is a closed rule in place – the prime minister is presumed in this case to control the party fully.

Data and Methodology

by Ted Gurr and associates (Eckstein and Gurr 1975; Gurr 1974; Jaggers and Gurr 1995; Marshall and Jaggers 2001).[38] Although not generally high-lighted as a measure of *Veto* within the literature because of the common practice of aggregating diverse components contained within the Polity data, it seems clear that it in fact functions in this manner (see, for example, Keefer and Stasavage 2003, 415). As designed, the indicator "[r]efers to the extent of institutionalized constraints on the decision-making pow-ers of chief executives, whether individuals or collectivities" (Marshall and Jaggers 2001, 21). Any "accountability groups" (for example, legislatures, political parties, councils of nobles or powerful advisers, private corpora-tions, the military, and independent judiciaries) may impose such limita-tions.[39] Indeed, the only distinctive characteristic of this measure as drawn from most discussions of *Veto* is the fact that accountability groups can exist both within government and outside of it.

Specifically, the Executive Constraints variable was created on a seven-point scale. Derived from a systematic analysis of a wide range of historical records, media sources, and government reports, the first value represents a situation of "unlimited authority."[40] Here, "there are no regular limitations on the executive's actions" (Marshall and Jaggers 2001, 21). Evidence of this category exists where legislatures and other groups within society are unable to control important government appointments or to influence policy deci-sions. The second value represents an intermediate category, bridging the gap between value 1 (discussed earlier) and value 3, where there is "slight to moderate limitation on executive authority" (Marshall and Jaggers 2001, 21). Value 4 constitutes another intermediate category, bridging the gap between categories 3 and 5. At the latter value, substantial limitations on the executive exist in this situation, and evidence of this category can be found where legislatures counteract directives issued by executives or when other groups within the society are able to control important appointments to government as well as various policy decisions. Value 6 represents another

---

[38] These data have been used quite frequently within political science and sociology. Indeed, many have suggested that this political measure is the most frequently employed indicator of political democracy in the social sciences (see, for example, Jaggers and Gurr 1995, 470; Ward 2002, 49).

[39] As they state, "[t]he concern is . . . with the checks and balances between the various parts of the decision-making process" (Marshall and Jaggers 2001, 21).

[40] In this situation, constitutional restrictions on executive action are ignored, no legislative assembly exists, and decrees are repeatedly used as the means to govern.

intermediary category, between 5 and 7. At the highest value, accountability groups are able to counteract the executive completely or initiate decisions on their own.

Summary

In this chapter, I presented the data for the statistical analysis of how democracy influences state repression (the domestic democratic peace). This included a discussion of the dependent variable (repressive lethality), which represented a combination of political restrictions and state violence. Additionally, I also included diverse independent variables commonly used in the literature to account for variation in repressive action: socioeconomic development/modernization (per capita GNP and population size) as well as political conflict (state behavior directed against its citizens (that is, lagged repression and deviation from regional repressive activity) and nonstate activity (that is, violent dissent, civil war and interstate war).

In preparation for the analysis of the peace proposition, I examined a basic model that did not include measures of democracy. As found, GNP and divergence from the regional mean encouraged lower-level repressive behavior while discouraging more lethal repressive action. In contrast, violent dissent, civil war, interstate war, and lagged repression had the opposite effect; encouraging higher level coercive activity while discouraging lower level applications. Lagged repression was by far the most powerful variable in the model.

The chapter concluded with the presentation of the data used to operationalize different aspects of political democracy: *Voice* – suffrage and competition weighted by participation and *Veto* – the official number of veto players as well as the unofficial presence of sociopolitical actors with oversight capability. In the next chapter, I use these measures to analyze how *Voice* and *Veto* influence repressive behavior, incorporating them into the basic model examined here. In Chapter 5, I interact these different aspects of democracy with political conflict so that I can gauge the robustness of the peace proposition in situations where political authorities are directly being challenged.

4

Democratic Pacification

THE DIRECT EFFECTS OF *VOICE* AND *VETO*

My statistical analysis is designed in two parts. As reported in this chapter, one section examines the direct influence of four aspects of democracy on state repression. Another section, presented in Chapter 5, examines the interactive influence of democracy on repression amid varying types of societal and interstate conflict. In investigating relationships, I first analyze each of the democratic characteristics individually. I then build a model using the significant variables from all the models investigated in order to evaluate the effect of diverse democratic characteristics competitively.

The Pacifying Effect of Democracy on Repression

I begin in this section with an examination of *Voice*: the *Suffrage* measure provided by Bollen (1998) and Paxton et al. (2003), as well as the *Competition/Participation* measure provided by Vanhanen (2000) and subsequently modified by Gates et al. (2003). This is followed by an analysis of *Veto*: the *Veto Players* measure as provided by Keefer (2002) and an indicator of *Executive Constraints* provided by Gurr (1974).

The Influence of Voice

Voice refers to those elements of a political system that afford citizens influence over those who govern. In line with existing research, I consider two of the more prominent characteristics highlighted in the theoretical literature as well as in public policy circles, NGOs, and democratic social movements around the world.

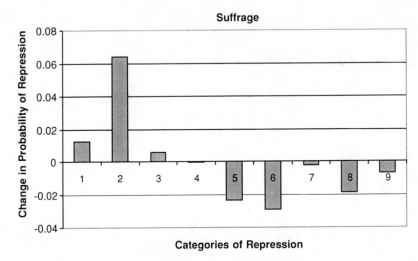

Figure 4.1 The Influence of *Suffrage* on Repressive Lethality

Suffrage

In order to understand how Suffrage influences repression, I introduce the Bollen and Paxton indicator into the basic model discussed in Chapter 3. All of these results are presented in Table 1, column 1 in Appendix 2. To focus the discussion and present the statistical findings parsimoniously, in the next two chapters I do not provide the ordered probit results for the variables in the basic model nor do I provide graphic representations of predicted probabilities for the base model in the equations estimated.[1]

What does the analysis reveal? Mere statistical tables are not sufficient for understanding causal influences on ordinal variables, I provide in Figure 4.1 the predicted change in probabilities (i.e., the probability of being in different categories of repression as *Suffrage* moves from its minimum to its maximum).[2]

Recall from the last chapter that one reads these figures by simply looking at a specific category of repression (i.e., 1–9) – the *x*-Axis, with reference to the independent variable of interest (*Suffrage* in this case). One then

---

[1] Those interested in how the base model varies across equations can view the general similarities of the results by observing the tables in Appendix 1.

[2] A likelihood ratio test shows that the model including *Suffrage* is "better" than the basic model (that is, the one that excludes *Suffrage*). This aspect of *Voice* thus diminishes state repressive behavior.

identifies the corresponding change in the probability of achieving this category derived from moving the relevant explanatory variable from its minimum to its maximum – the y-axis. If the value is positive, then, given an increase in the relevant independent variable, the likelihood of a government using a particular strategy of repression is increased. Correspondingly, if the value is negative, then, given an increase in the independent variable, the likelihood of a government using a particular strategy of repression decreases.

When Figure 4.1 is considered, the empirical findings are clear. Supporting Hypothesis 1 that *Voice* encourages the likelihood of lower level repression while discouraging the likelihood of higher level repressive activity, the results suggest that at higher levels of *Suffrage*, a country has a higher probability of being in a lower repressive category, all other variables held constant. The magnitude of these influences, however, is quite small. Comparatively, for example, the influence of GNP per capita on achieving the lowest three categories was 5 percent, 25 percent, and 1 percent, respectively. Overall, these findings offer weak support for the peace proposition.

The influence of *Suffrage* across values of the dependent variable is important to identify, for it is somewhat more complex than my hypothesis suggests. According to the earlier discussion, democracy should increase the probability of achieving low-level repression (category 1 and/or 2 on the dependent variable), which decreases the probability of achieving repressive behavior that was more lethal (3–9). From the statistical results, the probability of achieving the least repressive category (1) and the probability of achieving the next category (2) are increased by *Suffrage*, but the influence of this variable is not particularly strong (yielding a 1 percent chance of achieving category 1 and a 6 percent chance of achieving category 2). Against expectations, *Suffrage* also increases the probability of achieving repression where violence is low but restrictions are high (category 3); the magnitude of influence is lower than that exhibited in categories 1 and 2 (approximately less than half a percent). The first two findings are directly consistent with the pacification argument provided above (Hypothesis 1), but the third is not. Indeed, the latter finding provides preliminary support for Hypothesis 5, which suggests that state violence is more likely than political restrictions to be reduced by democratic characteristics of the political system.

The model provides no insight into repression where violence is moderate and restrictions are limited because of the low number of cases (category 4) – this is similar to category 7. The results are largely consistent

Table 4.1. *The Influence of* Suffrage *on the Most Likely Current Value of Repression*

1 Lag Repression	2 Most Likely Value of Current Repression When *Suffrage* = 0	3 Most Likely Value of Current Repression When *Suffrage* = 100
1	1	1
2	2	2
3	2▲–	2
4	2▲–	2
5	5	2▲–
6	5▲–	5
7	5▲–	2▲–
8	6▲–	6
9	9	8▲–

Legend: ▲ = change; – = negative change; + = positive change.

above this category, however, in terms of the expectations of Hypothesis 1: the most lethal forms of repression are consistently reduced by *Suffrage*. Again, these influences are relatively marginal – albeit somewhat variable. For example, when the level of state violence and restrictions is moderate (category 5), the influence of *Suffrage* is somewhat weak at approximately 2 percent as compared where the level of state violence is moderate but where restrictions are high at approximately 3 percent (category 6). Above this category, the influence of *Suffrage* decreases. Thus, where violence is high and restrictions are moderate (in category 8), the probability of attaining this value of repression is decreased to below 2 percent when *Suffrage* is increased from its minimum to its maximum, whereas in category 9 (where both violence and restrictions are high), the negative influence is even weaker.

These results also convey additional information. For example, the previous discussion assesses the influence of Suffrage on repressive lethality as the former increases from its minimum to its maximum, but this does not consider the fact that governments start at different levels of repression. Some governments might be at level 2 (low political violence but moderate restrictions) during the previous year, whereas others might be at level 8 (high violence but moderate restrictions). These very different contexts represent extremely different scenarios within which democracy is expected to have an impact. To address this situation, I consider in Table 4.1 the most likely value of current repression, at time t (in the column), given a specific value of previous repression at time $t - 1$, and *Suffrage* set to 0 (in the row). This is compared with the most likely value of current repression, given a specific value of previous repression at time $t - 1$ and *Suffrage* set to 100.

It is clear from these findings that electoral participation is fairly weak at decreasing state repression. For example, the second column reveals that in situations where there is no Suffrage at time $t - 1$, there is a natural drift downward in repressive behavior within the following year. This acknowledges that it is difficult for states (even relatively authoritarian ones) to sustain repressive behavior and that they reduce the magnitude of this application soon after it is employed. Thus, when prior repression was at low to mid-range values (levels 3 and 4), the next period repression is relatively low (in category 2); when previous repression was in the middle to upper range (categories 6 and 7), repression in the next year is likely moderate (in category 5); and when prior repression was quite high (category 8), the next year repression was likely to be closer to moderate values (in category 6).

Revealing the weak pacifying influence, movement in *Suffrage* from its lowest value (0) to its highest (100) in column 3 does very little to alter the results. Indeed, only three categories of repression are reduced by such a change: when previous repression was in categories 5 (moderate violence and restriction) and 7 (high violence, low restriction), these are reduced to category 2 (low violence, moderate restriction); and, when previous repression was in category 9 (high violence and restriction), this is reduced to category 8 (high violence, moderate restriction). *Suffrage* does have an influence, therefore, but compared with what simply happens naturally over time in the most autocratic of contexts, the magnitude of this influence is quite weak. In line with this, it should come as no surprise that during a period when *Suffrage* was particularly high in El Salvador (the legislative elections of 1976 and constitutional assembly of 1982), observers noted a consistent application of political assassinations, disappearances, and state prosecution of citizens. This led to numerous individuals referring to "demonstration" elections being nothing more than a show for foreigners.

Of course, other aspects of *Voice* may be relevant to repressive lethality. An additional measurement is considered later.

Competition and Participation

To investigate the impact of electoral competition and participation on repression, I use the variables collected by Vanhanen (2000) and modified

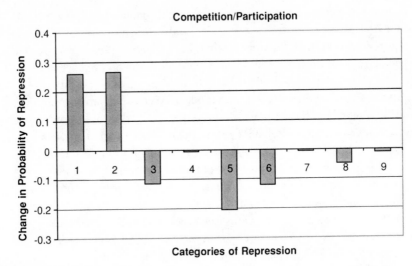

Figure 4.2 The Influence of *Competition/Participation* on Repressive Lethality

in Gates et al. (2003); this is referred to hereafter as the Vanhanen/Gates democracy measure, or *Competition/Participation*.[3] As with *Suffrage*, I include this variable in the basic model provided earlier. This model as well as some fit statistics are provided in Table 1, column 2 of Appendix 2.

Once again, the likelihood ratio statistics and their corresponding *p*-values suggest that the model including *Competition/Participation* is better than the model excluding it (i.e., the base model). Similar to the *Suffrage* model, Hypothesis 1 is again supported, and *Voice* is deemed statistically significant in determining the form repression takes. Indeed, findings reveal that, across categories of repression, the influence of this variable is several times larger than *Suffrage* as well as most variables in the basic model. Figure 4.2 presents the predicted probabilities.

From the results, *Competition/Participation* exhibits an influence that is generally similar to that identified with *Suffrage*, but with some important differences. First, only repressive categories 1 and 2 are influenced positively in this analysis whereas the others (3–9) are decreased, supporting the weak variant of the domestic democratic peace (Hypothesis 1). Second, when one increases *Competition/Participation* from its minimum to its maximum, the magnitude of change in predicted probabilities is much higher

---

[3] Recall that this measure privileges the competition component but hedges it by the proportion of the population enfranchised (over 30 percent).

than that identified when *Suffrage* is similarly altered. For example, in the context of enhanced *Competition/Participation* one observes an increase of approximately 26 percent in categories 1 and 2 repression (where violence is low but restrictions are respectively low and moderate). This amounts to an increase of approximately six times that provided by *Suffrage*. Third, the influence of *Competition/Participation* is negative in higher values of the dependent variable as suggested by the domestic democratic peace, but the magnitude of influence declines as the lethality of repression increases from category 5 to 9. Thus, the change in probability of achieving category 5 repression (where violence and restrictions are both applied at moderate levels) is decreased by about 20 percent when *Competition/Participation* is increased from its minimum to its maximum. When one considers repression where moderate values of violence but high values of restrictions are found (category 6), the change in probability is 12 percent; when one considers repression where violence is high but restrictions are moderate (category 8), the change in probability is 5 percent. Finally, at the highest value of repression (where both violence and restrictions are high), the change in predicted probability is 1 percent, indicating a very limited influence. *Voice* thus pacifies quite significantly, but the influence is substantially more important with regard to the least repressive techniques as well as with regard to those that emphasize restrictions (supporting the argument that democracy is better at diminishing violence than at diminishing restrictions on civil liberties).

It is useful to consider the results in a different form (see Table 4.2). When one considers the most likely value of current repression when *Competition/Participation* is 0 and given a specific value of previous repression, the results show a more robust pacifying influence.

For example, we see that when there is no *Competition/Participation* (column 2), there is still a drift in repression in relatively autocratic governments away from higher values in the previous year to lower values in the subsequent period. Thus, when prior repression was in category 3 (where violence is low but restrictions are high), the next period repression is likely in category 2 (where violence is low but restrictions are moderate); when previous repression was in category 4 (where violence is moderate but restrictions are low), in the next year repression is likely in category 2; when prior repression was in categories 6 and 7 (where, respectively, violence is moderate but restrictions are high and violence is high but restrictions are low), in the next year repression is likely moderate. These results are similar to those in the *Suffrage* model. Findings differ when one considers

Table 4.2. *The Influence of* Competition/Participation *on the Most Likely Current Value of Repression*

1	2	3
Lag Repression	Most Likely Value of Current Repression When *Competition/ Participation* = 0	Most Likely Value of Current Repression When *Competition/ Participation* = 100
1	1	1
2	2	2
3	2 ▲ −	2
4	2 ▲ −	2
5	5	2 ▲ −
6	5 ▲ −	2 ▲ −
7	5 ▲ −	2 ▲ −
8	8	2 ▲ −
9	9	5 ▲ −

Legend: ▲ = change; − = negative change; + = positive change.

what happens when *Competition/Participation* increases to its maximum value.

When this aspect of *Voice* is enhanced, we see that the most likely values of current repression for categories 1–4 are identical to those achieved had *Competition/Participation* remained low. Within categories 5 (moderate violence and restriction) through 9 (the highest form of repressive lethality), however, significant changes can be identified above and beyond those achieved when Suffrage was nonexistent. For example, in situations of increased *Competition/Participation*, when previous repression was in categories 5, 6, 7, or 8, coercion in the next year moves downward to category 2 (low violence, moderate restriction). Similarly, when previous repression was at the highest level of repressive lethality, *Competition/Participation* moves repression downward to a moderate value (category 5). Here, *Voice* pacifies and in comparatively larger amounts to that revealed in the *Suffrage* model.

The difference between the two measures of *Voice* is relevant to this discussion because they reflect unique forms of pacification. Apartheid South Africa provides a useful illustration. For example, although *Suffrage* was increased in January 1986 when P. W. Botha "accepted the principle of universal citizenship in a single nation and the formation of a National Council that would include the Bantustan leaders, elected township representatives, representatives of the three houses of Parliament, and ten presidential appointees" (Wood 2000, 180), it is not until 1994 that *Competition/*

Participation was increased following the representation of diverse political parties.[4] It should come as no surprise that it was only after the latter change that the lethality of state repression decreased, in 1995. Interestingly, the change was not as significant as most would expect – at least not initially; from 1994 to 1995, lethality moved only from category 8 (high violence and moderate restriction) to category 7 (high violence and low restriction). This differs from what most would associate with the post-Apartheid South African situation but as the 1995 U.S. State Department country report indicates, deaths in political custody as well as torture remained matters of concern following the official end of Apartheid. Additionally, the report recounted that despite numerous changes within the legal system (improving the ability to unionize to engage in collective bargaining, and so forth), the government still retained significant powers over the freedom of the press and there were numerous instances of forced deportation.

I now turn to my investigation of *Veto*.

The Influence of Veto

In line with the argument outlined earlier, it may be the case that those aspects of political democracy that involve *Veto* also pacify repressive behavior. Prior research suggests that when political authorities and their policies are subject to the supervision and/or approval of others both within and outside government, they would be less inclined to use repression. I consider two measures in order to investigate this relationship: the number of *Veto Players* and the level of *Executive Constraints*.

Veto *Players*

One aspect of democracy that is highlighted in the literature as an important determinant of repression is the number of *Veto Players* in the legislative process. As expected, those governments with fewer *Veto Players* have fewer restrictions on the leader and thus are less constrained in behavior that leads to repression; those governments with larger numbers of *Veto Players* have greater restrictions on political authorities and are therefore more constrained in what they can and cannot do. The data used to examine this

---

[4] Blacks were allowed to vote for Bantustan leadership, which did receive some form of representation within the South African federal government after 1986. This likely accounts for the high Suffrage figure observed prior to 1994.

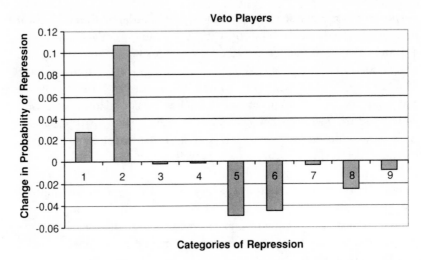

Figure 4.3 The Influence of *Veto Players* on Repressive Lethality

argument are taken from Keefer (2002). Table 1, column 3 in Appendix 2, presents the coefficients and model fit statistics for the ordered probit models of repression that include the *Veto Player* measure. Looking at the likelihood ratio test and supporting Hypothesis 2 that *Veto* decreases coercive action, it is again evident that the model including *Veto Players* is better than those that exclude the concept.

Observing the change in predicted probability across the nine values of repression (Figure 4.3), we see a trend similar to that found by *Suffrage* and *Competition/Participation*. The probability of achieving categories 1 and 2 – the least repressive strategies examined, is influenced positively, whereas the probability of the next seven is decreased. In short, low-level repressive activities are encouraged but more lethal forms of repression are discouraged by this aspect of democracy. Interestingly, influences on the first two categories are similar to *Suffrage* with the magnitude of impact on the second category far exceeding that of the first; recall that *Competition/Participation* influenced both categories in approximately the same way. The remaining seven values of the dependent variable closely resemble *Competition/Participation*. Here, the magnitude of influence wanes as one moves across repressive categories, so that by category 8, the impact of changing *Veto* is quite small (approximately 1 percent).

The different magnitudes of influence across aspects of democracy are particularly worthy of attention. For example, the effect for *Competition/*

Democratic Pacification

Table 4.3. *The Influence of* Veto Players *on the Most Likely Current Value of Repression*

1	2	3
	Most Likely Value of Current Repression	Most Likely Value of Current Repression
Lag Repression	Given *Veto Players* = 1	Given *Veto Players* ≥ 6
1	1	1
2	2	2
3	2 ▲ −	2
4	2 ▲ −	2
5	5	2 ▲ −
6	5 ▲ −	5
7	5 ▲ −	2 ▲ −
8	8	5 ▲ −
9	9	9

Legend: ▲ = change; − = negative change; + = positive change.

Participation is generally about eight times that of *Suffrage* in the most influenced category (2) and the effect of *Veto Players* is about two times that of *Suffrage* but less than half that of *Competition/Participation*. This establishes a clear hierarchy of influence. The findings present somewhat mixed results regarding the relative importance of *Voice* and *Veto*, however, because one aspect of *Voice* (*Competition/Participation*) is stronger in its effect compared with one aspect of *Veto* (*Veto Players*) but another is weaker (*Suffrage*). Given that *Competition/Participation* wields the greatest influence of any variable examined thus far, I conclude that *Voice* generally exceeds *Veto* in terms of its pacific capabilities, which support Hypothesis 4.

Continuing a practice established in the other statistical analyses, I also consider the influence of *Veto* on repression noting the previous level of repressive behavior. From Table 4.3, I find that the most likely value of current repression when *Veto Players* is set to its lowest value and given a specific value of previous repression (column 2) is more or less comparable to that revealed above. Specifically, results disclose that there was a natural diminishment in repression from one year to the next within autocratic systems. For example, when repressive behavior was previously low in violence but high in restrictions and where violence was moderate but restrictions were low (in categories 3 and 4), subsequent repression is reduced to low violence, moderate restriction (category 2). Additionally, when repression was previously moderate in violence but high in restrictions and where violence was high but restrictions were low (in categories 6 and 7), in the next year repressive behavior was reduced to moderate values (category 5).

Moving the number of *Veto Players* to its maximum value (column 3), there are a few changes in the results, in line with the domestic democratic peace. Within repressive categories 1 through 4, there are no changes at all. With regard to these strategies, it does not matter if the number of *Players* is low or high. When repression is previously in categories 5 and 7 and *Veto Players* are enhanced, however, subsequent repression is reduced to a relatively low value (category 2). Prior use of moderate to high values of repression were diminished when the number of *Veto Players* was increased. Additionally, when previous repression was in category 8 (high violence but moderate restriction) and *Veto Players* were increased in number, subsequent repressive activity is again reduced to moderate values (category 5).

The other type of *Veto* I consider looks beyond the political actors that officially play a role in influencing the government. This is considered next.

Executive Constraints

To investigate the impact of this variable on repression, I use the (XCONST) indicator collected by Ted Gurr and his research team. Drawing upon Davenport and Armstrong (2004), I created a series of dummy variables to measure this regime characteristic, each representing the seven categories of the indicator, including the highest six in the model.[5] Table 1, column 4 in Appendix 2, presents the coefficients and fit statistics for the models of repression, including the six dummy variables representing the categories of *Executive Constraints*. Again, the likelihood ratio statistics and their associated p-values show that the model containing *Executive Constraints* is better than the model excluding this variable (supporting Hypothesis 2 which maintained that *Veto* decreased repressive behavior).

From the empirical results presented in Figure 4.4, the predicted probabilities show that the effects of *Executive Constraints* on repressive lethality are similar to the other aspects of democracy examined previously, especially the other *Veto* measure. Again, movement of *Executive Constraints* from its minimum to maximum generally increases the likelihood of low-level repression while decreasing the likelihood of more lethal activity. Additionally, once more, the greatest positive impact is observed in category 2 (low violence, moderate restriction) – an influence that is comparable to

[5] The lowest was left out as a control.

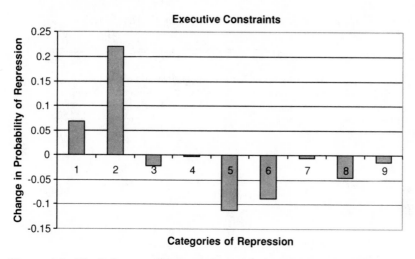

Figure 4.4 The Influence of *Executive Constraints* on Repressive Lethality

the other aspects of democracy. The greatest negative influence is found in category 5, diminishing as more lethal forms of repression are considered. This is also similar to the other aspects of democracy examined previously.

The magnitude of the *Executive Constraints* variable in the most influential category is lower than *Competition/Participation* but higher than *Veto Players* and *Suffrage*. Again, this presents something of a mixed finding considering the hypotheses identified in Chapter 2. The most influential variable concerns *Voice* (*Competition/Participation*), the next two concern *Veto* (*Executive Constraints* and *Veto Players*), and the weakest concerns the other measure of *Voice* (*Suffrage*). Given the magnitude of difference between *Competition/Participation* and others, I still draw the conclusion that the empirical results generally support the argument that *Voice* is more pacific than *Veto* (Hypothesis 4); I say this noting that the indicators of *Veto* are more consistent in their negative influence.

I acknowledge that the results reported here are potentially misleading because they do not allow us to address the issue of distinct starting points: the idea that democracy might function more or less effectively given different levels of previous repression. To address this, I consider the most likely value of current repression when *Executive Constraints* are set to 0 (column 2 in Table 4.4), given a specific value of previous repression. Under these circumstances, I again find that there is a downward drift in repressive activity from one year to the next even in a relatively autocratic context. Thus,

Table 4.4. *The Influence of* Executive Constraints *on the Most Likely Current Value of Repression*

1 Lag Repression	2 Most Likely Current Repression Given *Executive Constraints* = 1	3 Most Likely Current Repression Given *Executive Constraints* = 7
1	1	1
2	2	2
3	2 ▲ −	2
4	5 ▲ −	2 ▲ −
5	5	2 ▲ −
6	5 ▲ −	2 ▲ −
7	5 ▲ −	2 ▲ −
8	8	5 ▲ −
9	9	8 ▲ −

Legend: ▲ = change; − = negative change; + = positive change.

when previous repression was in category 3 (low violence, high restriction), subsequent repression was likely to move to category 2, and when previous repression was in categories 6 and 7, subsequent repressive activity was likely to move to category 5 (moderate violence and restriction). Interestingly, when previous repression was in category 4 (moderate violence and low restriction), there is a general tendency for this to increase to category 5 in the next year.

Moving *Executive Constraints* from their minimum to their maximum (column 3), there were numerous changes that reveal strong support for the domestic democratic peace. For example, when previous repression was in categories 1–3, the results were similar to what occurred had there been no change in regime type. When prior repression was in categories 4–7, however, I find that increasing *Executive Constraints* uniformly reduced subsequent repressive activity to low violence, moderate restriction (category 2). Even the most lethal forms of repression were pacified. Thus, when previous repression was in category 8 (high violence, moderate restriction) and *Executive Constraints* increased, subsequent repressive behavior decreased to category 5 (moderate violence and restriction). Similarly, in the most lethal of categories (9), after *Executive Constraints* increased, subsequent repressive behavior decreased to category 8. Here, we see that *Veto* reduces repression in a manner directly in line with the domestic democratic peace and quite significantly across categories of previous repression.

The differences between the two measures of *Veto* are useful to highlight with a historical example. During the first free elections in Bulgaria after nearly four decades of communist rule and the fall of Todor Zhivkov's regime (in 1990), official *Veto Players* were essentially absent from a political system still influenced by the Bulgarian Socialist Party (formerly the Bulgarian Communist Party). Nevertheless, civil society organizations began to wield a significant influence over government authorities, thereby serving as unofficial *Veto Players* more in keeping with what Gurr and associates refer to as *Executive Constraints*. This development was facilitated by the institutionalization of twenty-one measures of constitutional reform, including the end of political monopolization of the Bulgarian Communist (Socialist) Party and, in the wake of this action, the fractionalization of many political organizations. The influence of civil society was so significant at this time that a legislative review board referred to as "the round table" took on an unofficial but prominent role. This informal structure was formalized in the Political Consultant Council in late 1990–1 (under President Zhelyu Zhelev), and by 1991–2 there was an increase in the number of official *Veto Players*.

The influence of *Veto* on repression was apparent rather quickly. Across a wide range of repressive behavior, by 1992–3, most human rights organizations viewed the Bulgarian government as quite tolerant. Despite deadlocks, the persecution of former communist leaders for repressive action and significant competition within as well as between parties, most forms of repression were diminished over this time, moving repressive lethality from moderate violence and high restriction (category 6) to low violence and moderate restriction (category 2). This was very different from the 1980s, when state sanctions against Muslim movements and political challengers were significant.

Of course, the pacification of state coercion was not complete; there were still some problems. Several instances of police abuse were reported (especially against Gypsies). Restrictions applied against Muslims still existed (for example, language rights). During this time, several hundred people affiliated with the Communist Party were banned from diverse government and civil service positions in what is commonly referred to as "lustration" (a ruling handed down by the constitutional court in 1992). Finally, although press freedom had improved, a new penal code was passed, making it illegal to discuss the internal security police, an obvious instance of censorship with far-reaching consequences. At no point did anyone suggest that the situation was anything close to what it was under communist rule.

Combining Models

In the first part of this chapter, I examined the effects of diverse aspects of democracy, looking at them individually. This provides useful information, as many who are interested in creating domestic peace (for example, policymakers, funding organizations, activists, and ordinary citizens) seek to identify the most effective aspect of democracy in which to invest, relative to the alternatives. It is more appropriate, however, to evaluate the importance of diverse aspects of democracy in a competitive fashion. Toward this end, I develop a more complete model containing all relevant indicators: *Suffrage, Competition/Participation, Veto Players*, and *Executive Constraints*. The model is presented in Table 1, column 5 of Appendix 2.

To select the variables for inclusion, I considered diverse tests. A single measure is employed to represent *Suffrage* and *Competition/Participation*, these variables were rather easy to assess. Both were tested simply by observing the p-value on their coefficient in the relevant table. When examined competitively, only the latter achieved statistical significance. To assess whether the *Veto Player* and *Executive Constraint* variables were worthy of inclusion, I used a Wald test. If either variable was equivalent to zero, it was dropped from the final model. I found that when examined competitively only *Executive Constraints* were significant, and the coefficients for *Veto Players* were indistinguishable from zero. Based on these findings, I examined a reduced model containing only *Competition/Participation* and *Executive Constraints*.

While reconfirming the results obtained in the earlier examination, the coefficients from the analysis, again, provide only incomplete understanding. To investigate the impact of each variable more fully, I use predicted probabilities (Figure 4.5).

Reconfirming the preceding analyses, Figure 4.5 shows that both *Competition/Participation* (the first bar in the figure) and *Executive Constraints* (the second bar in the figure) generally increase the probability of being in the least repressive categories while decreasing the probability of being in the next seven. The lone exception here is the statistically significant but substantively unimportant positive influence of *Executive Constraints* on the achievement of category 3. These findings support the weak version of Hypotheses 1 that *Voice* decreases repression but challenges Hypothesis 2 that *Veto* decreases repression (though only in a small way given the magnitude of influence achieved in category 3). With the significance of both

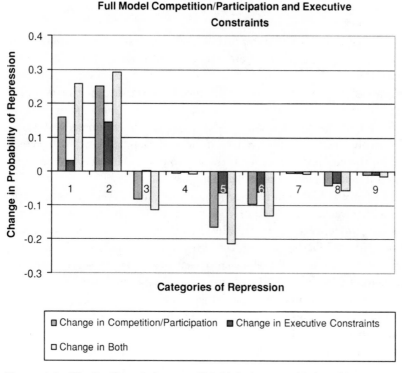

Figure 4.5 The Pacifying Influence of Multiple Aspects of Political Democracy

variables in categories 1 and 2 (where political violence is low but restrictions are low and moderate, respectively) as well as the significance of *Executive Constraints* in category 3, support is also provided for the argument that state violence is somewhat better pacified than political restrictions (Hypothesis 5).

The results are generally weaker when diverse democratic components are considered simultaneously but still stronger than all of the variables in the base model. Within the individual analyses, the influence of *Competition/Participation* on category 2 (low violence and moderate restriction) was approximately 27 percent, while the influence of *Executive Constraints* on achieving this category was approximately 23 percent. Considering the competitive model, these influences decline to about 25 percent and 14 percent, respectively; that is, democratic pacification of each component is less powerful when multiple aspects of democracy are considered at the same time.[6]

Results also reveal significant differences across values of repression. For example, the margin of difference between *Competition/Participation* and *Executive Constraints* was greater in lower and middle-range categories of repression (generally in favor of the former). Consistent with earlier findings, therefore, we see that *Competition/Participation* generally exceeds the influence of *Executive Constraints*, thus supporting Hypothesis 4. In short, the involvement and effectiveness of the mass population in participating within the political system holds the key to domestic peace. Interestingly, this difference in influence wanes in higher categories. Thus, where political violence is high and restrictions are moderate (level 8), both *Competition/Participation* and *Executive Constraints* wield approximately the same negative influence on the probability of achieving repression (approximately 5 percent). While the involvement of the mass population with the political system holds the key to domestic peace, promoting low-level repressive behavior, the existence of *Veto Players* is as capable as this other aspects of democracy in discouraging more lethal repressive activities.

The relative importance of *Voice* is revealed in yet another way. Considering situations in which both *Competition/Participation* and *Executive Constraints* were simultaneously increased from their minimum to maximum (the last bar in Figure 4.5), the familiar pattern of the previous investigations is found with the probability of lower level repression being increased while the probability of higher level repression is decreased. An example of this simultaneous occurrence includes the period after President (and General) Muhammed Zia-Ul-Haq of Pakistan died in a plane crash in 1988, freeing the country from military rule and facilitating the ascendance of the former chairman of the senate,[7] Ghulam Ishaq Khan to the presidency.

As found, the influence of the *Competition/Participation–Executive Constraints* combination is larger than when either variable is viewed by itself. Anyone interested in decreasing repressive behavior, would be well advised to increase both at the same time. It is clear, however, that if one were

---

[6] This does not mean that interactive relationships are not important, but they are not considered in this analysis.

[7] According to available data, *Suffrage* was increased in 1984 from 0 to 95.6 percent – staying there through 1996. The number of *Veto Players* increased in 1989 from 1 to 5, decreasing in 1992 to 4, increasing to 6 in 1994 through to the end of the period under examination (1996).

to alter only one/aspect of the political system, it should be *Competition/Participation*. This variable comes closest to the influence reached by the combination of democratic characteristics at every single value of repressive behavior. Interestingly, where coercion is most lethal (at the highest levels of repression), all three measures (*Competition/Participation, Executive Constraints,* and the combination of both aspects of democracy) wield approximately the same influence – an admittedly small amount in terms of substantive impact. This suggests that when repression is most lethal, none of the system characteristics function particularly well as mechanisms of pacification.

Similar to the earlier analyses, in an effort to better contextualize the empirical results, I also consider the influence of three different variants of system characteristics amid diverse starting points (that is, values of lagged repressive behavior): one where *Executive Constraints* is held constant at its mean but where *Competition/Participation* is increased from its minimum to its maximum, one where this is reversed, and one where both *Executive Constraints* and *Competition/Participation* are increased from their minimum to maximum.

It is clear from Table 4.5 that *Competition/Participation* carries the bulk of the explanatory weight in the model. Holding *Executive Constraints* constant at its median and *Competition/Participation* at its minimum (column 2) and viewing the most likely value of current repression given diverse values of past repression, there are several noteworthy results. For example, one can see a decrease in repressive behavior from one year to the next, even in a generally inhospitable political environment (limited *Competition/Participation* and *Executive Constraints*). Thus, when previous repression was in category 3 (low violence, high restriction), the following year decreases to category 2 (low violence, moderate restriction). When previous repression was in categories 6 and 7, subsequent repression decreases to category 5 (moderate values). And, when past repression was category 8 (high violence, moderate restriction), subsequent repressive behavior decreases to category 6 (moderate violence, high restriction). Again, I find that category 4 escalates to category 5.

Moving *Competition/Participation* to its maximum but retaining *Executive Constraints* at its median (column 3), I find that the domestic democratic peace is well supported. In this context, the influence on categories 1–3 is the same as what would have happened had *Competition/Participation* not been increased, but in categories 5–9 there are significant differences. For

Table 4.5. *The Influence of Diverse Aspects of Democracy Viewed Simultaneously on the Most Likely Current Value of Repression*

1	2 *Executive Constraints = Median; Competition/ Participation = Minimum*	3 *Executive Constraints = Median; Competition/ Participation = Maximum*	4 *Executive Constraints = Minimum; Competition/ Participation = Median*	5 *Executive Constraints = Maximum; Competition/ Participation = Median*	6 *Executive Constraints = Minimum; Competition/ Participation = Minimum*	7 *Executive Constraints = Maximum; Competition/ Participation = Maximum*
Lag Repression						
1	1	1	1	1	1	1
2	2	2	2	2	2	1▲–
3	2▲–	2	2▲–	2	2▲–	2
4	5▲+	2▲–	5▲+	2▲–	5▲+	2▲–
5	5	2▲–	5	2▲–	5	2▲–
6	5▲–	2▲–	5▲–	5	5▲–	2▲–
7	5▲–	2▲–	5▲–	5	5▲–	2▲–
8	6▲–	5▲–	8	5▲–	8	2▲–
9	9	5▲–	9	9	9	5▲–

Legend: ▲ = change; – = negative change; + = positive change.

example, when prior repression was between categories 4 and 7 – encompassing regimes that employ moderate values of violence with a range of political restrictions or high political violence with low restrictions – enhanced *Competition/Participation* uniformly decreases repression to category 2 (low violence, moderate restriction). Even the highest categories of repressive lethality (8 and 9) are reduced to moderate values (5) when *Competition/Participation* is increased.

The situation is different when *Competition/Participation* is held at its median but *Executive Constraints* is increased from its minimum (column 4) to its maximum (column 5). In this case, a comparable amount of pacification is observed when *Executive Constraints* was limited (comparing columns 1 and 3). When previous repression is found in categories 3, 6, and 7, subsequent repressive behavior is decreased (the first to category 2 and the remaining two to category 5). Again, a positive influence is found when prior repression was in category 4, which subsequently increased to moderate violence and restriction (category 5). When *Competition/Participation* is held constant and *Executive Constraints* is increased (column 4), there are few additional instances of pacification (compared to column 3). For example, under these circumstances previous repressive behavior in categories 4 and 5 is further reduced to category 2 in the following year. Additionally, when prior repressive behavior is in category 8 (one of the most lethal categories), this is decreased to category 5 in the following year (moderate activity). The differences between high *Competition/Participation* and high *Executive Constraints* (between columns 2 and 4) are significant, revealing the greater pacifying capability of the former.

When both aspects of democracy are changed simultaneously (column 7), the results reconfirm what was identified earlier: *Competition/Participation* carries the bulk of the explanatory weight. Observing the table, one can see that the results look almost identical to those derived when the value of *Competition/Participation* was manipulated by itself. Indeed, there are only two changes between these two models. First, countries that previously were in repressive category 2 (where violence is low but restrictions are high) are subsequently moved to the least repressive category (1). Second, countries that were previously in the second most lethal category (8) are reduced to category 2 instead of category 5 (where both forms of repression are at moderate levels). This suggests that *Competition/Participation* is by far the most important aspect of democracy in decreasing the state's lethal repressive activity.

Summary

Upon examining diverse democratic characteristics individually as well as competitively, my research discloses an influence on repression that is consistent with the expectations of the domestic democratic peace: different aspects of democracy (*Voice* and *Veto*) promote lower level coercive activity while discouraging more lethal forms. The magnitude of this influence varies across types of democracy as well as across repressive strategies. As found, *Voice* (*Competition/ Participation*) is more effective than *Veto* (*Executive Constraints*) in reducing state repression. Generally, the influence of *Voice* and *Veto* is quite strong in its ability to influence the adoption of different strategies of repression. At their best, these variables are able to influence the probability of achieving one repressive category (2) at approximately 30 percent; at their worst (categories 8 and 9), they still function better than almost any other variable used in the standard explanatory model, including GNP per capita, population size, violent dissent, and civil and interstate war.

From this analysis, we thus see that the argument of Schumpeter and Dahl generally outweigh those of Madison and Montesquieu. Although settling one debate within the literature regarding the relative importance of mass-based as compared with elite-based aspects of democracy, however, another remains: the ability of distinct components of the domestic democratic peace to function in times of political conflict. I turn to this issue in Chapter 5.

5

Peace under Fire

THE INTERACTIVE EFFECT OF
DEMOCRACY AND CONFLICT

In the last chapter, I examined the influence of diverse aspects of institutional democracy on state repression. This included mass-oriented characteristics such as suffrage and competition weighted by participation referred to as _Voice_, as well as elite-oriented characteristics such as the number of official and unofficial political actors that wield an influence on central authorities referred to as _Veto_. Results disclose that repressive behavior is generally decreased in lethality when these aspects of the political system are enhanced. As suggested earlier, however, it might be more appropriate to evaluate the effect of democracy on repressive behavior as conditioned by different forms of political conflict (both intrastate and interstate). Indeed, this may be the strongest test of the domestic democratic peace. If, despite the presence of behavioral threats, _Voice_ and _Veto_ can still reduce the lethality of repression, this speaks to the power of the relationship. If, in the face of conflict behavior, however, _Voice_ and _Veto_ cannot reduce repressive behavior, then this identifies an important limitation of the peace proposition. In an effort to understand the democracy-repression nexus, I now reexamine the models discussed in Chapter 4 and introduce different interactions between democracy and political conflict.

Measures of Voice

I begin my reassessment of the peace proposition with an examination of _Suffrage_ and _Competition/Participation_. Specifically, I evaluate three models where the particular aspect of democracy under consideration is interacted with three measures of political conflict: violent political dissent, civil war, and interstate war. To facilitate the exposition, two graphs accompany each analysis: one represents the influence of a particular aspect of democracy when specific forms of conflict are not present, and one represents the influence of a particular aspect of democracy when conflict is present. Following this, I consider the impact of relevant interactions while incorporating information about exactly what level of repression the government previously employed.

Suffrage

Considering the results (provided in Table 1 in Appendix 3), it is clear that the ability of *Suffrage* to decrease repression is lost in the presence of conflict. This supports Hypothesis 6, which suggests that when domestic and international conflict exists, *Voice* would be unable to reduce repressive behavior. To determine exactly how much conflict alters the influence of suffrage, I again provide the change in predicted probabilities. This reveals exactly how likely it is that a particular category of repression will be achieved given a movement in *Suffrage* from its minimum to its maximum value within periods of peace and conflict, respectively. These are presented in Figure 5.1.

Recall that one reads the figure by simply looking at a specific category of repression (that is, 1–9 along the *x*-axis) with reference to the independent variable of interest (generally identified on the legend along the top or at the right side of the figure). The focus then becomes the corresponding change in the probability of achieving this category, derived from moving the relevant independent variable from its minimum to its maximum (indicated along the *y*-axis). If the value is positive, then the likelihood of a government using a particular combination of repressive tactics is increased. Correspondingly, if the value is negative, then the likelihood of a government using a particular combination of repressive strategies is reduced.[1]

---

[1] Of course, this is somewhat easier said than done. Despite clear explanations in political science journals (see Freidrich 1982), the interpretation of interaction terms is frequently misinterpreted in statistical results. To facilitate clear as well as accurate discussion, I interact the diverse democracy variables identified in the text with a series of conflict dummy variables (coded 0 when conflict is not present and 1 when it is), thus making interpretation somewhat easier. The interpretation of these variables is rather straightforward because the coefficient and standard error on the democracy term are the value and standard error of democracy when violence is equal to zero. The coefficient and standard error on the multiplicative term are the effect and standard error of the difference between democracy when violence equals zero and when violence equals one. If this term is significant, the effect of democracy when violence equals one is different from when violence equals zero. To obtain the effect of

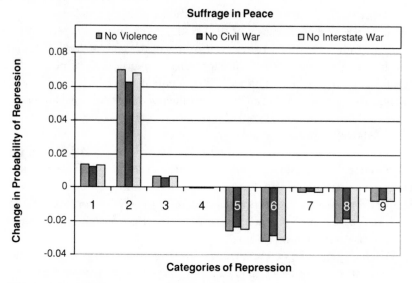

Figure 5.1(a) *Suffrage* in Peace and Conflict

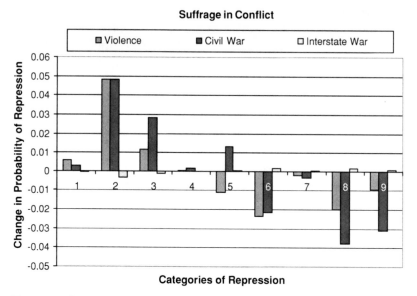

Figure 5.1(b)

Mirroring the results from the noninteractive model provided in Chapter 4, the graphic presentation of the results reveals that *Suffrage* has only marginal influences on repression, regardless of the type of conflict being considered. Specifically, results disclose that during periods of peace (the top figure) the influence of *Suffrage* is generally comparable to the earlier analyses: in the absence of conflict, lower values of repressive behavior (categories 1–3) were increased by *Suffrage*, while higher values of repression (5 and above) were decreased by it. Here, the absence of violent dissent slightly outweighs the absence of all other forms of conflict followed by the absence of interstate war and finally civil war. Although this generally supports the argument that *Voice* decreases repression (Hypothesis 1), the support for this conclusion is weakened because repressive category 3 is increased by *Suffrage* in the absence of political conflict. The influence however is substantively marginal.

When one considers the influence of *Suffrage* in periods of conflict (the bottom part of Figure 5.1), the results change significantly with regard to both causal direction and the relative importance of different interactions. Overall, the domestic democratic peace is weakened, but the results themselves are quite mixed across types of conflict and repressive strategies.

For instance, compared with the results obtained when conflict is absent, when violent dissent exists and *Suffrage* is increased from its minimum to its maximum, the likelihood of achieving lower level (categories 1–3) as well as mid-level repressive behavior (category 5) is diminished by a decent amount, while the likelihood of attaining higher level repression (categories 6–9) is reduced by a somewhat lesser amount. In other words, when violent dissent takes place and *Suffrage* is increased, governments are much less likely to employ lower level repression, and they are less likely to employ more lethal repressive behavior; the democratic peace is weakened in the least lethal situations. This supports the argument that political threats overwhelm democracy (Hypothesis 6) while revealing that it is inappropriate to view all repressive categories in the same manner.

In the case of civil war, causal relationships are less definitive. Similar to violent dissent, the probability of achieving the first three repressive

democracy when violence equals zero, I add the coefficients of the democracy and the multiplicative term. The variance of this term is a linear combination of the variances of the democracy and multiplicative terms and two times the covariance of the democracy and multiplicative terms. A z-value can then be calculated and evaluated on the standard normal distribution. This will suggest whether the effect of democracy is significant under conditions of conflict.

categories decreases when civil war exists and *Suffrage* increases from its minimum to its maximum (compared with when these conditions do not exist). At each value of repression, given the same enhancement of *Suffrage*, the probability of achieving the relevant value is much higher when civil war is not present. The magnitude of influence across these categories varies, however. While the probability of attaining the least repressive strategy (category 1) is greater in the violent dissent-*Suffrage* interaction, the situation is reversed in categories 2 and 3 (where political violence is low and restrictions are moderate and high, respectively). The probability of observing repression in these contexts is much greater when civil war and *Suffrage* interact, suggesting that high-level threats are more likely to prompt higher level repressive behavior. Very different in terms of causal impact are categories 4 and 5 (where political violence is moderate but restrictions are low and moderate, respectively). In these circumstances, when civil war exists and *Suffrage* increases, the probability of achieving these categories is enhanced. This moves against the hypothesis that *Voice* decreases repression during conflict. Again, the magnitude of the influence is marginal, but the direction of the influence is not in line with anticipated results. Moving with the expectations of the peace proposition, the likelihood of lethal repression is decreased when civil war and *Voice* interact at the highest values of the dependent variable; indeed, within categories 8 and 9, the negative influence is about twice what it is when there is no civil war – showing that democratic peace functions best in the most violent situations.

Finally, in the case of interstate war, the findings generally support Hypothesis 6, which stipulates that *Voice* is unable to diminish repression when conflict is present. In the absence of war, *Suffrage* increases the probability of achieving the lowest forms of repression while decreasing the likelihood of more lethal coercive behavior. When interstate war occurs, however, the pacifying influence of *Suffrage* is completely eliminated. In the context of international conflict and increased *Suffrage*, the likelihood of achieving lower level conflict decreases, and the probability of more lethal repressive activity is increased. Now, it is clearly the case that the magnitude of influence is still substantively unimportant, but the reversal of causal impact is worthy of attention.

To better understand the results, I consider in Table 5.1 the most likely value of current repression (at time t), given a specific value of repression at time $t - 1$, no *Suffrage*, and varying violent dissent (columns 2 and 4). This is compared with the most likely value of current repression (at time t), *Suffrage* and varying violent dissent (columns 3 and 5).

Table 5.1. *Most Likely Value of Current Repression for* Suffrage

1 Lag Repression	2 Given Suffrage = 0; Violent Dissent = 0	3 Given Suffrage = 100; Violent Dissent = 0	4 Given Suffrage = 0; Violent Dissent = 1	5 Given Suffrage = 100; Violent Dissent = 1
1	1	1	1	1
2	2	2	2	2
3	2▲−	2	5▲+	2▲−
4	2▲−	2	5▲+	2▲−
5	5	2▲−	5	5
6	5▲−	5	8▲+	6▲−
7	5▲−	2▲−	5▲−	5
8	6▲−	6	8	8
9	9	9	9	9

Lag Repression	Given Suffrage = 0; Civil War = 0	Given Suffrage = 100; Civil War = 0	Given Suffrage = 0; Civil War = 1	Given Suffrage = 100; Civil War = 1
1	1	1	1	1
2	2	2	2	2
3	2▲−	2	5▲+	5
4	2▲−	2	5▲+	5
5	5	2▲−	6▲+	5▲−
6	5▲−	5	8▲+	8
7	5▲−	5	6	5▲−
8	8	5▲−	9▲+	9
9	9	9	9	9

Lag Repression	Given Suffrage = 0; Interstate War = 0	Given Suffrage = 100; Interstate War = 0	Given Suffrage = 0; Interstate War = 1	Given Suffrage = 100; Interstate War = 1
1	1	1	1	1
2	2	2	2	2
3	2▲−	2	5▲+	2▲−
4	2▲−	2	5▲+	2▲−
5	5	2▲−	5	5
6	5▲−	5	6	6
7	5▲−	5	5▲−	5
8	6▲−	6	8	8
9	9	9	9	9

Legend: ▲ = change; − = negative change; + = positive change.

Consistent with the earlier investigation, results disclose that *Suffrage* is generally unable to influence repressive behavior, especially the most lethal combinations. For example, the most likely value of current repression when *Suffrage* as well as violent dissent is set to 0 (column 2 in the top of Table 5.1), reveals that there is a decrease in state coercive behavior from one year to the next in situations of no suffrage and no dissent. Specifically, where violence is low but restrictions are high and where violence is moderate but restrictions are low (categories 3 and 4), repression is reduced in the following year to low violence but moderate restriction (category 2). Similarly, where violence is moderate but restrictions are high and where violence is high but restrictions are low (categories 6 and 7), repression is reduced in the following year to moderate repressive activity (category 5). Even one of the most lethal combinations of repression is diminished amidst situations of no suffrage and no dissent (category 8), decreasing to category 6 in the following year.

Increasing *Suffrage* to its highest value but retaining dissent at 0 (column 3) does not change the results much. Indeed, there are only two changes when this is done. For example, when prior repressive behavior was moderate in both violence and restrictions (category 5), there is no dissent but *Suffrage* is enhanced, and subsequent repression is decreased to category 2 (low violence, moderate restriction). Similarly, when prior repressive behavior is high in violence but low in restrictions (category 7) and *Suffrage* is increased, subsequent repression is decreased beyond where it would have been had *Suffrage* not been enhanced, again to category 2.

When violent dissent is introduced, results are altered, but again the influence of *Suffrage* is found to be minimal. For example, given a particular value of prior repression, *Suffrage* set to 0 (at time *t*) and dissident activity (also at time *t*) several values of current repression are increased (column 4). Under these circumstances, mid-level coercive strategies (3 and 4) in the previous year are increased to category 5 in the following year, while category 6 in the previous year is increased to category 8 (high violence, moderate restriction). Interestingly, under the same conditions, category 7 in the previous year decreases to category 5. Dissent thus compels a previously repressive regime to diminish its efforts, not completely but noticeably.

During violent dissent, enhancing *Suffrage* to its highest value again does not change the results very much (column 5). In this case, there are only three changes, all consistent with the domestic democratic peace but substantively minor. When violent dissent (at time *t*) and prior repression are in categories 3 and 4, increasing *Suffrage* reduces repressive behavior to category 2 the next year (low violence, moderate restriction). Similarly, when repression was previously moderate in violence and high in restriction (category 6), increasing *Suffrage* in periods of violent dissent tends to keep the subsequent value of repression at the same level (6) instead of increasing it to category 8, as is observed when *Suffrage* is not increased.

When the form of political conflict considered is changed from violent dissent to civil war (the middle grouping in Table 5.1), the results change in important ways. Again, however, *Suffrage* has little to no impact on repressive behavior. For example, the most likely value of current repression given diverse values of lagged repression, *Suffrage* set to 0, and no civil war (column 2) is essentially the same as that found when there is no violent dissent. Here, categories 3, 4, 6, and 7 reveal a tendency to decline in the next year. During these relatively peaceful periods, increasing *Suffrage* (column 3) reduces repression only within two categories: moderate violence and restriction (category 5) – which is reduced to low violence, moderate restriction (category 2) – and high violence, moderate restriction (category 8) – which is reduced to category 5. While consistent with the domestic democratic peace, this suggests that the influence of this aspect of *Voice* is limited, as all other categories are not influenced.

In line with expectations, when civil war takes place but *Suffrage* is set at its minimum (column 4), repression is increased across almost all values. For example, when prior coercion is in categories 3 and 4 (where, respectively, violence was low but restrictions were high and violence was moderate but restrictions were low) in the face of civil war, subsequent repressive activity increases to value 5. When previous repression is in categories 5 and 7 (where, respectively, violence as well as restrictions are moderate and violence is high but restrictions are low) in the face of civil war, subsequent coercive activity increases to level 6. Finally, during episodes of large-scale domestic conflict, prior repressive level 6 increases to level 8, while prior repressive behavior 8 increases to 9, leading to the most lethal forms of state repression.

Within contexts of civil war, the impact of *Suffrage* is minimal. In fact, raising this aspect of democracy to its highest value (column 5) only diminishes repressive activity in two situations compared to what was found if suffrage did not exist. First, when prior repression was moderate (in category 5), *Suffrage* maintains this level in the following year instead increasing to category 8, which occurs when *Suffrage* is minimal. Second, when prior

140

violence is high and restrictions are low (in category 7), *Suffrage* decreases repression to category 5.

Comparatively, the pacifying capabilities of *Suffrage* in the face of inter-state war are limited (the bottom part of Table 5.1). In viewing the results, it is clear that the most likely value of current repression in the absence of *Suffrage* and interstate war is comparable to the results obtained in the absence of dissent (column 2). Increasing *Suffrage* to its highest value (column 3), changes only one category. As found, when previous repression is moderate in both violence and restrictions, when there is no war, and when *Suffrage* is increased from its minimum to its maximum, then subsequent repressive behavior is decreased to category 2 (low violence, moderate restriction).

In situations of war but limited *Suffrage* (column 4), changes are again limited. The most likely value of current repression in the absence of *Suffrage* but in the presence of interstate war is directly comparable to the results obtained in the presence of dissent. Indeed, there is only one difference (the increase from category 6 to 8). Increasing *Suffrage*, during interstate conflict (column 5), changes only two categories, thus revealing the weak pacifying capability of this aspect of *Voice*. Here, enhanced *Suffrage* tends to reduce repression when prior levels were in low-to-middle range values of repressive lethality (either category 3 or 4). All other categories are the same as they would have been had no adjustment been made to regime type.

I now turn to the other aspect of *Voice*, *Competition/Participation*.

Competition and Participation

Observing the results for the Vanhanen/Gates et al. measure (provided in Table 2 in Appendix 3), it is clear that despite political conflict, *Competition/Participation* influences repression in a manner consistent with the domestic democratic peace. Relationships during periods of peace as well as during periods of conflict are provided in Figure 5.2.

Without conflict (the top half of Figure 5.2), we see Figure 4.2, which was derived from the direct analysis of the last chapter. When *Competition/Participation* is increased and conflict does not exist, the probability of the lowest two values of repression is increased whereas the likelihood of the next seven is diminished. There is some variation across types of conflict absence below category 6 (where state violence is moderate and restrictions are high). For example, the greatest impact on repressive category 1 exists

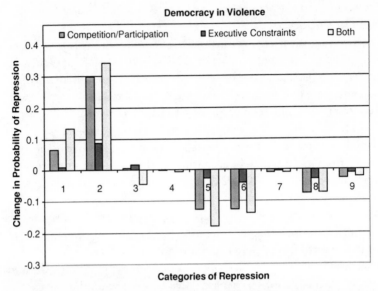

Figure 5.2(a) *Competition/Participation* in Peace and Conflict

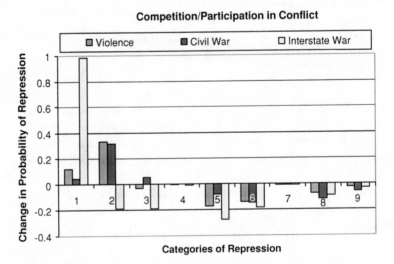

Figure 5.2(b)

when violent dissent is not present, followed by the absence of interstate war and the absence of civil war. This same pattern of effects is also found in categories 3–5, albeit with a negative instead of positive effect on the dependent variable. Differing from this, the highest probability for repressive behavior in category 2 (low in violence but moderate in restrictions) exists when interstate war absence is considered, followed by civil war and violent dissent. Higher values of repressive lethality (6, 8, and 9) reveal similar influences, although with somewhat different magnitudes.

When one considers the influence of *Competition/Participation* in periods of conflict (the bottom half of Figure 5.2), the results change significantly, but they are consistent with the domestic democratic peace. For instance, one is immediately struck by the interstate war–*Competition/Participation* interaction. When war is present and this measure of *Voice* increases from its minimum to its maximum, the probability of achieving the lowest level of repression (category 1) is near 100 percent – three times the influence when war is not present. In the context of war, enhanced *Voice* almost always leads to the least amount of repressive behavior. In line with the strong version of the pacification argument, the remaining categories are negative in their effects, at more or less comparable amounts (around 2 percent), until the highest values of the repression measure when they diminish. A decent example of this influence is provided in Morocco in 1977. In this year, parliamentary elections were held, ending the on-again, off-again constitutional monarchy[2] and, in this context, the degree of *Competition/Participation* is significantly increased. A year earlier, Morocco had annexed the northern part of the former Spanish territory of the Western Sahara and in resistance to this effort a loose band of guerrillas (the Polisario) engaged both Moroccan and Mauritania's government in battle – aid was also received from Saudi Arabia, Kuwait, and Abu Dhabi. Given the remote location of the war, the lack of connection between the rebels and those within Morocco as well as the "opening" of the Moroccan government, it makes sense that there would be essentially no effect of the war on repression in the home country. According to the data consulted for the analysis, this influence lasted throughout the conflict.

Comparatively, the other two forms of conflict (violent dissent and civil war) wield different as well as weaker influences on state coercive action, but they are still consistent with the domestic democratic peace. For instance,

---

[2] Despite the change, the central authorities (especially King Hassan II) still retain some power.

when violent dissent takes place and *Competition/Participation* is increased from its minimum to its maximum, the likelihood of attaining the least repressive categories is increased: where state violence and restrictions are low (1) and where violence is low and restrictions are moderate (2). Although the impact on the remaining categories of repression is negative, several diminish in their magnitude (3–5) while several are increase (7–9) relative to the situation when conflict is not present. Under threat, governments with enhanced *Competition/Participation* function quite well as mechanisms of peace.

This influence is very apparent within the example of Uruguay in 1993. Eight years after a transfer of power from military rule to a democratically elected government (1985) and four years after the second electoral transfer of power (1989), Uruguayan political authorities faced isolated violent attacks and general strikes. Despite these challenges, however, government officials did not generally resort to more than lower level repressive behavior (category 1). The only activities noted by human rights monitors at the time concerned a few instances of police abuse directed against prisoners and detainees. This was very different from the large-scale activities identified during the years of the "dirty war" (1972–83), when, under military rule, the use of lethal repressive behavior against violent dissent was extensive.

One can also see the relevant influence in the case of Nicaragua in 1990. Three years earlier (in 1987, during the Arias peace accord), representatives of the military force that removed General Anastasio Somoza from power, the Sandinista government,[3] negotiated a cease-fire that called for eliminating political violence and for national elections. One of the combatant groups, the Contras (former supporters of Somoza who were covertly supported by the United States and who fled to Costa Rica and Honduras), did not agree to the cease-fire, and thus hostile interactions continued between them and the Sandinista army. In February 1990, with civil war still under way, the presidential election took place and brought National Opposition Union candidate Violetta Chamorro into office, with the Sandinistas retaining control of the military, police, and secret service. By March, however, the Contras put down their arms, the Sandinistas accepted Chamorro's political victory, and peace was restored, if only temporarily. During this period, intimidation, censorship, arrest, torture, armed attacks, and even killing were reported (5 on my repressive measure), but despite the presence of

[3] Formally, they were called the Sandinista National Liberation Front (FSLN).

state-sponsored political violence, the lethality of repressive behavior had significantly decreased from where it was (8 on the repression scale in 1989, which represents high violence but moderate restrictions). This is also better than where state behavior quickly moved within the next few years, as the delicate balance between the Chamorro government, the Sandinista coercive agents, and the Contras once again fell apart (again, moving back to 8 on the repression scale). Within a period of political opening and civil instability, repressive behavior was pacified.

Examining the most likely value of current repression given lagged repression, *Competition/Participation* at its lowest value, and no political conflict (column 2 in the upper part of Table 5.2), all influences are generally similar to the results found in the *Suffrage* analysis with minor differences. In this context, when prior repression is characterized by low violence, high restriction (category 3), current *Competition/Participation* is limited and there is no violent dissent, repressive behavior is decreased to low violence, moderate restriction (category 2). In contrast, during a time of low *Competition/Participation* and no violent dissent, when previous repression is characterized by moderate violence, low restriction (category 4), repression is subsequently increased to category 5 (moderate violence and restriction). Under the same circumstances, several combinations of higher level repression are diminished, though only slightly. For example, where prior violence is moderate but restrictions are high and where prior violence is high but restriction is low (when prior repression is in categories 6 and 7, respectively), subsequent repressive action tends to decrease to moderate values (category 5). Finally, when previous state repression is high in violence and moderate in restriction (category 8), in situations where *Competition/Participation* is low and there is no violent dissident activity, subsequent repression decreases to moderate violence and high restriction (category 6).

Significantly differing from the *Suffrage* model, results disclose that when *Competition/Participation* increases but violent dissent is still absent (column 3 in the top part of Table 5.2), the domestic democratic peace is strongly supported. Here, seven out of nine categories are influenced in a negative direction (the lethality of repression is diminished at substantively important values). For example, when previous repressive behavior was in category 2 (low violence, moderate restriction) and *Competition/Participation* increases to its maximum, subsequent repressive activity is decreased to the least coercive strategy (category 1). When previous repression is in categories 4–8 and *Competition/Participation* increases to its maximum, subsequent repression

Table 5.2. *Most Likely Value of Current Repression for* Competition/Participation

1	2	3	4	5
Lag Repression	Given Competition/Participation = 0; Violent Dissent = 0	Given Competition/Participation = 100; Violent Dissent = 0	Given Competition/Participation = 0; Violent Dissent = 1	Given Competition/Participation = 100; Violent Dissent = 1
1	1	1	1	1
2	2	1▲−	2	2
3	2▲−	2	5▲+	2▲−
4	5	2▲−	5▲+	2▲−
5	5	2▲−	5	2▲−
6	5▲−	2▲−	5▲−	2▲−
7	5▲−	2▲−	5▲−	2▲−
8	6▲−	2▲−	8	5▲−
9	9	5▲−	9	6▲−
Lag Repression	Given Competition/Participation = 0; Civil War = 0	Given Competition/Participation = 100; Civil War = 0	Given Competition/Participation = 0; Civil War = 1	Given Competition/Participation = 100; Civil War = 1
1	1	1	2▲+	1
2	2	1▲−	2	2
3	2▲−	2	5▲+	2▲−
4	5▲+	2▲−	5▲+	2▲−
5	5	2▲−	5	2▲−
6	5▲−	2▲−	8▲+	5▲−
7	5▲−	2▲−	8▲+	5▲−
8	6▲−	2▲−	9▲+	5▲−
9	9	5▲−	9	9
Lag Repression	Given Competition/Participation = 1; Interstate War = 0	Given Competition/Participation = 100; Interstate War = 0	Given Competition/Participation = 0; Interstate War = 1	Given Competition/Participation = 100; Interstate War = 1
1	1	1	1	1
2	2	1▲−	2	1▲−
3	2▲−	2	5▲+	1▲−
4	5▲+	2▲−	5▲+	1▲−
5	5	2▲−	5	1▲−
6	5▲−	2▲−	5▲−	1▲−
7	5▲−	2▲−	5▲−	1▲−
8	6▲−	2▲−	9▲+	1▲−
9	9	5▲−	9	1▲−

Legend: ▲ = change; − = negative change; + = positive change.

is reduced to low violence, moderate restriction (category 2). Further, even when previous repression is in the most lethal category (9), pacification occurs; in this context, increased *Competition/Participation* diminishes subsequent coercive activity to category 5 (moderate repressive action). Regardless of a country's starting point, domestic democratic peace works. This is by far the most pacific influence yet identified in the empirical investigation.

As expected, the findings change when political conflict is introduced. For example, when *Competition/Participation* is at its lowest value and violent dissent exists (column 4 in the top part of Table 5.2), prior repression where, respectively, violence is low but restrictions are high and violence is moderate and restrictions are moderate (categories 3 and 4) increases to moderate violence and restriction (category 5). Under the same circumstances (low *Competition/Participation* and violent dissent), when previous repression is in categories 6 and 7, coercive behavior in the next year decreases to category 5 as well.

Civil war has a much greater influence (column 4, middle part of Table 5.2). Here, repression is increased across different values of prior repression. Thus, when civil war exists, *Competition/Participation* is minimal, and previous repression is in the least repressive category (1), subsequent repression is increased to category 2 (low violence, moderate restriction). Under the same circumstances, when previous repression is relatively low to moderate (in categories 3 and 4), later repressive activity is increased to category 5 (moderate violence and restriction). Additionally, when prior repression is highly violent but moderately restrictive (category 8), civil war prompts subsequent repressive activity to increase to the most lethal form of repression (category 9).

When *Competition/Participation* is at its lowest value and interstate war exists (column 4, bottom of Table 5.2), the results are almost identical to those achieved when violent dissent is considered. Again, we find that political conflict increases repression when it had been relatively low in the previous year (categories 3 and 4). At the same time, subsequent repressive activity diminishes when prior levels were somewhat higher (categories 6 and 7). Different from the violent dissent model, we find that in situations of interstate war, when prior repression was lethal (category 8, high violence, moderate restriction), subsequent activity is increased yet further (to category 9).

Consistent with the results obtained earlier, when political conflict exists and *Competition/Participation* increases from its minimum to its maximum (from column 4 to 5 in Table 5.2), the domestic democratic peace is again supported. *Competition/Participation* pacifies and does so quite well relative to *Suffrage*. There is some variation, however, across types of political conflict.

For example, in the context of violent dissent (column 5, top of Table 5.2), *Competition/Participation* decreases five out of nine categories to one of the least repressive strategies, category 2 (low violence, moderate restriction). The most lethal coercive categories (8 and 9) diminish to categories 5 and 6, respectively. *Competition/Participation* thus reduces repression even in the face of violent dissent but achieves this at different levels of effectiveness according to the value of prior repressive activity. When confronting civil war (the middle of Table 5.2), the results are not as strong as those found in the case of violent dissent, but the results still support the peace proposition. For example, when civil war exists and *Competition/Participation* is at its maximum (column 5), prior repression in category 1 is not increased to category 2, as it was when *Competition/Participation* was limited; rather, it is maintained at category 1. When prior repression is in low to mid-range values (3–5), despite civil war, *Competition/Participation* decreases subsequent repression to low violence, moderate restriction (category 2). Similarly, in the face of large-scale domestic conflict, when prior repression is in high to mid-range values (6 and 8), subsequent coercive activity decreases to moderate repression (category 5). Without question, the most pacific influence of *Competition/Participation* is found in situations of interstate war (the bottom of Table 5.2). Here, we find that from one year to the next eight out of nine categories decrease in this context. Results disclose that regardless of the category of prior repression, when interstate war exists and *Competition/Participation* increases to its maximum level, repression decreases to its lowest value.

Up to this point, the discussion has focused on the pacifying influence of *Voice* and its interaction with diverse forms of conflict. I now shift the discussion to the other aspect of political democracy commonly highlighted in research and policy circles.

Veto Measures of Democracy

I continue my reassessment of the peace proposition with an examination of *Veto Players* and *Executive Constraints*. I again evaluate three models, including the particular aspect of democracy under consideration interacted with three conflict variables: violent political dissent, civil war, and interstate war. Again accompanying each analysis are two graphs representing the influence of a particular aspect of democracy when specific forms of conflict are not present as well as when conflict does exist. Additionally, I consider the influence of democratic-conflict interactions while incorporating information about exactly what level of repression was used in the past.

Veto Players

As expected, when conflict is absent, the influence of *Veto Players* on repression is comparable to the model examined in Chapter 4 (provided in Table 3 in Appendix 3). In periods of peace (see Figure 5.3), when the number of players increases from its minimum to its maximum, the probability of being in the least repressive categories (1 and 2) increases,[4] while the probability of achieving the next seven categories decreases. Similar to earlier results, the magnitude of influence wanes as the values of repression become more lethal. The influence of the two conflict variables examined is about the same, with the absence of violent dissent holding a slight advantage over the absence of civil war. Essentially, there is no influence where repression is highly restricted but not violent, moderately violent but not restrictive and highly violent but not restrictive, in order (categories 3, 4, and 7). It should be noted that given the limited number of wars in the period and small number of cases across categories of the dependent variable, I was not able to estimate the influence of interstate war.

When one considers the influence of *Veto Players* in periods of conflict, the findings are different from situations in which conflict is absent, and they generally counter the domestic democratic peace. For example, when violent dissent exists and the number of *Veto Players* increases, the probability of achieving the least repressive categories (1 and 2) is still positive, but the impact decreases in magnitude. Further challenging the peace proposition, when violent dissent takes place and the number of *Veto Players* is increased, the probability of achieving category 3 repression is increased (not decreased) – albeit marginally. Compared with the influence found when there is no political conflict, the negative influence on achieving categories 4–6 is weakened by violent dissent. The pacifying influence of *Veto Players* increases at the highest levels of repression (7–9); within the context of the interaction between *Veto Players* and violent dissent, the probability of achieving the most lethal forms of repression is diminished, decaying in magnitude as the lethality of repression becomes more severe.

---

[4] Because of the number of cases, interstate war was too small to be estimated dependably.

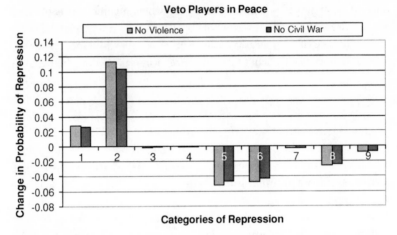

Figure 5.3(a) *Veto Players* in Peace and Conflict

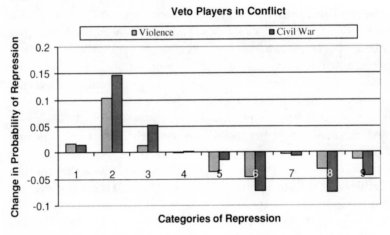

Figure 5.3(b)

Exemplifying this impact is Chile in 1991. To understand the influence, however, one must step back a bit further, to 1989. During this year, the military leader General Augusto Pinochet agreed to fifty-four constitutional changes, including presidential and legislative elections, an increase in the number of congressional members, an end to the ban against Marxist political organizations, and a reduction of the president's term from eight to four years. The electoral victory of Patricio Aylwin for the presidency in 1990 was also accompanied by a commitment to investigate and openly discuss the human rights abuses of the past regime. Not all changes, however, were completely in the direction of political democracy. For example, Pinochet initially remained commander-in-chief of the army (the largest coercive organization in the country), and, equally as important, the outgoing government was allowed to select nine senators, a number that prevented any majority from forming in the senate. While this seems like a formidable veto power, almost completely undermining the checks and balances built into the new government, two elements were important: (1) there was a growing rift between Pinochet and many of the younger officers who favored civilian rule as well as the withdrawal of the army from political activity, and (2) the judiciary was able to maintain a certain degree of independence.[5] By the time extensive strikes and terrorism broke out in 1991 (the latter undertaken by the Manuel Rodriguez Patriotic Front), there were enough *Veto Players*,[6] each with an interest in preventing repressive action from being increased beyond the levels already adopted (category 4 in my measure of repressive lethality: moderate violence and low restriction). Once violent dissent diminished (in 1992), this strategy of state coercion was sustained until 1994, when it decreased further to category 1 – the lowest repressive technique possible.

Within the context of civil war and increased *Veto Players*, the results are somewhat different from those found with the violent dissent model. As found, the probability of achieving the least repressive category (1) is diminished when civil war takes place and the number of *Veto Players* is enhanced. The likelihood of achieving category 2 is increased, however, suggesting that during interactions between large-scale conflict and restrictions on executive power, authorities are more likely to use low levels of violence and moderate levels of restriction. Against expectations, the probability of achieving low violence but high restrictions (category 3) and moderate violence but low restrictions (category 4) are increased during civil war. Large-scale challenges within a country increase the likelihood that authorities will employ a wider range of coercive activities. Under the same circumstances, the likelihood of achieving moderate violence and restriction (category 5) is significantly weakened. In line with the peace proposition, however, we see that the negative influence of *Veto Players* on higher level values

---

[5] This continued a trend established even under authoritarian rule.
[6] On the Keefer measure, this is coded as a four, up from one the previous year – staying at this level until 1996, when my study ends.

of repression is increased in its pacifying influence when the civil war – *Veto Players* interaction is considered (further diminishing the possibility of achieving these values had there been no conflict). This effect exceeds those situations where violent dissent is taking place and *Suffrage* is increased, but it does not exceed the influence wielded by *Competition/Participation*. Even confronting the most threatening form of domestic conflict, therefore, *Veto Players* are still capable of reducing the lethality of state repression.

The strength but limitation of *Veto*'s pacifying capability during civil war is revealed in the Philippines during the mid-to-late 1980s. In 1986, following the removal of Ferdinand Marcos as president by a combination of national election and mass uprising (commonly referred to as People Power), Corazon Aquino was elected president, and her administration quickly embarked on restructuring the political system in the direction of veto. A major component of this effort was the development of the 1987 constitution (replacing the Freedom Constitution that was put in place immediately after Marcos was removed). This document included adjustments to both the president's and the legislature's terms of office and the establishment of a Commission on Human Rights to oversee trends and developments. In addition to this, the new government sought to reestablish a presidential system with a bicameral legislature and an independent legislature[7] with emphasis on the former. Despite the many limitations of this effort, the impact on repression was immediate. Indeed, although the civil war being waged by the New People's Army and the Moro Islamic Liberation Front was underway as well as the political instability associated with the democratic transition, repressive behavior was generally diminished (from category 7 in 1986, where violence is high and restrictions are low, to 4 in 1987, where violence is moderate and restrictions are low – the level maintained until 1989).

Unfortunately, the veto powers identified in the constitution did not, and many suggested were not designed to (Ruland 2003, 464), effectively counter centralized authority. The possibility of diminishing repressive action with *Veto* was further undermined in other ways as well. For example, creating distance from the previous government, which largely favored repressive behavior, was difficult to achieve because many of the individuals affiliated with it simply changed sides and supported Aquino, however briefly (see, for example, Boudreau 2004). Thus, it is not surprising that "[m]any of the congressmen elected in 1987 were also successful

---

[7] This was first enacted after the 1935 constitution, but it was dismissed by Marcos.

candidates in 1984, 18 were members of Marcos' 1978 Interim Batasan Pambasa [parliament] and another 30 ran in the 1984 elections and lost" (Freedom House 1991–2, 371). This brings home the criticism of *Veto* discussed earlier as certain elements within the society spent more time trying to overthrow the new government than trying to counterbalance the public policies of rival elites. In addition to this, the veto power that did exist was limited because of excessive factionalization within political organizations that could have been directed against those with coercive power like the executive (see, for example Casper 1995). Consequently, in the face of continued insurgency, government intrigue, and ineffectual veto players,[8] coercion increased again in 1990.

Examining the most likely value of current repression, we see that the results are generally similar to the *Suffrage* model. There is an influence consistent with the domestic democratic peace; however, the value of this impact is limited both in terms of the range of categories decreased and in terms of the magnitude of the change. Once again, given the limited number of wars in the period of interest and the small number of cases across categories of the dependent variable, I was not able to estimate the influence of interstate war.

Largely comparable to both models of *Voice*, we again find that when *Veto* power is limited and there is no political conflict, several categories are reduced from one year to the next. For example, when prior repression is low in violence but high in restrictions or moderate in violence but low in restriction (categories 3 and 4, respectively) and violent dissent is absent (the upper part of Table 5.3), subsequent repressive activity decreases to low violence, moderate restriction (category 2). Similarly, when previous repression is moderate in violence but high in restriction or high in violence but low in restriction (categories 6 and 7, respectively), subsequent repressive action decreases to category 5 (moderate violence and restriction). When prior repression is in category 8 (high violence, moderate restriction), subsequent repression decreases to category 6 (moderate violence, high restriction).

Significantly differing from the *Competition/Participation* model but similar to *Suffrage*, it is clear that the number of *Veto Players* has a limited impact

[8] According to a recent article in the *Economist* (2004 – www.economist.com/displayStory. cfm?story_id/2876966), the 1987 constitution includes checks and balances galore to prevent a return to strongman rule. In practice, however, it actually promotes power grabs by leaving the government in a near-constant state of gridlock.

Table 5.3. *Most Likely Value of Current Repression for* Veto Players

1	2	3	4	5
Lag Repression	Given *Veto Players* = 1; *Violent Dissent* = 0	Given *Veto Players* ≥ 6; *Violent Dissent* = 0	Given *Veto Players* = 1; *Violent Dissent* = 1	Given *Veto Players* ≥ 6; *Violent Dissent* = 1
1	1	1	1	1
2	2	2	2	2
3	2▲−	2	5▲+	2▲−
4	2▲−	2	5▲+	2▲−
5	5	2▲−	5	5
6	5▲−	5	5▲−	5
7	5▲−	5	5▲−	5
8	6▲−	5▲−	8	5▲−
9	9	9	9	9
Lag Repression	Given *Veto Players* = 1; *Civil War* = 0	Given *Veto Players* ≥ 6; *Civil War* = 0	Given *Veto Players* = 1; *Civil War* = 1	Given *Veto Players* ≥ 6; *Civil War* = 1
1	1	1	1	1
2	2	2	2	2
3	2▲−	2	5▲+	2▲−
4	2▲−	2	5▲+	2▲−
5	5	2▲−	5	5
6	5▲−	5	8▲+	5▲−
7	5▲−	2▲−	6▲−	5▲−
8	7▲−	5▲−	9▲+	8▲−
9	9	9	9	9

Legend: ▲ = change; − = negative change; + = positive change.
Note: * = Interstate wars could not be examined because of the low number of cases.

on repressive behavior during periods of peace. Increasing the number of *Veto Players* when conflict is not present (column 3) results change in only two categories. For example, when prior repression is moderate in both violence and restriction (category 5), subsequent repressive action is reduced to category 2. Similarly, when repression is in category 8 (high violence, moderate restriction) and violent dissent is not present, subsequent repression is reduced to category 5.

Considering civil war (the bottom part of Table 5.3), essentially the same results are identified. The only difference concerns the reduction of repressive behavior when prior repression is in category 8 (high violence, moderate restriction), which in the absence of civil war and low *Veto Players* (column 2), is reduced to category 7 in the following year.

Given the most likely value of current repression given low number of *Veto Players* and political conflict (column 4), there are some differences across categories, again largely similar to those found with the *Suffrage* model. For instance, when the number of *Veto Players* is low and violent dissent exists (the top part of Table 5.3), past repressive behavior in the low-middle range (categories 3 and 4) increases to moderate values (category 5). Interestingly, when state coercive activity is previously in category 6 in the face of violent dissent but low *Veto Players*, it decreases to moderate values (category 5). In contrast, when civil war exists and the number of *Veto Players* is low, four out of nine categories increase. Civil war thus prompts authorities to increase repression but not uniformly. Thus, when previous repression is in the lower-to-middle range (categories 3 and 4), subsequent coercive activity increases to category 5; when previous repression is in the middle-to-upper range (category 6), it increases to high-value repression (category 8); and, when previous repressive behavior is in one of the second highest values of repression (category 8), in the face of civil war it increases to the most lethal strategy of repression (category 9). One category is influenced negatively, however, when civil war exists, and the number of *Veto Players* is low. Specifically, when previous repression is high in violence but low in restriction (category 7), the subsequent value on the repression measure decreases to category 6 (moderate violence and high restriction). Faced with large-scale violent domestic conflict, authorities who previously applied at high levels of repression change their approach to one that was not as lethal (moderate violence, high restriction).

Increasing the number of *Veto Players* during political conflict, we again see support for the domestic democratic peace but only in a limited manner. For example, in the case of violent dissent and increased *Veto Players* (column 3 at the top of Table 5.3), only three categories are influenced. Thus, when prior repression is in lower-to-middle range values (categories 3 and 4), subsequent repressive behavior is diminished to category 2 (low violence, moderate restriction). Similarly, when prior repression was high in violence but moderate in restriction (category 8), subsequent coercive behavior decreases to moderate values (category 5). During civil war (column 5 on the bottom of Table 5.3), the influence of *Veto Players* as a mechanism of peace is even greater. In this context, the number of categories reduced in lethality is increased from three to five.

Comparable to the earlier findings, the impact of *Veto Players* is not as strong as that wielded by *Competition/Participation*, but it is greater than *Suffrage*. For example, when prior repression is in categories 3 and 4, civil war is present, and *Veto Players* is increased to its maximum value, subsequent repressive behavior is decreased to category 2 (low violence, moderate restriction). The situation is somewhat different for more lethal values of repression. For example, under the same circumstances as those discussed previously, when prior coercive behavior was in the middle to upper range (categories 6 and 7), the government's approach to coercion is reduced in the next year but only to moderate violence and restriction (category 5). As an indication of the pacifying capability, even the most lethal form of repression is decreased by the civil war–*Veto Player* interaction, but only from category 9 to 8 – the most lethal to the second most lethal.

Executive Constraints

Our final analysis brings us to the less formal indicator of *Veto – Executive Constraints*. When this system characteristic is examined (Table 4 in Appendix 3), the results are different from those within the *Veto Player* model – distinct, that is, from the results in Chapter 4. Generally, *Executive Constraints* is overwhelmed by conflict and unable to reduce repression, except in very specific circumstances.

In periods of peace the results look similar to those identified earlier. When there is no conflict and *Executive Constraints* is increased from its minimum to its maximum, then the likelihood of achieving the first two categories of repression is increased, while the remaining seven are diminished – declining in the magnitude of influence as the lethality of repressive behavior increases. Again, results for interstate war could not be estimated because of the small number of cases across values of the dependent variable. Similar to the investigation of *Veto Players*, the influence when violent dissent is absent exceeds that of situations where civil war is not present. This effect holds in all repressive categories. Also similar to the *Veto Players* investigation, repression in categories 4 and 7 is not well accounted for because of the sheer number of cases.

Although comparable to the other measure of *Veto* in the direction of influence, the magnitudes are different (see Figure 5.4). For example, in category 2 (again, the repressive category that is the most likely influenced), when violent dissent was absent, the effect of *Veto Players* is about half of that revealed within the analysis of *Executive Constraints*. The difference

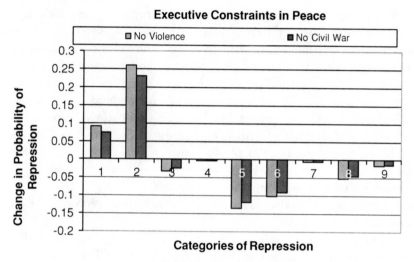

Figure 5.4(a) *Executive Constraints* in Peace and Conflict

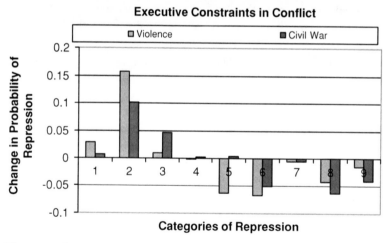

Figure 5.4(b)

in category 1 repression is even larger (that is, the influence of *Executive Constraints* given the absence of violent dissent is several times that wielded by the other indicator of *Veto*). Finally, the difference between the two *Veto* measures in categories 5–9 still favors *Executive Constraints*, suggesting that this aspect of democracy is generally more effective at reducing these forms of repression.

When situations of conflict are considered, the results again change. Here we see that while the same influence across repressive categories is identified, the strength of *Executive Constraints* is diminished. For example, when violent dissent exists and *Executive Constraints* is increased from its minimum to its maximum, the probability of achieving low-level repression is still increased, but the magnitude of this influence is much less than that when conflict is absent; violent dissent simply overwhelms the pacifying influence of this aspect of democracy. Similar to the *Veto Player* results (in Figure 5.3), the probability of observing category 3 (where violence is low but restrictions are high) is increased by the simultaneous presence of lower-level conflict and *Constraints*. The remaining categories are negatively influenced, decaying in magnitude as the form of repression being considered is more lethal.

An ideal example of this situation is found in Bulgaria during 1996. Immediately after the first multiparty election of 1989, following the collapse of communist rule, Bulgaria's constraints on the executive were enhanced dramatically (from 3 to 7). As designed by the 1991 constitution, this was largely attributed to the creation of a parliamentary system in which power was shared equally among three actors: the executive, the legislature, and the judiciary. In addition to this, a constitutional court was established, distinct from the regular court system that had powers of judicial oversight and review. In terms of political representatives, only two political parties were legal initially (the Bulgarian Communist Party and the Bulgarian Agrarian Union), but this quickly grew to include a wide range of political orientations as well as organizations, thereby increasing the number of political actors who could constrain the central authorities. Even though the constitution forbade organizations that threatened the integrity of the nation-state and "political strikes," a robust civil society quickly came into being, serving as yet another source of constraint.

As expected, these developments decreased repression quickly after the political transformation (from category 6 – moderate violence and high restriction in 1988 – to something ranging between categories 1 and 4 afterward). Even amidst the massive strikes and demonstrations that took place in 1996 (involving approximately one million people at its highest point), repression was still kept at relatively low levels. Clearly, it is the case that political authorities applied some repressive action. The key for this discussion is that the magnitude of this application never exceeded a particular low to middle range threshold.

From the results, the influence of civil war on the peace proposition is much greater than that wielded by dissent. Indeed, in these situations, we find a major reduction in the probability that either lower level repressive strategy will be applied (for example, categories 1 and 2). Again, the probability of achieving category 3 is increased by the civil war–*Executive Constraint* interaction – this moves against the domestic democratic peace. Different from the violent dissent model, we also see that the likelihood of achieving mid-level repressive behavior (categories 4 and 5) is now increased (in the case of violent dissent, these influences were negative, as the domestic democratic peace would expect). Civil war thus simultaneously decreases the magnitude of achieving the least repressive strategies and increases the range of repressive actions that states apply, albeit at relatively small amounts. The weakened pacifying influence of *Executive Constraints* during civil war is further revealed in mid-to-upper range repression (categories 6, 8, and 9). Given large-scale domestic conflict, at the highest levels of state repression, the influence of *Executive Constraints* is weakened relative to the impact when conflict is absent, and this result is lower than that wielded by *Veto Players*. Interestingly, there are some differences between veto measures. For instance, the pacifying influence of violent dissent interacting with *Executive Constraints* is greater across values of repression than that found when violent dissent interacts with *Veto Players*. The situation is reversed in the context of civil war where the interaction with *Veto Players* is greater than that with *Executive Constraints*, again across values of repression. Regardless, in neither case is the influence greater than that wielded by the *Competition/Participation* interactions.

Sierra Leone in 1996 provides an interesting example of this *Executive Constraint*–political conflict interaction. For example, three years into a civil war involving the Revolutionary United Front, the National Provisional Ruling Council (which had assumed power via a coup in 1992) acceded to popular demand, adhered to the 1991 constitution, and held multiparty elections. To ensure that the diverse political organizations would not be excluded, the government adopted a system of proportional representation, providing five different political parties with seats. This increased the number of executive constraints from one to five, which prompted a reduction in the lethality of repression from the most lethal form of repression (category 9, observed the previous year) to the second most lethal form of repression (category 8). This democratic peace was short-lived, however, for one year later the president (Ahmed Tejan Kabbah of the Sierra Leone

People's Party) was removed by a group of military officers, the constitution was suspended (as it had been in 1992), all political parties as well as diverse forms of expression were banned, and diverse forms of restriction as well as violence were enacted by the regime.

Examining the most likely value of current repression, we again see that the results support the domestic democratic peace. Additionally, we see a similar hierarchy of causal relationships to that identified earlier, but with some important differences. For example, results disclose that the greatest influence is wielded by *Competition/Participation*, but this is now followed by *Veto Players*, *Executive Constraints*, and *Suffrage*. The basic findings are similar when political conflict is absent and *Executive Constraints* is kept at its lowest value (column 2 top of Table 5.4). In this context there is a general downward shift identified with prior repression in categories 3, 6, and 7 being reduced in the next year to categories 2, 5, and 5, respectively. Additionally, the empirical findings show that when previous repression is in category 4, *Executive Constraints* is limited, and violent dissent is not present, repressive behavior in the next year increases to category 5.

Enhancing *Executive Constraints* in the absence of violent dissent tends to diminish state repression (column 3 in the top of Table 5.4). Indeed, in six of nine categories, coercive behavior is reduced. For example, when prior repression is in middle-to-upper range values (categories 4–7) and *Executive Constraints* is increased, subsequent coercive action is decreased to low violence, moderate restriction (category 2). Under the same circumstances (increased *Executive Constraints* but no dissent), *Executive Constraints* reduces category 8 to 5 and category 9 to 8 from one year to the next. Domestic democratic peace thus works even at the highest values of repression. The results are nearly identical in the context of no civil war and increased *Executive Constraints* (column 3 bottom of Table 5.4). The only difference concerns category 9, which is no longer diminished.

Introducing political conflict changes the results in important ways (column 4 in Table 5.4). For example, when *Executive Constraints* is limited but violent dissent takes place (top of Table 5.4), previous levels of lower level repression are increased (from categories 3 and 4 at time $t - 1$ to category 5 at time t). Under the same circumstances, moderate-to-high values of coercive behavior are reduced (from categories 6 and 7 to the moderate repressive behavior in category 5). Consequently, when prior repressive action was in category 1, *Executive Constraints* are low, and civil war exists (bottom of Table 5.4), repression in the next year is increased to category 2. Similarly, under the same circumstances, categories 3 and 4 (at time $t - 1$)

Table 5.4. *Most Likely Value of Current Repression for* Executive Constraints

1	2	3	4	5
	Given *Executive* Constraints = 1;	Given *Executive* Constraints = 7;	Given *Executive* Constraints = 1;	Given *Executive* Constraints = 7;
Lag Repression	*Violent Dissent* = 0	*Violent Dissent* = 0	*Violent Dissent* = 1	*Violent Dissent* = 1
1	1	1	1	1
2	2	2	2	2
3	2 ▲ −	2	5 ▲ +	2 ▲ −
4	5 ▲ +	2 ▲ −	5 ▲ +	2 ▲ −
5	5	2 ▲ −	5	2 ▲ −
6	5 ▲ −	2 ▲ −	5 ▲ −	5
7	5 ▲ −	2 ▲ −	5 ▲ −	5
8	8	5 ▲ −	8	5 ▲ −
9	9	8 ▲ −	9	9
	Given *Executive* Constraints = 1;	Given *Executive* Constraints = 7;	Given *Executive* Constraints = 1;	Given *Executive* Constraints = 7;
Lag Repression	*Civil War* = 0	*Civil War* = 0	*Civil War* = 1	*Civil War* = 1
1	1	1	2 ▲ +	1 ▲ −
2	2	2	2	2
3	2 ▲ −	2	5 ▲ +	5
4	5 ▲ +	2 ▲ −	5 ▲ +	5
5	5	2 ▲ −	6 ▲ +	5 ▲ −
6	5 ▲ −	2 ▲ −	9 ▲ +	6 ▲ −
7	5 ▲ −	2 ▲ −	6 ▲ −	5 ▲ −
8	8	5 ▲ −	9 ▲ +	9
9	9	9	9	9

Legend: ▲ = change; − = negative change; + = positive change.
Note: * = Interstate wars could not be examined because of the low number of cases.

are increased to category 5 (at time *t*); category 5 (at time *t* − 1) is increased to category 6 (at time *t*); category 6 (at time *t* − 1) is increased to category 9 (at time *t*); and category 8 (at time *t* − 1) is increased to category 9 (at time *t*). Yet, in the presence of civil war, when previous repression is in category 7 (where violence is high and restrictions are low), subsequent repression decreases to category 6 (moderate violence, high restriction). These all reveal an increased repressive effort in periods of political challenge.

When conflict exists and *Executive Constraints* is increased from its minimum to its maximum (column 5), the results are again consistent with the domestic democratic peace, but it is generally not as strong as either the results for *Competition/Participation* or the results for *Veto Players*. For example, when violent dissent exists and *Executive Constraints* is increased (the top of Table 5.4), four out of nine categories of repression are reduced. Specifically, when previous repressive behavior assumed low-to-middle range values (3, 4, and 5), subsequent activity decreases to category 2. Similarly, when coercion was in one of the highest categories (8, which represents a situation of high and moderate repression), subsequent repressive behavior is decreased to moderate violence and restriction (category 5).

The difference between *Executive Constraints* and *Veto Players* is even clearer in the context of civil war (bottom of Table 5.4). When this form of political conflict is present and *Executive Constraints* is increased (column 5), only three categories of repressive behavior are reduced (compared with the five in the *Veto Player* model); all appear in the middle range of the repression measure. Specifically, results disclose that when prior repression was in the upper-middle range (5, 6, or 7), subsequent repressive action is maintained at moderate values (level 5 or 6). It is clear that if repression is previously at level 5 and current coercive behavior is at this same level, this does not represent a decrease, but it should be recalled that these findings are compared against situations where conflict exists but *Executive Constraints* is limited (column 4). I conclude from this analysis that *Executive Constraints* does have a pacifying influence on repressive lethality but that relative to other aspects of democracy (*Competition/Participation* and *Veto Players*), the scope and magnitude of this influence is limited.

Combining Models

It is extremely informative to estimate the influence of each aspect of democracy independent of the others, but it is more important to investigate them competitively. Acknowledging that it is somewhat unwieldy to do this when all forms of conflict are constrained at once, I report here on models in which each form of conflict is interacted with the statistically significant aspects of democracy identified previously but viewed one at a time (Table 5 in Appendix 3). The two aspects of democracy considered here include *Competition/Participation* and *Executive Constraints*, which were selected following an assessment of statistical significance similar to that used in Chapter 4. Given the limitations discussed with reference to the usefulness of consulting results provided in statistical tables, I identify changes in predicted probability for each form of conflict, beginning with violent dissent and then civil war.

Interactions Concerning Violent Dissent

When violent dissent is absent (Figure 5.5), the results are almost identical to those found in earlier analyses. For example, when one observes the now familiar increased probability of attaining the two lowest categories and the decreased probability of attaining the next seven, the influence of both *Competition/Participation* and *Executive Constraints* is slightly lower in the lowest as well as highest categories (1, 6, 8, and 9) than that identified when each is viewed individually. These influences are higher in the second lowest and middle range categories (2 and 5). Additionally, the impact of *Competition/Participation* is slightly higher in category 3 (where violence is low and restrictions are high), but *Executive Constraints* wields no influence at all. In contrast, *Executive Constraints* wields a somewhat greater influence on reducing higher level behavior (categories 8 and 9) compared with the influence identified when it was evaluated individually, but these differences are only slight. This suggests that the individual effects identified earlier are robust and that these aspects of democracy function as suggested by the domestic democratic peace with *Competition/Participation* (*Voice*) wielding a greater influence over *Executive Constraints* (*Veto*). Also similar to the earlier results, the influence exhibited when violent dissent is absent as well as when *Competition/Participation* and *Executive Constraints* are increased from their minimum to their maximum is greater than when these aspects of democracy are increased individually. This said, the magnitude of difference between the combination and *Competition/Participation* by itself is greater in lower and moderate categories of repression (1, 2, 5, and 6, where violence tends to be limited) than in others (3, 4, 7, 8, and 9, where violence is generally more prominent).

When violent dissent exists, the basic structure of relationships is generally the same, but there are numerous changes within the empirical findings. For example, the probability of achieving the least repressive strategies (categories 1 and 2) is still increased by *Competition/Participation* and *Executive Constraints* compared with the examination of these characteristics viewed individually. The magnitude of this effect decreases in the case of the least repressive strategy (category 1) but increases in the next repressive category (2). Again when political violence is low but restrictions are high (category 3), support for the peace proposition is mixed. In the face of violent dissent, both aspects of democracy increase the likelihood of achieving this repressive category when they are increased from their minimum to their maximum. When political violence is moderate but restrictions are either

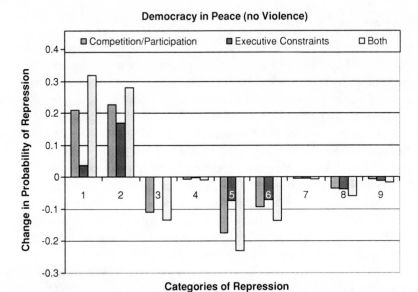

Figure 5.5(a) Democracy in Peace and Conflict: The Case of Violent Dissent

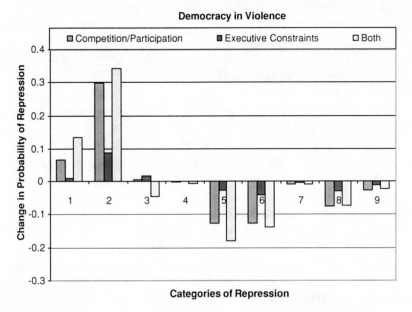

Figure 5.5(b)

moderate or high (categories 5 and 6, respectively), results disclose that the pacifying influence of *Competition/Participation* is weakened in the case of the former but strengthened in the case of the latter. By contrast, the pacifying influence of *Executive Constraints* is weakened in both categories (5 and 6). In the most lethal strategies of repression where political violence is high but restrictions are moderate and high (8 and 9, respectively), we again see that the negative influence of *Competition/Participation* on attaining these categories is enhanced but the influence of *Executive Constraints* is weakened. In support of the domestic democratic peace, therefore, the pacifying influence of *Competition/Participation* is shown to increase during periods of violent dissent, but contrary to the expectations of the peace proposition, the influence of *Executive Constraints* is weakened under the same circumstances.

Of course, individuals might also consider the joint application of *Competition/Participation* and *Executive Constraints* (the third bar in the graph). Investigating situations in which there is violent dissent and both aspects of democracy are increased from their minimum to maximum simultaneously, we see that the influence of this interaction exceeds that of each aspect of democracy viewed individually. The magnitude of difference is greatest in the lower categories of repression, but when political violence is high and restrictions vary (categories 7–9), the influence of *Competition/Participation* by itself and the interaction between *Competition/Participation* and *Executive Constraints* are about even.

This again supports the argument that *Voice* is the most influential mechanism of democratic peace considered in this study. We also see that the pacifying influence identified when distinct aspects of democracy are viewed individually is further enhanced when both aspects are increased at the same time, exactly as the domestic democratic peace would suggest. It should be noted, however, that the influence is small.

Continuing the practice of the earlier analysis, I discuss the most likely current value of repression given diverse conditions. To present results in a less cumbersome manner than considering all possible scenarios, I focus on three situations: (1) where there is violent dissent, *Executive Constraints* moved from its minimum to its maximum, and *Competition/Participation* held at its median; (2) where there is violent dissent, *Executive Constraints* holds at a value in its middle range (specifically 3/4), and *Competition/Participation* moves from its minimum to its maximum; and (3) where there is civil war and both *Executive Constraints* and *Competition/Participation* move from their minimum to their maximum. In earlier versions of this research, I explored diverse combinations of these variables at different values, but the three selected are the most informative.[9]

From the analysis, I find that joint enhancement of both aspects of democracy is generally more effective at diminishing repression than either characteristic individually (column 6 in Table 5.5). Nonetheless, if one had to select one aspect to modify, it would be *Competition/Participation* because of the sheer magnitude of its influence. Once again, therefore, *Voice* is found to be more effective at decreasing repression than *Veto*.

For example, when *Executive Constraints* is held at values 3/4 but *Competition/Participation* is increased to its maximum (column 3), seven out of nine repressive categories are influenced negatively. Specifically, when previous repression is in category 2, violent dissent exists, *Executive Constraints* is held constant, and *Competition/Participation* is enhanced, subsequent repressive behavior is decreased to the least repressive category (1) instead of staying at category 2, which it does without the change in political institutions (column 2). Similarly, under the same circumstances, past repression in low- to middle-range values (categories 3–5) subsequently decreases to low violence, moderate restriction (category 2), and prior middle- to upper-range values of repression (7 and 8) are reduced to moderate values (category 5). Even the most lethal form of repression is decreased when *Competition/Participation* is enhanced, from high violence and restriction (category 9) to moderate violence, high restriction (category 6).

Comparatively, *Executive Constraints* has less of a pacifying influence as fewer categories are decreased when this regime characteristic is enhanced. For example, we see that when previous repression is in category 3 (low violence, high restriction), violent dissent exists, *Executive Constraints* is increased to its maximum, and *Competition/Participation* is held at its median (column 5), subsequent repressive action is decreased to low violence, moderate restriction (category 2). Had *Executive Constraints* been limited and all other conditions been applied, subsequent repressive action would have increased to category 5 – a clear indication of the pacifying influence of *Executive Constraints*. Similarly, under the same circumstances of modified *Constraints*, violence, and stable *Competition/Participation*, we see that *Executive Constraints* reduce middle- to upper-range values of repression (categories 6 and 7) subsequently to moderate violence and restriction (category 5). Comparatively, one of the most lethal categories is diminished from high

---

[9] For example, I have not provided the results for how different aspects of democracy function in the absence of conflict because by now this influence is well understood.

Table 5.5. *Most Likely Value of Current Repression for Competition/Participation and Executive Constraints during Violent Dissent*

Lag Repression	Given Executive Constraints = 3/4; Competition/ Participation = Minimum; Violent Dissent = 1	Given Executive Constraints = 3/4; Competition/ Participation = Maximum; Violent Dissent = 1	Given Executive Constraints = Minimum; Competition/ Participation = Median; Violent Dissent = 1	Given Executive Constraints = Maximum; Competition/ Participation = Median; Violent Dissent = 1	Given Executive Constraints = Maximum; Competition/ Participation = Maximum; Violent Dissent = 1
1	2	1	1	1	1
2	2	2	2	2	2
3	5▲+	2▲−	5▲+	2▲−	2
4	5▲+	2▲−	5▲+	5	2▲−
5	5	2▲−	5	5	2▲−
6	5▲−	5	6	5▲−	2▲−
7	6▲−	5▲−	6▲−	5▲−	2▲−
8	8	5▲−	9▲+	8▲−	5▲−
9	9	8▲−	9	9	6▲−

Legend: ▲ = change; − = negative change; + = positive change.

violence, moderate restriction (category 8) to high violence, low restriction (category 7).

Joint enhancement of both *Competition/Participation* and *Executive Constraints* yields even greater reductions in state repression (column 6). Essentially, the results are similar to those found in the *Competition/Participation* model column 3. For example, with regard to coercive strategies 1–5, we see that in the face of violent dissent, *Competition/Participation* is just as effective at reducing lethality as when *Competition/Participation* and *Executive Constraints* are considered at the same time. The combination of democratic characteristics is generally more effective at the upper range of the repressive scale. For instance, when previous repression is in categories 6 and 7, violent dissent exists, and both *Competition/Participation* and *Executive Constraints* are increased from their minimum to maximum, subsequent repression is reduced to low violence, moderate restriction. This is far greater than the value reached by either democratic characteristic viewed individually (category 5 in both cases). The result for the second most lethal form of repression (category 8) is similar to that found in the *Competition/Participation* model, and thus joint consideration does not really add much in this case. A major difference here is the fact that the most lethal repressive category is influenced when both characteristics are enhanced at the same time. Specifically, results disclose that when previous repression is in category 9, violent dissent exists, and both democratic characteristics are enhanced, subsequent repressive action is reduced to moderate violence, high restriction (category 6). This improves upon the values reached by *Competition/Participation* (8) and *Executive Constraints* (9), thus revealing the value added of joint consideration.

Interactions Concerning Civil War

In this case, it is clear that when civil war is absent and both *Voice* and *Veto* are increased, the influence on repressive lethality is comparable to that derived from the model examined in Chapter 4 (see also Table 6 in Appendix 3). In the context of civil war, however, relationships are very different across aspects of democracy.

For example, when civil war is under way and *Competition/Participation* is increased from its minimum to maximum (see Figure 5.6), the probability of achieving the least repressive category (1) is again positive, revealing that this aspect of democracy encourages the least repressive combinations of state violence and restriction. At the same time, research also

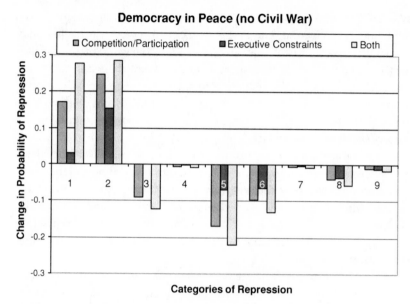

Figure 5.6(a) Democracy in Peace and Conflict: The Case of Civil War

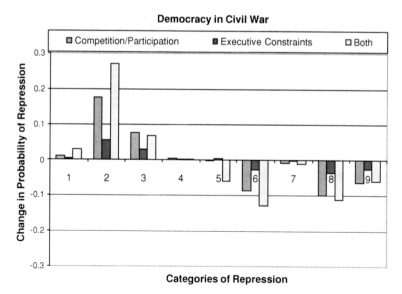

Figure 5.6(b)

discloses that the magnitude of this influence is reduced significantly from when there is no civil war. Under the same circumstances, the likelihood of attaining the next repressive category (2, where violence is low and restrictions are moderate) is decreased compared with earlier investigations but not nearly as much as the reduction in the first category. Both findings undermine the domestic democratic peace but to different degrees. Further challenging the peace proposition, civil war changes the influence of *Competition/Participation* in attaining category 3 from negative (which was the case when civil war was not present) to positive. In other words, civil war moves *Competition/Participation* from discouraging to promoting the likelihood that repressive behavior will be highly restrictive but low in terms of violence. Moreover, the civil war–*Competition/Participation* interaction significantly reduces the negative influence of achieving moderate repression (category 5) while also reducing the negative influence of achieving higher values (categories 6 and 7).

As found, the results for *Executive Constraints* generally follow those derived from *Competition/Participation*. Here, in the presence of civil war, the pacifying influence of *Executive Constraints* is reduced in lower and middle to upper repressive categories (1, 2, 6, and 7). At the same time, repression in middle-range categories (3, 4, and 5) are changed from negative to positive, suggesting that when confronting civil war the influence of *Executive Constraints*, which normally discourages these activities, ends up encouraging them. In contrast to these dampening influences, when civil war is present and *Competition/Participation* is increased from its minimum to its maximum, the probability of achieving the two most lethal forms of repression is reduced in comparison with a situation in which civil war is not present. Overall, one must conclude, the domestic democratic peace does not fare well under situations of high-level domestic threat.

One could argue that the effectiveness of pacification would be improved if distinct aspects of democracy were simultaneously improved. I consider this situation as well (that is, where civil war is present along with an increase in *Executive Constraints* and *Competition/Participation*). This is observed in the third bar of Figure 5.6.

Essentially, the interaction yields the same results as those obtained within the previous analyses (closely approximating the individual examinations of *Competition/Participation* and *Executive Constraints*). The influence of joint movement increases the probability of achieving lower level repression (categories 1–4) but decreases the probability of achieving middle to upper-level coercive behavior (categories 5–9). Interestingly, the influence on moderate repression (category 5) is weaker than the higher categories and, unlike the individual aspects of democracy, the influence wanes as one increases repressive lethality from categories 6–9. The individual components decrease categories 8, 6, and then 9 (in order) but joint consideration decreases categories 6, 8, then 9 (in order).

Finally, in line with the earlier analyses, I consider the most likely current value of repression given diverse conditions (Table 5.6). Again, three scenarios are considered: (1) where there is civil war, *Executive Constraints* moves from its minimum to its maximum, and *Competition/Participation* holds at its median; (2) where there is civil war, *Executive Constraints* is held at a value in its middle range (specifically 3/4), and *Competition/Participation* is moved from its minimum to its maximum; and (3) where there is civil war and both *Executive Constraints* and *Competition/Participation* are moved from their minimum to their maximum.

Similar to the earlier analysis, results disclose that joint enhancement of both democratic characteristics is generally more effective at diminishing repression than either considered individually [if both *Voice* and *Veto* are increased simultaneously, the influence is greater than if either characteristics is modified independent of the other (column 5)]. Distinct from the earlier findings, however, results disclose that the pacifying influence of *Competition/Participation* and *Executive Constraints*, viewed individually, are basically equivalent. During civil war, one can decrease repression by improving either *Competition/Participation* and *Executive Constraints*, for approximately the same impact.

For example, when *Executive Constraints* is held at values 3/4, civil war exists, and *Competition/Participation* is increased to its maximum value (column 3), again seven out of nine categories are influenced negatively. This is derived after comparing the results against a situation where the other conditions stay the same but *Competition/Participation* is not modified (column 2). Specifically, I find that civil war does not increase category 1 to category 2 but is sustained at the original value. Similarly, in the face of civil war, countries applying repression at category 3 (low violence, high restriction) are decreased to category 2 (low violence, moderate restriction) when *Competition/Participation* increases. Middle-and upper-range values of coercive behavior (categories 5–7) are stabilized or reduced to moderate violence and restriction (category 5); this value is lower than that identified had *Competition/Participation* not been enhanced. Even repression in the second most lethal category (8) is diminished from where it would be had no enhancement in *Voice* occurred (staying at category 8 instead of increasing in the

Table 5.6. *Most Likely Value of Current Repression for* Competition/Participation *and* Executive Constraints *during Civil War*

Lag Repression	Given Executive Constraints = 3/4; Competition/ Participation = Minimum; Civil War = 1	Given Executive Constraints = 3/4; Competition/ Participation = Maximum; Civil War = 1	Given Executive Constraints = Minimum; Competition/ Participation = Median; Civil War = 1	Given Executive Constraints = Maximum; Competition/ Participation = Median; Civil War = 1	Given Executive Constraints = Maximum; Competition/ Participation = Maximum; Civil War = 1
1	2	1	2▲+	2	1
2	2	2	2	2	2
3	5▲+	2▲−	5▲+	5	2▲−
4	6▲+	5▲−	5▲+	5	2▲−
5	6▲+	5▲−	6▲+	5▲−	2▲−
6	9▲+	5▲−	8▲+	8	5▲−
7	9▲+	5▲−	8▲+	8	5▲−
8	9▲+	8▲−	9▲+	8▲−	6▲−
9	9	9	9	9	9

Legend: ▲ = change; − = negative change; + = positive change.

face of civil war to category 9). Comparatively, when *Executive Constraints* is enhanced and *Competition/Participation* is held constant (column 5), there is very little different from when *Executive Constraints* are low (column 4); in other words, changing *Constraints* by itself has very little influence on repressive activity.

There is a slightly more pacific influence revealed when both democratic characteristics are raised to their maximum value at the same time (column 6) compared to when *Competition/Participation* was enhanced (column 3). In the former situation, several differences can be found. For example, improved pacification can be observed in two middle-range category (5). For instance, when *Competition/Participation* and *Executive Constraints* are viewed individually, repressive behavior is reduced from category 6 to category 5. When both aspects of democracy are enhanced at the same time, however, we see that subsequent repressive activity is decreased even lower to low violence, moderate restriction (category 2). The only other difference concerns a more lethal form of coercion (category 8). With both democratic characteristics at their minimum and civil war, prior repression in this category is increased to the most lethal form of state repression (category 9). When both aspects of democracy are increased to their maximum, even in the face of civil war, this value is diminished to moderate violence, high restriction (category 6) – a value that is two categories lower and significantly less lethal because it involves moderate amounts of violence.

Summary

Considering the full range of interactions examined in this chapter, results are generally supportive of the domestic democratic peace, but they are very specific about the conditions within which they work. When viewed in terms of their general influence (that is, without considering exactly where countries are starting in terms of their applications of repression), the impact of diverse democratic characteristics is consistent with what was identified in Chapter 4: as each characteristic is increased in value, the probability of achieving the least repressive categories increases, while the probability of achieving the most lethal decreases. The results vary, however, by the aspect of democracy as well as by the type of conflict considered.

On the one hand, the empirical results for *Voice* are clear and consistent. For example, across analyses (whether examined individually or competitively against other aspects of democracy) *Suffrage* is consistently overwhelmed by conflict – regardless of the form that the conflict takes. In this situation, the argument of "Domestic Realism" is supported. By contrast, again across analyses, the pacifying influence of *Competition/Participation* is repeatedly strengthened within contexts of violent dissent and interstate war but weakened in contexts of civil war. This follows the argument referred to earlier as Political Integrity, where repression was diminished only in contexts where the sheer magnitude of domestic political threat divided the populous.

On the other hand, the results for *Veto* are less definitive. When examined by itself (without other aspects of democracy being considered), results show *Veto Players* diminished in their pacifying capability when facing violent dissent but strengthened in the face of civil war (what I referred to as Conflict Scale). This highlights the fact that repressive behavior is likely to respond differently to lower levels of conflict than to higher levels. In a model with other aspects of democracy, however, *Veto Players* fails to achieve statistical significance. Results for *Executive Constraints* are different from those concerning *Veto Players*. Examined alone, in the face of both violent dissent and civil war, *Executive Constraints* is diminished in its pacifying capabilities. When examined competitively, this variable maintains its statistical significance, but its influence varies. In contexts of violent dissent, its influence is much lower than that wielded by *Competition/Participation*. In contexts of civil war, however, the influence is about the same.

In all situations, enhancing both aspects of democracy at the same time is better than enhancing any single aspect individually. Interestingly, the magnitude of difference between the joint consideration and the individual components is greater in situations of civil war than in violent dissent. Within the former (civil war), the magnitude of influence wielded by joint consideration is far greater than that wielded by either *Competition/Participation* or *Executive Constraints* viewed individually. Within the latter (violent dissent), the magnitude of influence wielded by joint consideration is approximately the same as that wielded by *Competition/Participation* viewed by itself but much greater than that wielded by *Executive Constraints*. Although the key to domestic peace appears to lie in enhancing both elements simultaneously, results suggest that Schumpeter and Dahl, who advocate mass-oriented aspects of political democracy, are generally favored over Madison, Montesquieu, and Tsebelis, who advocate elite-oriented aspects of political democracy.

6

(Re)considering Domestic Peace

Over the last half century, democratic political institutions have emerged as the principal means for reducing state coercive power. To advance this approach to domestic peace, individuals have requested, lobbied, boycotted, protested, revolted, invaded, and occupied – on hundreds of occasions; they have spent billions of dollars on democratic preparation and promotion (for example, voter awareness campaigns); and they have (re)designed constitutions and held elections at local as well as national levels, involving millions of people.

The work of these activists and policymakers notwithstanding, the question of the efficacy of democratic institutions remains open. Are democratic institutions, the best of an imperfect set of choices as Dahl and others argue? Does democracy pacify state repression? Over the past thirty-five years, research in international relations and comparative politics has led us to believe that, yes, democracy does reduce repressive behavior. Unfortunately, however, it is also clear from this work that the conclusion is potentially misleading because three limitations plague the literature. It is not clear whether all types of repression are equally susceptible to the influence of democratic political institutions (the problem of repressive variation). It is not clear whether all aspects of democracy are equally capable of reducing repressive behavior (the problem of democratic variation). And it is not clear whether different aspects of political democracy are equally capable of reducing repression in circumstances of varying types of political threat (the problem of conflictual variation). These are the issues that motivated the current research.

I have discussed the diverse ways that democracy can influence different types of repressive behavior and also the confounding influence that political conflict can have on this relationship (Chapters 1 and 2). To examine several hypotheses, I operationalized the different components of this argument (Chapter 3) and conducted statistical analyses of the direct influence of democracy on repression (Chapter 4), as well as the interactive influence of democracy on repression by considering distinct types of political conflict (Chapter 5). In this concluding chapter, I offer a brief overview of the theoretical argument and review my empirical findings. I then revisit the two cases with which the book opened – Rwanda and the United States – utilizing the insights gained from the statistical investigation for a deeper exploration of what took place in these countries as well as what is likely to take place in the future given current trajectories. I conclude by identifying some future lines of inquiry for further pursuing the influence of democracy on repressive behavior.

State Repression and Democratic Domestic Peace

Individuals have spent a great deal of time talking about how democracy influences political outcomes, and they have also spent much time and resources attempting to create democracies that could achieve the desired effects. One such outcome is the reduction of state repression (restrictions on civil liberties such as political bans as well as limits on association and violations of personal integrity such as torture and mass killing). The argument underlying this approach is straightforward. When authorities are accountable to those within their territorial jurisdiction, they are less inclined to use coercion against them because they could lose mass support, be removed from office, or face increased difficulty getting legislation passed/implemented because of delays, negotiations, or some form of investigation. Political authorities therefore resort to repressive behavior in order to avoid the costs normally associated with coercion and to maintain the position, status, and resources that accompany public office. Drawing upon research in international relations concerned with interstate war, this relationship has been labeled the "domestic democratic peace."

Over a thirty-five-year period, dozens of quantitative investigations have supported the expectations of the peace proposition discussed here. In every investigation across time, space (countries), measurements, and statistical methods, increasing levels of democracy correlate with diminished levels of state repression. Indeed, the only debate within the literature appears to be about the precise point at which the relationship has an impact. For instance, most research concludes that any movement toward full democracy decreases repression and that all higher values on a democracy measure are likely to reduce repressive action. A few scholars maintain that not all movements and levels of democracy have an impact (e.g., Davenport and Armstrong 2004; Bueno de Mesquita et al. 2005). Specifically, this work finds that democracy reduces state coercive behavior at only the highest values of the system characteristic. Below this threshold, there is no influence. Movements up the scale of democracy or particular levels of democracy that do not cross this boundary therefore have no impact on repressive action; only above this threshold is there a statistically significant reduction in state repression. The findings of this research bode well for those engaged in building democratic political institutions as a means of reducing human rights violations. Nevertheless, the threshold finding establishes a somewhat greater hurdle to overcome before repressive action is pacified.

Recent years have seen the emergence of several challenges to the domestic democratic peace, challenges that earlier research ignored.

First, some research suggests that democracy is effective at reducing state-sponsored violence but not the restrictions on civil liberties employed by political authorities (see, for example, Davenport 2004). The former is outside the realm of legitimate political behavior within a system of governance in which citizens are given a place to exist as well as a role to play. By contrast, the latter is well within the bounds of democratic governance as it serves to keep individuals within specific parameters without removing them completely.

Second, some research suggests that certain aspects of democracy might be better at decreasing repression than others. Supported by individuals such as Schumpeter and Dahl, some focus on those aspects of the political system concerned with the mass population (Suffrage and the relative degree of participation in the political system weighted by the competitiveness of the outcome), arguing that because authorities fear being removed from office, they reduce repressive activities. I refer to this as *Voice*. Others supported by individuals such as Montesquieu and Madison, focus on those aspects of the political system concerned with political elites (official and unofficial actors that can delay, oversee, or overturn the decisions of government officials). Authorities, fearing the retribution of other elites and attempting to avoid the imposition of sanctions, reduce repressive activity. This is *Veto*.

Third, it is possible that democracy is effective at decreasing repression but that this ability is weakened, if not completely eliminated, within contexts of political conflict. Specifically, there are four hypotheses. The peace proposition maintains that the pacifying influence of democracy never diminishes regardless of political conflict. The argument of Domestic Realism suggests just the opposite – that whenever authorities are confronted with politically threatening behavior, they increase the application of repression in an effort to maintain order. Acknowledging that the influence of democracy works best when populations are unified in their opinion about the merits of state coercive action, the Conflict Scale argument advances a different position. Thus, when political threats are less threatening and there is likely a difference of opinion about how citizens should be treated, it is less likely that democracies will use repression. When political threats are highly threatening and there is likely minimal disagreement about how citizens should be treated, however, repressive behavior increases. Finally, the argument of Political Integrity suggests that democracy is less likely to employ repressive action when conflict is either domestic and low level (for example, riots, strikes, and guerilla warfare) or international (war). In both cases, the degree of division within the population about appropriate responses is not large. When the form of political conflict is large scale and domestic, however (that is, during civil war), then there is less likely to be a difference of opinion about appropriate responses within the population, and authorities are more likely to use repressive behavior.

An Overview

To understand the influence of democracy on state repression and address the three limitations within the current literature, I engaged in a statistical analysis of 135 countries from 1976 to 1996. This period was selected for a number of reasons. In part, I chose it because of the important changes that were taking place in the world. This period saw a global shift toward democracy in many countries, as well as extensive discussion of human rights violations (who did what to whom). In part, I chose this period because of the confusion regarding what was happening at the time and the varied opinions that emerged about the meaning of the global movement toward democracy [what Huntington (1991) referred to as the Third Wave]. In the mid-1970s, for example, there was great hope for the prospects of democracy diminishing state repression; it was the "end of history," when all dreams were about to be fulfilled. By the mid-1990s, however, there was a high degree of skepticism about the ability of democracy to deliver various outcomes, including a reduction in repressive behavior. Indeed, it is at this time that individuals began to speak of the end of the movement toward democracy as they noted reverse waves (movement back in the direction of autocracy) and the potential for a new type of change in the world's political systems (a fourth "wave" of democracy). It is also at this time that individuals began speaking of illiberal democracy – the persistence of state repression despite political democracy. The peace proposition came under challenge as what was generally seen as a straightforward association was revealed to be anything but straightforward. Indeed, the anecdotal investigation of the phenomena that emerged during the 1980s and 1990s suggested that we understood very little about what took place during this critical period in history.

After employing a wide variety of data to examine the identified hypothe- *Findings* ses, several findings emerge to shed light on the domestic democratic peace.

① First, in support of the peace proposition, I find that <u>democracy generally decreases the lethality of state repression</u>. Specifically, democracy generally increases the likelihood that authorities will employ less lethal combinations of violence and restriction while decreasing the likelihood that more lethal combinations will be adopted. Regarding the relative effectiveness of democracy in pacifying distinct forms of repressive behavior, I find that democracy significantly diminishes the probability that state-sponsored violence will be applied, and that there is less of an impact on political restrictions. Although unlikely, then, democracies do sometimes impose significant restrictions on civil liberties.

② Second, results consistently reveal that (Voice) (specifically participation weighted by competition) exceeds the influence of *Veto* (executive constraints and veto players) in its ability to decrease state repression; it is more important for the South African case for example that the white population supported F. W. de Klerk in a referendum concerning the reduction of repression directed against blacks than that diverse social and economic groups quietly pushed for the same outcome. The most influential mechanism of domestic peace thus resides with citizens and their connection to those who represent them in political parties. Nevertheless, it is generally the case that coercive activity is most likely decreased when both *Voice* and *Veto* are enhanced at the same time. Together they are most likely to produce domestic peace. And in South Africa white electoral participation worked in conjunction with the activities of diverse social and economic groups to reduce state repression. If, however, only one aspect of democracy can be modified, it should be *Voice*.

③ Third, the results suggest that the <u>domestic democratic peace is generally not able to withstand the confounding influences of political conflict</u>. Investigating the interactive effect of conflict and democracy on repressive

179

behavior, again I find that in the face of conflict *Voice* is more effective than *Veto* at pacifying repression, but there are significant differences across types of conflict and aspects of democracy. For example, across analyses (where the relevant explanatory variable was considered by itself and also competitively against other aspects of democracy), *Voice* is consistently strengthened in its pacifying influence when confronting violent dissent (riots and guerrilla warfare), but it is weakened in the face of civil war. This supports the Political Integrity argument. The results for *Veto* tend to be less consistent across analyses. When examined individually, both *Veto Players* and *Executive Constraints* are statistically significant. The influence of the former is weakened, however, in situations of violent dissent and strengthened in situations of civil war (supporting the Conflict Scale argument), whereas the influence of the latter is weakened in both contexts (supporting the Domestic Realism argument). When examined against other aspects of democracy, *Veto Players* have no significant influence at all but the impact of *Executive Constraints* is weakened in the face of violent dissent (to a level lower than that wielded by *Competition/Participation*) and civil war (about the same influence as that wielded by *Competition/Participation*). These results again support the Domestic Realism argument. It is thus clear that the peace proposition is not bulletproof (invulnerable). At the same time, it is also clear that the nature of the wound inflicted by conflict on the pacifying influence of democracy is variable.

A Sober Second Look

With the empirical findings from my statistical analysis, I revisit the two cases with which this book opened, in an effort to better flesh out exactly how the peace proposition does and does not function. I begin with Rwanda and then move to the United States.

Rwanda Between 2001 and 2003, seven years after the civil war and genocide that devastated the country, the small East African nation began a process of political democratization. With extremely high levels of participation, Rwandans participated in local, parliamentary, and presidential elections as well as in a constitutional referendum on how the government, laws, and society should be structured. The outcome of the latter effort established clear distinctions between the executive, legislature, and judiciary – giving priority to the first – and it laid out the fundamental principles essential to the rule of law (for example, it explicitly identified how things would be done and who would do them). These efforts were initially outlined in the Arusha Accords – the deal brokered between the Rwandan government (the last vestiges of which currently reside in the Congo) and the Rwandan Patriotic Front (then a rebel organization and currently the ruling authority). Following 1994, these changes also became a matter of major interest to the international community. To facilitate the transition to democracy, governments and NGOs gave or invested tremendous amounts of money and training. Unable and unwilling to assist directly in the prevention of political violence, the international community set itself to assist Rwandans on the path to "good governance." The Rwandan government itself maintained an interest in these objectives that at best could be described as ambivalent. Their attitude was best captured by the idea that "it would happen when the time was right."

In line with the expectations of the domestic democratic peace, there was a fundamental reduction in the lethality of state repression, as the government democratized. Between 1994 and 1997, it was commonplace for the government to engage in widespread assassinations, disappearances, torture, large-scale imprisonment, and mass killing. For example, in 1994,

[t]he government responded to attacks (from anti-government forces in Northern Rwanda) with an excessive and indiscriminate use of force, by October killing an estimated 3,500 unarmed civilians in the course of military operations. These operations generally followed attacks on government soldiers, Tutsi civilians, and local government officials or the reported presence of insurgents in a community. Soldiers and government officials also killed hundreds of civilians in circumstances other than military operations. In August, soldiers reportedly executed some 150 detainees at the communal jails in Kanama and Rubavu in northwestern Rwanda. In the southern prefecture of Butare, two soldiers killed eleven detainees in Muyira commune in January and an RPA guard killed another eleven at Maraba commune in May. A prison guard in the commune of Rutongo killed eight detainees in early August. On January 24, at a public meeting in Karengera commune, Cyangugu prefecture, soldiers carried out the extrajudicial execution of two persons suspected of murder, repeating violations from the previous month when four persons were shot dead by soldiers in the presence of civilian authorities in Satinsyi commune, Gisenyi prefecture, and Mubuga commune, Gikongoro prefecture. (Human Rights Watch 1998)[1]

By the time the movement toward democracy was under way, the government rarely engaged in such behavior anymore, although such activities

---

[1] This is taken from the World Report: *http://www.hrw.org/worldreport/Africa-10.htm#TopOfPage*

did not cease entirely, according to numerous human rights organizations inside as well as outside the country. It appears, however, that the coercive strategies employed by the Rwandan government shifted to something less violent. As to why repressive behavior was being applied against the population at all, the answer is simple: the continuing security situation, both inside and outside the country.

It seems clear from my statistical analysis that there are no grounds for optimism about Rwanda's prospects for reducing political repression in the future. This is especially the case if we accept that (1) *Voice* is more effective than *Veto* in reducing repressive action (especially violent behavior), (2) the simultaneous development of *Voice* and *Veto* is generally better at pacification than either component alone, and (3) the pacifying influence of democracy (particularly *Voice*) is most likely to work during periods of violent dissent and interstate war. In large part, this is because the democratic political institutions are so weak that they are not able to prevent the repression from being turned on the society seeking to regulate state coercion.

First, *Voice* in Rwanda is very much in peril because of political conflict. Although there were numerous elections, held at diverse levels and with significant levels of participation from the population, the degree of competitiveness within these contests was extremely limited. Indeed, before each of the elections identified earlier, in an effort to eliminate the possibility of conflict and "divisionism," local-level campaigning was officially banned. Despite the restriction on activity, however, the ex-ruling party (the Rwandan Patriotic Front) engaged in significant canvassing for candidates affiliated with the existing leadership, leaving them essentially alone in the field. In addition, there was widespread criticism about the intimidation of other candidates, their political parties, and those supporting them. One week before the 2003 presidential election several members of the major opposition party were arrested for threatening the peace. This worked against the creation of an environment conducive to the emergence of an opposition and to open debate.

Second, *Veto* is also in jeopardy. For example, a recent parliamentary commission assessed the extent of support for a genocidal ideology. As an outgrowth of this effort, one now sees extensive monitoring of political parties and religious activities by state-sponsored "forums"[2] and even by the parliamentary commissions. One also sees the banning of individuals and

---

[2] These identify and monitor the individuals and organizations that exist, as well as the content of the messages that are put forward.

organizations that challenge the existing government. There are relatively tight controls over all political discussion by means of intimidation (frequently through the state-controlled militia, the Local Defense Force) and of various legal prohibitions (for example, outlawing local-level organizing). Indeed, what is most dangerous about the current government's behavior is its all-encompassing nature. It is simply not obvious, from the available information, what is meant by "divisionism" and fomenting genocide (for example, raising particular topics and engaging in any form of speech that challenges the existing government and in specific forms of association or assembly). In this context, the search for subversion and the systematic targeting of almost any politically oriented individuals and/or organizations within as well as outside the country (for example, the MDR, national universities, secondary schools, churches) effectively eliminates all official and unofficial *Veto Players* – thereby eliminating yet another mechanism of accountability (*Veto*). And targeting foreigners as also fomenting "divisionism" and violence (for example, Norwegian People's Aid and the Dutch government) only serves to further intimidate the domestic population.

The most ominous indication of the state's new strategy of repression is the Rwandan version of truth and reconciliation effort – Gacaca. This community-based system of confession, public denunciation, and prosecution represents a relatively innovative way for the Rwandan government to deal with individuals who may have played a role in the genocide of 1994, but at the same time, it allows the government to control the population with little interference from the international community (indeed, they have become quite supportive of this effort).[3] Understanding that anyone can be accused of divisionism and genocide, all political opposition has effectively been silenced. As this system has recently been extended to one million individuals who will be investigated (one-eighth of the population, with no upper limit established for this figure), the comments of Reyntjens (2004), a preeminent scholar of the Great Lakes conflict, captures the situation perfectly. Essentially, he says, "the (Rwandan) government is holding $7\frac{1}{2}$ million hostages."

The third factor undermining domestic peace in Rwanda concerns the intersection of different aspects of democracy and political conflict. At

[3] As the crimes considered in these proceedings are much less severe than those dealt with elsewhere in the Rwandan government (for example, Gacaca only considers property crimes and the like), the severity of punishment meted out is minimal but the message is nevertheless clear.

present, as the government confronts challengers both outside and inside the country, the levels of *Voice* and *Veto* in Rwanda are quite low. Outside (in Congo in particular) are the remaining troops who participated in the civil war against the existing government as well as those who participated in the genocide against moderate Hutu and ethnic Tutsi. In addition, the Rwandan government faces a growing number of alliances among former Hutu political leaders, Tutsi survivors of the genocide, and former members of the ruling government who have all left the country in an effort to modify or overthrow the existing regime. On the inside, there are other potential opponents. By most accounts the ideological and structural foundation that lay behind the mass killing of 1994 still exists. There is, for example, the lingering animosity between the dominant ethnic groups that at different times have directed discriminatory and violent policies against one other. Additionally, those who have challenged the governments of Rwanda historically have not fared very well. At no time since independence (1960–1) has there been a period within which nonviolent challenges could be put forward and sustained for long periods. Regarding the structural foundation of the movement that facilitated mass killing, rumors have persisted both within and outside of government that the network of militias, neighborhood associations, kin groups, and party affiliations that facilitated the activities in 1994 still exists. This poses an immense challenge for the ruling government. Given the severity of this situation, it is anticipated that the positive influence of conflict on repression will outweigh the negative influence of democracy.

In light of these dynamics, the future of state-induced domestic peace in Rwandan looks bleak. The aspects of democratic rule built over the last few years (such as they are) have all been gutted of any substance in terms of their capacity to pacify state repression. Additionally, the existing political threats to the state and society are believed to be so pervasive that no other political factor appears likely to make any headway.

The United States The Rwandan case compels me to be extremely skeptical about the prospects of democratic domestic peace; however, the U.S. case leads me to be somewhat less pessimistic, at least in the medium to long term. The reasons are fairly straightforward. In the former case, the low levels of political democracy rather easily allow the mechanisms of accountability to be overcome by conflict, whereas in the latter case, the higher levels of political democracy have produced several counterbalancing forces to reduce repressive behavior. Unfortunately, these forces seem slow, partial, and largely unable to challenge the hold of future conflict over the political system and society.

Immediately after the terrorist attacks on September 11, 2001, in an effort to counter the threat, the U.S. government produced a sweeping series of legislative and behavioral responses. Legislatively (in the U.S. Patriot Act along with several other legal actions),[4] the government increased its powers to establish wiretaps, obtain private records, engage in searches of all kinds, detain and deport citizens, ignore habeas corpus in a variety of circumstances, and identify individuals and organizations as "domestic terrorists" because of their intent to influence government through violating state or federal law or coercing civilians. Behaviorally, the government rounded up large numbers of suspects and arrested them, subjected large numbers of individuals to surveillance and physical searches, seized records of a wide variety of individuals and organizations, militarized airports as well as other targets that were deemed worthy of protection (for example, dams and nuclear plants), and generally increased its aggressiveness in policing protest in the United States.

The Bush administration's activities made sense. The attacks of 9/11 represented the first large-scale attack on U.S. soil in nearly forty years, and its perpetrators indicated that it would not be an isolated incident. Quite the contrary, Osama bin Laden portrayed the attacks on New York City and Washington, D.C., as the first volley in a series of attacks intended to send the United States into a downward spiral of insecurity and chaos.

---

[4] The list of relevant legislation is actually quite long: Anti-Terrorism Intelligence Tools Improvement Act of 2003; Antiterrorism Tools Enhancement Act; Benjamin Franklin True Patriot Act; Citizens' Protection in Federal Databases Act of 2003; Civil Liberties Restoration Act; Domestic Security Enhancement Act of 2003 (Patriot Act II); Domestic Surveillance Oversight Act of 2003; Freedom to Read Protection Act; Homeland Security Act of 2002; Homeland Security Enhancement Act of 2003; Intelligence Authorization Act for Fiscal Year 2004; Joint Terrorism Task Force Enhancement Act of 2003; Justice Enhancement and Domestic Security Act of 2003; JTTF Enhancement Act of 2003; Library, Bookseller, and Personal Records Privacy Act; Library and Bookseller Protection Act of 2003; Patriot Oversight Restoration Act of 2003; Pretrial Detention and Lifetime Supervision of Terrorists Act; The Protecting the Rights of Individuals Act; Our Lady of Peace Act; Reasonable Notice and Search Act of 2003; Safety and Freedom Ensured (SAFE) Act of 2003; The Space Preservation Act of 2001; Uniting and Strengthening America by Providing Appropriate Tools Required to Intercept and Obstruct Terrorism (Patriot) Act of 2001; Surveillance Oversight and Disclosure Act of 2003; Terrorist Penalties Enhancement Act; Universal National Service Act of 2003; and the Vital Interdiction of Criminal Terrorist Organizations (Victory Act).

Unlike the Rwandan case, however, the highly institutionalized nature of U.S. democracy tempered the government's behavior. For example, there were no public pronouncements in support of directing violence against American citizens, even though Congress authorized the president to use all necessary force to counter the threat. Instead, what was discussed and enacted was a relatively nonviolent repressive effort to root out, identify, monitor, and hinder the capabilities and actions of terrorist operatives in the United States. Invariably this involved diverse restrictions on American civil liberties (speech, association, assembly, due process, and so forth), but it did not generally involve more lethal forms of state repression. Of course, violent activities did take place in other countries, and there were numerous isolated incidents within the United States in which individuals were treated violently when arrested. No such patterns, however, were consistently or explicitly part of U.S. domestic policy.

In addition to the structure of the government's response, one can also see a reaction of the countervailing forces discussed by advocates of the peace proposition both within and outside of government, revealing the influence of both *Voice* and *Veto*. The timing of the response was much slower than what the domestic democratic peace and my research suggests, but nonetheless it occurred.

For example, after 9/11, the Congress, which was believed by critics of the government to be largely deferential to the executive's wishes, initially disregarded the first effort brought forward – the Mobilization against Terrorism Act. This was a much more ambitious effort containing even fewer constraints on state coercive power. By contrast, the U.S. Patriot Act passed without substantial opposition. Members of the civil society were largely quiescent. Over the next few years, however, there were successive waves of resistance to the government's repressive actions, largely during periods when legislation was being constructed but eventually also going beyond this rather limited domain. At each juncture the mechanisms of accountability discussed in the domestic democratic peace were shown to be functioning.

At the time the Domestic Security Enhancement Act (commonly known as Patriot Act II) was being discussed in 2003, diverse political pundits began speaking out against the government and its behavior. Opponents included the usual suspects (for example, the ACLU and Bill O'Reilly), but they also included individuals and organizations that generally did not take such a stand (for example, city councils from hundreds of towns and a handful of states around the country, lesser known NGOs such as the Center for

Democracy and Technology). There were also conferences such as "Grass-roots America Defends the Bill of Rights," which brought together activist organizations from around the United States in Washington, D.C., during October 2003. Without much fanfare, several legislative efforts were put forward to rein in the coercive power of the state. For example, on July 31, 2003, the Protecting the Rights of Individuals Act (S. 1552) was introduced in an effort to revise several provisions of the Patriot Act, expanding the degree of judicial review so that wiretaps would be authorized against actual crimes and not for fishing expeditions with no specific activities or individuals in mind. Additionally, the Benjamin Franklin True Patriot Act introduced on September 24, 2003, attempted to review various sections of the Patriot Act relevant to the searches for types of records. This amendment initially obtained a tie vote in the House but was later defeated when several individuals changed their vote.

At the end of 2005, when fifteen "sunsetting" (temporally limited) provisions of the Patriot Act came up for renewal, an even larger battle ensued, and a bipartisan vote in the Senate blocked passage of a bill that would extend some hotly contested provisions. The attorney general and president sought to have these provisions made permanent, but amidst a barrage of criticism, all they could obtain was a four-year extension. Opponents of the bill attempted to get a three-month extension. This activity came on the heels of efforts some months earlier when the Senate had unanimously supported an extension of the Patriot Act but with several checks and balances built into the extension, that were subsequently removed in committee. Although the provisions were extended, these two instances signaled a growing dissatisfaction with the power and behavior of the state. These developments had support across large sections of the political spectrum, including explicit defections from the president's party. Additionally, it identified a potential key issue in the next electoral contests – the states' repressive power.

Not only were diverse politicians increasingly exerting efforts in a direction consistent with the democratic peace, but American civil society was increasing its pacifying activities as well. For example, grassroots efforts in American universities, towns, and states continued to grow. There was almost weekly news of yet another ordinance or statement being issued against the Patriot Act and related legislation. In an important move invoking *Veto*, the ACLU brought lawsuits against President Bush and the FBI for misuse of the powers associated with the Patriot Act, specifically highlighting wiretapping. Furthermore, the number of prominent individuals taking a stand against government repressive activity continued to expand, including democratic senator Hillary Clinton (a potential candidate for the 2008 presidential race), former Vice President Al Gore, and human rights activist Harry Belafonte.

All told, the diverse mechanisms of accountability discussed within the domestic democratic peace have functioned as they are supposed to. And with no additional instances of political conflict within the country, it appears that repression will be diminished in the near future. Of course, there has been conflict in Afghanistan and Iraq, but according to the analysis presented here, this does not interfere with the peace proposition – especially not within a country with a high degree of *Voice* and *Veto* such as the United States. This having been said, there is a disturbing aspect to the case. Seemingly, there is an imbalance between the relatively small amount of civil liberties restrictions undertaken after 9/11 and the extensive leeway given to authorities to expand their efforts in the future. The limited number of restrictions are consistent with the peace proposition, but the unlimited potential for other activities is not. Of course, this is precisely where the legal and political battles have been and are going to be fought and here an important similarity to Rwanda exists. At some level, the appointment of individuals to the Supreme Court who would be sympathetic to the behavior of the authorities undermines the role believed to be played by the judiciary, as well as the system of checks and balances.

Whenever yet another tape and threat from bin Laden emerges, it is clear that actual political conflict is the key. It does not appear that the American public and its political officials view terrorist videotapes as being equivalent to terrorist behavior, so they do not accept restrictions on their civil liberties every time another virtual challenge is made. If there were another attack, however, then the situation would be changed significantly. Indeed, given the existing momentum, it is likely that those in favor of extending U.S. repressive power will manage to do so with little resistance.

Future Questions

The overview of the quantitative study and brief revisiting of historical cases is important for it reveals that our understanding of the domestic democratic peace is still incomplete.

It is clear, for example, that the meaning and operationalization of threats is crucial. Not only are there important differences between forms, but the potential for threat is consistently found to be an important factor in an of itself. How are threats defined? How does one know a threat when he or she sees one? It is also clear that the existing concepts for political conflict are deficient. Is it more appropriate to consider the threats to the current regimes of Rwanda or Iraq as domestic, international, or both? Are the domestic threats better thought of as violent dissent or civil war? The statistical results show that these differences matter a great deal, even as the cases show us that making these distinctions is difficult.

Related to this, it is clear that some effort must be extended to conceptualize and understand political repression. For example, in the U.S. case, we see civil liberties restrictions (detention and aggressive protest policing) – behavior we are well aware of and for which existing measurements are adequate – but we also see the use of other forms of repression that were not well accounted for in this study and that prove to be difficult to detect (wiretapping and torture). This problem is important for a case can be made that, in an effort to decrease the detection of repressive action and the negative consequences of being caught, democratic political leaders will employ forms of coercion that are less obvious. Such a practice threatens the domestic democratic peace because the function of this argument presumes that citizens have some idea about what is taking place. Without this knowledge, they cannot take action, and without this possibility, the behavior of political leaders will not be controlled.

Following on this point, another crucial assumption of the peace proposition that needs to be explored concerns the connection made between repressive behavior and electoral accountability. As conceived, it is expected that politicians fear retrospective voting (the idea that citizens will hold leaders responsible for previous repressive behavior at a future electoral contest). Do citizens hold political authorities responsible for coercive activity? What forms of activity do they hold them responsible for – wiretaps, arrests at a protest event, an instance of torture in some distant prison, mass killing? What authorities are held accountable for different types of activities? Is it possible for government officials to make challengers like Al-Qaida responsible for repressive behavior thereby diffusing the primary mechanism of influence within the democratic peace? These are some of the questions to which future research must be directed.

Other topics are worthy of attention as well. For example, from the analysis, we see that previous contentious activities are important. Not only does past political conflict influence subsequent repressive behavior but past characteristics of the political system influence the activities of the government later. The resonance of the civil war and genocide in Rwanda has cast a dark shadow over all political life in the country that persists to the present day, domestically and internationally. The Rwanda of the early to mid-1990s established a context within which an extremely far-reaching security policy was created and in its wake all other political developments appeared to wither – especially those like democracy that could rein in this power. Similarly, the resonance of 9/11 in the United States has cast a dark shadow over American policy (again both domestically and internationally). The importance of this lagged influence is clearly smaller than in the Rwandan case, and the degree of violence prompted by political conflict is accordingly much lower. Nevertheless the injuries sustained still motivate politicians and coercive agents years after the violence subsided. Indeed, to date, the provisions extended by the U.S. government have not been substantively withdrawn, and discussion is still taking place about making them permanent. This important factor, missed in the current project, is a matter worthy of additional consideration.

The concern with contemporaneous and lagged influences of political conflict, democracy, and prior repression highlights a topic of importance within policy and activist circles. It is generally acknowledged that during the Cold War the concern for political order (eliminating domestic threats) took precedent over all other objectives (democracy, for example). Repression would be employed to eliminate challenges, and little else was deemed more important. Following the Cold War, however, some have argued that this prioritization has been reversed, with democracy/democratization given priority over political order (especially in the West and in the United States in particular). In this context, efforts would be undertaken to "open" the political system, and only subsequently would other issues be addressed (for example, political conflict).

This approach is problematic because of the role played by state repression. On the one hand, political conflict increases repressive behavior; on the other hand, democracy decreases repression. This places the domestic democratic peace as well as the confounding influence of political conflict on this peace (what I refer to as the bulletproof nature of the proposition) at the center of the current debate. It is not only here that the topic is central. Indeed, the issues addressed in this book also belong in discussions about human rights and conflict studies, democratic theory, new institutionalism, and democratic outcomes/performance. Only twenty years ago John McCamant (1984, 11) remarked that "[o]ne searches in vain through the thousands of articles and books written by political scientists, political sociologists, economists, and anthropologists for references to the awful

and bloody deeds of governments and for explanations of how a
these deeds are done." We are clearly beyond the point highlig
McCamant: we now know a great deal about repressive behavior. Bu
is still a ways to go, for we are unclear about how the relevant behavior and
our understanding of it fit with other concerns, other ideas, and other behavior. Every day we hear about some new disclosure regarding state-sponsored
torture, surveillance, mass arrests and killing somewhere in the world. In
addition, every day we hear about some individual, organization, or nation
that aspires to be free from repression, very frequently in the context of a
movement to democracy or within a democratic state. It is time to give these
events and these efforts our full attention. Indeed, either there is a connection and our world is rendered more peaceful because of it, or there is no
connection and we need to get on with the business of identifying new and
better approaches to dealing with state coercive activity. Having completed
the analyses reported here, I feel that Bertrand Russell was on to something
when he remarked that "democracy, while not a complete solution, is an
essential part of the solution." Exactly how far does this thinking take us?
How can we improve upon this pacifying influence such as it is? These are
the questions to which we must now turn. Indeed, these are perhaps the
only questions worthy of any attention at all.

Appendix I

Table AI.1. *Models with Diverse Aspects of Democracy*

Lag Repression 2	1.615**	2.052**	1.952**	1.812**	1.578**
	(0.000)	(0.000)	(0.000)	(0.000)	(0.000)
Lag Repression 3	2.415**	2.971**	2.789**	2.596**	2.320**
	(0.000)	(0.000)	(0.000)	(0.000)	(0.000)
Lag Repression 4	2.540**	2.773**	2.765**	2.803**	2.616**
	(0.000)	(0.000)	(0.000)	(0.000)	(0.000)
Lag Repression 5	2.691**	3.185**	3.075**	2.928**	2.654**
	(0.000)	(0.000)	(0.000)	(0.000)	(0.000)
Lag Repression 6	3.178**	3.848**	3.628**	3.440**	3.113**
	(0.000)	(0.000)	(0.000)	(0.000)	(0.000)
Lag Repression 7	2.984**	3.164**	3.168**	3.300**	3.105**
	(0.000)	(0.000)	(0.000)	(0.000)	(0.000)
Lag Repression 8	3.692**	4.154**	4.097**	3.950**	3.687**

(*continued*)

Table AI.1 *(continued)*

	(0.000)	(0.000)	(0.000)	(0.000)	(0.000)
Lag Repression 9	4.515**	5.173**	5.034**	4.850**	4.485**
	(0.000)	(0.000)	(0.000)	(0.000)	(0.000)
Difference from Region	−0.041*	−0.068**	−0.067**	−0.068**	−0.049**
	(0.025)	(0.000)	(0.000)	(0.000)	(0.007)
Violent Dissent	0.320**	0.249**	0.274**	0.269**	0.313**
	(0.000)	(0.000)	(0.000)	(0.000)	(0.000)
Civil War	0.728**	0.709**	0.744**	0.757**	0.730**
	(0.000)	(0.000)	(0.000)	(0.000)	(0.000)
Interstate War	0.302**	0.416**	0.344**	0.314**	0.278**
	(0.004)	(0.000)	(0.001)	(0.002)	(0.008)
Log Population	0.066**	0.051**	0.053**	0.062**	0.074**
	(0.000)	(0.001)	(0.001)	(0.000)	(0.000)
Log Per Capita GNP	−0.085**	−0.137**	−0.121**	−0.118**	−0.092**
	(0.000)	(0.000)	(0.000)	(0.000)	(0.000)
Gates Democracy Measure	−0.015**				−0.011**
	(0.000)				(0.000)
Bollen Suffrage		−0.002**			
		(0.000)			
Veto Players 2			−0.159		

Appendix I

			(0.068)		
Veto Players 3			−0.447**		
			(0.000)		
Veto Players 4			−0.322**		
			(0.000)		
Veto Players 5			−0.437**		
			(0.000)		
Veto Players 6+			−0.349*		
			(0.023)		
Executive Constraint 2				−0.200*	−0.191*
				(0.012)	(0.019)
Executive Constraint 3/4				−0.151*	−0.151*
				(0.013)	(0.014)
Executive Constraint 5				−0.572**	−0.325**
				(0.000)	(0.002)
Executive Constraint 6				−0.385**	−0.110
				(0.001)	(0.377)
Executive Constraint 7				−0.750**	−0.459**
				(0.000)	(0.000)
Observations	2732	2707	2769	2769	2732
Null % Predicted	0.239	0.241	0.238	0.238	0.239
Model % Predicted	0.554	0.551	0.551	0.557	0.558

Table AI.2. *Models Interacting Suffrage with Conflict*

Lag Repression 2	2.001**	2.004**	2.002**
	(0.000)	(0.000)	(0.000)
Lag Repression 3	2.857**	2.862**	2.862**
	(0.000)	(0.000)	(0.000)
Lag Repression 4	2.612**	2.613**	2.613**
	(0.000)	(0.000)	(0.000)
Lag Repression 5	2.954**	2.958**	2.954**
	(0.000)	(0.000)	(0.000)
Lag Repression 6	3.558**	3.559**	3.553**
	(0.000)	(0.000)	(0.000)
Lag Repression 7	2.843**	2.842**	2.842**
	(0.000)	(0.000)	(0.000)
Lag Repression 8	3.731**	3.740**	3.735**
	(0.000)	(0.000)	(0.000)
Lag Repression 9	4.682**	4.680**	4.674**
	(0.000)	(0.000)	(0.000)
Difference from Region	0.061**	0.061**	0.062**
	(0.000)	(0.000)	(0.000)
Violent Dissent	0.202*	0.249**	0.250**
	(0.043)	(0.000)	(0.000)
Civil War	0.708**	0.733**	0.705**

Appendix I

	(0.000)	(0.000)	(0.000)
Interstate War	0.412**	0.414**	0.241
	(0.000)	(0.000)	(0.205)
Log Population	0.049**	0.050**	0.049**
	(0.002)	(0.002)	(0.002)
Log Per Capita GNP	−0.137**	−0.137**	−0.137**
	(0.000)	(0.000)	(0.000)
Bollen Suffrage	−0.002**	−0.002**	−0.002**
	(0.001)	(0.001)	(0.000)
Suffrage * Violent Dissent	0.001		
	(0.573)		
Suffrage * Civil War		−0.000	
		(0.829)	
Suffrage * Interstate War			0.002
			(0.282)
Observations	2707	2707	2707
Null % Predicted	0.241	0.241	0.241
Model % Predicted	0.550	0.552	0.550

p values in parentheses
* significant at 5%; ** significant at 1%

Table AI.3. *Models Interacting Participation/Competition with Conflict*

Log Per Capita GNP	−0.085**	−0.085**	−0.084**
	(0.000)	(0.000)	(0.000)
Log Population	0.063**	0.063**	0.066**
	(0.000)	(0.000)	(0.000)
Lag Repression 2	1.561**	1.572**	1.573**
	(0.000)	(0.000)	(0.000)
Lag Repression 3	2.316**	2.333**	2.337**
	(0.000)	(0.000)	(0.000)
Lag Repression 4	2.440**	2.440**	2.430**
	(0.000)	(0.000)	(0.000)
Lag Repression 5	2.535**	2.543**	2.541**
	(0.000)	(0.000)	(0.000)
Lag Repression 6	2.981**	2.995**	2.990**
	(0.000)	(0.000)	(0.000)
Lag Repression 7	2.797**	2.782**	2.775**
	(0.000)	(0.000)	(0.000)
Lag Repression 8	3.414**	3.410**	3.429**
	(0.000)	(0.000)	(0.000)
Lag Repression 9	4.204**	4.218**	4.206**
	(0.000)	(0.000)	(0.000)
Difference from Region	0.037*	0.036*	0.035*

Appendix I

	(0.029)	(0.033)	(0.037)
Violent Dissent	0.250**	0.323**	0.326**
	(0.000)	(0.000)	(0.000)
Civil War	0.735**	0.675**	0.723**
	(0.000)	(0.000)	(0.000)
Interstate War	0.297**	0.299**	0.356**
	(0.004)	(0.004)	(0.001)
Gates Democracy Measure	−0.017**	−0.015**	−0.015**
	(0.000)	(0.000)	(0.000)
Gates Democracy Measure * Violent Dissent	0.005*		
	(0.026)		
Gates Democracy Measure * Civil War		0.004	
		(0.325)	
Gates Democracy Measure * Interstate War			−0.033
			(0.153)
Observations	2732	2732	2732
Null % Predicted	0.239	0.239	0.239
Model % Predicted	0.553	0.555	0.556

p values in parentheses
* significant at 5%; ** significant at 1%

Table AI.4. *Models Interacting Veto Players with Conflict*

Log Per Capita GNP	−0.119**	−0.121**
	(0.000)	(0.000)
Log Population	0.050**	0.050**
	(0.002)	(0.002)
Lag Repression 2	1.879**	1.883**
	(0.000)	(0.000)
Lag Repression 3	2.646**	2.658**
	(0.000)	(0.000)
Lag Repression 4	2.584**	2.604**
	(0.000)	(0.000)
Lag Repression 5	2.825**	2.824**
	(0.000)	(0.000)
Lag Repression 6	3.319**	3.326**
	(0.000)	(0.000)
Lag Repression 7	2.839**	2.839**
	(0.000)	(0.000)
Lag Repression 8	3.648**	3.653**
	(0.000)	(0.000)
Lag Repression 9	4.528**	4.535**
	(0.000)	(0.000)
Difference from Region	0.058**	0.064**
	(0.000)	(0.000)

Appendix I

Violent Dissent	0.205**	0.276**
	(0.001)	(0.000)
Civil War	0.760**	0.680**
	(0.000)	(0.000)
Interstate War	0.345**	0.341**
	(0.001)	(0.001)
Veto Players 2	−0.239*	−0.139
	(0.046)	(0.135)
Veto Players 3	−0.529**	−0.484**
	(0.000)	(0.000)
Veto Players 4	−0.328**	−0.364**
	(0.002)	(0.000)
Veto Players 5	−0.782**	−0.448**
	(0.000)	(0.000)
Veto Players 6+	−0.358	−0.328*
	(0.074)	(0.039)
Veto Players 2 * Violent Dissent	0.177	
	(0.288)	
Veto Players 3 * Violent Dissent	0.202	
	(0.189)	
Veto Players 4 * Violent Dissent	0.003	
	(0.985)	

(*continued*)

Table AI.4 *(continued)*

Veto Players 5 * Violent Dissent	0.660**	
	(0.004)	
Veto Players 6+ * Violent Dissent	0.022	
	(0.941)	
Veto Players 2 * Civil War		−0.111
		(0.651)
Veto Players 3 * Civil War		0.317
		(0.177)
Veto Players 4 * Civil War		0.316
		(0.164)
Veto Players 5 * Civil War		−0.046
		(0.951)
Veto Players 6+ * Civil War		−0.231
		(0.673)
Observations	2769	2769
Null % Predicted	0.238	0.238
Model % Predicted	0.550	0.553
p values in parentheses * significant at 5%; ** significant at 1%		

Appendix I

Table AI.5. *Models Interacting Executive Constraints with Conflict.*

Log Per Capita GNP	−0.118**	−0.118**	−0.117**
	(0.000)	(0.000)	(0.000)
Log Population	0.056**	0.058**	0.061**
	(0.000)	(0.000)	(0.000)
Lag Repression 2	1.736**	1.742**	1.742**
	(0.000)	(0.000)	(0.000)
Lag Repression 3	2.434**	2.459**	2.467**
	(0.000)	(0.000)	(0.000)
Lag Repression 4	2.642**	2.631**	2.623**
	(0.000)	(0.000)	(0.000)
Lag Repression 5	2.673**	2.682**	2.680**
	(0.000)	(0.000)	(0.000)
Lag Repression 6	3.118**	3.138**	3.130**
	(0.000)	(0.000)	(0.000)
Lag Repression 7	2.989**	2.959**	2.958**
	(0.000)	(0.000)	(0.000)
Lag Repression 8	3.493**	3.489**	3.511**
	(0.000)	(0.000)	(0.000)
Lag Repression 9	4.337**	4.347**	4.332**
	(0.000)	(0.000)	(0.000)
Difference from Region	0.064**	0.062**	0.059**

(*continued*)

Table AI.5 *(continued)*

	(0.000)	(0.000)	(0.000)
Violent Dissent	0.087	0.271**	0.274**
	(0.299)	(0.000)	(0.000)
Civil War	0.771**	0.677**	0.751**
	(0.000)	(0.000)	(0.000)
Interstate War	0.322**	0.311**	0.377**
	(0.002)	(0.003)	(0.007)
Executive Constraint 2	−0.159	−0.170*	−0.194*
	(0.119)	(0.046)	(0.019)
Executive Constraint 3/4	−0.273**	−0.171**	−0.147*
	(0.000)	(0.007)	(0.019)
Executive Constraint 5	−0.610**	−0.578**	−0.563**
	(0.000)	(0.000)	(0.000)
Executive Constraint 6	−0.454**	−0.359**	−0.361**
	(0.007)	(0.003)	(0.001)
Executive Constraint 7	−0.912**	−0.789**	−0.748**
	(0.000)	(0.000)	(0.000)
Executive Constraint 2 * Violent Dissent	−0.057		
	(0.726)		
Executive Constraint 3/4 * Violent Dissent	0.382**		

Appendix I

	(0.002)		
Executive Constraint 5 * Violent Dissent	0.130		
	(0.469)		
Executive Constraint 6 * Violent Dissent	0.200		
	(0.355)		
Executive Constraint 7 * Violent Dissent	0.411**		
	(0.003)		
Executive Constraint 2 * Civil War		−0.215	
		(0.376)	
Executive Constraint 3/4 * Civil War		0.262	
		(0.203)	
Executive Constraint 5 * Civil War		0.136	
		(0.668)	
Executive Constraint 6 * Civil War		−0.063	
		(0.820)	
Executive Constraint 7 * Civil War		0.360	
		(0.124)	

(*continued*)

Table AI.5 *(continued)*

Executive Constraint 2 * Civil War			−0.050
			(0.872)
Executive Constraint 3/4 * Civil War			−0.012
			(0.961)
Executive Constraint 6 * Civil War			−8.104
			(1.000)
Executive Constraint 7 * Civil War			−7.601
			(1.000)
Observations	2769	2769	2769
Null%Predicted	0.238	0.238	0.238
Model%Predicted	0.550	0.554	0.555
p values in parentheses * significant at 5%; ** significant at 1%			

Appendix II

Table A II.1. *Out-of-Sample Prediction Statistics*

	Weak Out-of-Sample Prediction	Strong Out-of-Sample Prediction
Non-Interactive: In Sample	54.2%	46.0%
Non-Interactive: Out of Sample	54.3%	49.1%
Interactive Violence: In Sample	55.5%	51.0%
Interactive Violence: Out of Sample	53.1%	46.7%
Interactive Civil War: In Sample	54.9%	54.0%
Interactive Civil War: Out of Sample	53.5%	48.7%
Interactive Interstate War: In Sample	53.7%	52.0%
Interactive Interstate War: Out of Sample	53.4%	48.0%

Cell entries are % correctly predicted by the model
Weak OSP uses all countries on or before 1986 to predict all countries after 1986
Strong OSP uses a sample of randomly selected countries (roughly half, 66) on or before
1986 to predict the countries not in the sample (71) after 1986.

Bibliography

Adcock, R. and D. Collier (2001). "Measurement Validity: A Shared Standard for Qualitative and Quantitative Research." *American Political Science Review* **95**(3): 529–46.

Aflatooni, A. and M. P. Allen (1991). "Government Sanctions and Collective Political Protest in Periphery and Semiperiphery States – A Time-Series Analysis." *Journal of Political & Military Sociology* **19**(1): 29–45.

Agamben, G. (2005). *State of Exception*. Chicago, University of Chicago Press.

Alvarez, M., J. Ciheibub, F. Limongi and A. Przeworski (1996). "Classifying Political Regimes." *Studies in Comparative International Development* **31**(2): 1–37.

American Civil Liberties Union (2005). *Main Street America Fights Back: Anti-Patriot Act Community Resolutions Sweep the Nation.*

Ames, B. (1987). *Political Survival: Politicians and Public Policy in Latin America*. Berkeley, University of California Press.

Apodaca, C. (2001). "Global Economic Patterns and Personal Integrity Rights after the Cold War." *International Studies Quarterly* **45**: 587–602.

Apter, D. E. (1965). *The Politics of Modernization*. Chicago, University of Chicago Press.

Arat, Z. F. (1991). *Democracy and Human Rights in Developing Countries*. Boulder, Colorado, Lynne Rienner Publishers.

Arendt, H. (1951). *The Origins of Totalitarianism*. New York, Harcourt.

Ashcroft, J. (2001a). Testimony before the House Committee on the Judiciary. *House Committee on the Judiciary*.

(2001b). Department of Justice Oversight: Preserving Our Freedoms While Defending against Terrorism. *Hearing before the Senate Committee on the Judiciary*.

Bachrach, P. (1967). *The Theory of Democratic Elitism; A Critique*. Boston, Little.

Banks, A. S. (2001). Cross-National Time-Series Data Archive.

Barro, R. and J. Lee (1993). "International Comparisons of Educational Attainment." *Journal of Monetary Economics* **32**: 363–94.

Bay, C. (1958). *The Structure of Freedom*. Stanford, California, Stanford University Press.

Beetham, D. (1994). *Defining and Measuring Democracy*. London; Thousand Oaks, California, Sage Publications.

Blalock, H. M. (1989). *Power and Conflict: Toward a General Theory*. Newbury Park, California, Sage Publications.

Bollen, K. A. (1998). Cross-National Indicators of Liberal Democracy, 1950–1990, Inter-University Consortium for Political and Social Research (ICPSR) #2532. Ann Arbor, Michigan: ICPSR.

(1980). "Issues in the Comparative Measurement of Political Democracy." *American Sociological Review* **45**(3): 370–90.

(1986). "Political Rights and Political Liberties in Nations – An Evaluation of Human-Rights Measures, 1950 to 1984." *Human Rights Quarterly* **8**(4): 567–91.

Bollen, K. A. and R. W. Jackman (1985). "Political Democracy and the Size Distribution of Income." *American Sociological Review* **50**(4): 438–57.

Boudreau, V. (2004). *Resisting Dictatorship: Repression and Protest in Southeast Asia*. Cambridge, United Kingdom; New York, Cambridge University Press.

Bovard, J. (2003). *Terrorism and Tyranny: Trampling Freedom, Justice, and Peace to Rid the World of Evil*. New York, Palgrave Macmillan.

Bueno de Mesquita, B. (2003). *The Logic of Political Survival*. Cambridge, Massachusetts, MIT Press.

Bueno de Mesquita, B., G. W. Downs, A. Smith and F. M. Cherif (2005). "Thinking inside the Box: A Closer Look at Democracy and Human Rights." *International Studies Quarterly* **49**(3): 439–57.

Burkhart, R. E. and M. S. Lewisbeck (1994). "Comparative Democracy – The Economic-Development Thesis." *American Political Science Review* **88**(4): 903–10.

Bush, G. W. (2005). Second Inaugural Speech.

Carleton, D. (1989). "The New International Division of Labor, Export-Oriented Growth and State Repression in Latin America." *Dependence, Development, and State Repression*. George A. Lopez and Michael Stohl. New York, Greenwood Press.

Carleton, D. and M. Stohl (1985). "The Foreign-Policy of Human-Rights – Rhetoric and Reality from Carter, Jimmy to Reagan, Ronald." *Human Rights Quarterly* **7**(2): 205–29.

Casper, G. (1995). *Fragile Democracies: The Legacies of Authoritarian Rule*. Pittsburgh, University of Pittsburgh Press.

Charny, I. W. (1999). *Encyclopedia of Genocide*. Santa Barbara, California, ABC-CLIO.

Cingranelli, D. L. and D. L. Richards (1999). "Respect for Human Rights after the End of the Cold War." *Journal of Peace Research* **36**(5): 511–34.

Cnudde, C. F. and D. E. Neubauer (1969). *Empirical Democratic Theory*. Chicago, Markham Publishing Co.

Coleman, J. S. (1960). "Conclusion: The Political System of the Developing Areas." *The Politics of Developing Areas*. G. A. Almond and J. S. Coleman. Princeton, New Jersey, Princeton University Press.

Bibliography

Collier, D. and S. Levitsky (1997). "Research Note: Democracy with Adjectives: Conceptual Research in Comparative Politics." *World Politics* **43**(3): 430–51.

Congdon, P. (2003). *Applied Bayesian Modelling*. West Sussex, Wiley.

Coppedge, M. and W. H. Reinicke (1991). "Measuring Polyarchy." *On Measuring Democracy: Its Consequences and Concomitants*. L. Alex Inkeles. New Brunswick, Transaction Publishers.

Coser, L. A. (1956). *The Functions of Social Conflict*. Glencoe, Illinois, Free Press.

Crescenzi, M. J. C. and A. J. Enterline (1999). "Ripples from the Waves? A Systemic, Time-Series Analysis of Democracy, Democratization, and Interstate War." *Journal of Peace Research* **36**(1): 75–94.

Cutright, P. (1963). "National Political-Development – Measurement and Analysis." *American Sociological Review* **28**(2): 253–64.

Dahl, R. A. (1966). *Political Opposition in Western Democracies*. New Haven, Connecticut, Yale University Press.

(1971). *Polyarchy: Participation and Opposition*. New Haven, Connecticut, Yale University Press.

(1989). *Democracy and Its Critics*. New Haven, Connecticut, Yale University Press.

(1998). *On Democracy*. New Haven, Connecticut, Yale University Press.

Dallin, A. and G. W. Breslauer (1970). *Political Terror in Communist Systems*. Stanford, California, Stanford University Press.

Davenport, C. (1995a). "Assessing the Military's Influence on Political Repression." *Journal of Political & Military Sociology* **23**:119–44.

(1995b). "Multi-Dimensional Threat Perception and State Repression: An Inquiry into Why States Apply Negative Sanctions." *American Journal of Political Science* **39**(3): 683–713.

(1996a). "'Constitutional Promises' and Repressive Reality: A Cross-National Time-Series Investigation of Why Political and Civil Liberties Are Suppressed." *Journal of Politics* **58**(3): 627–54.

(1996b). "The Weight of the Past: Exploring Lagged Determinants of Political Repression." *Political Research Quarterly* **49**(2): 377–403.

(1997). "From Ballots to Bullets: An Empirical Assessment of How National Elections Influence State Uses of Political Repression." *Electoral Studies* **16**(4): 517–40.

(1998). "Liberalizing Event or Lethal Episode: An Empirical Assessment of How National Elections Affect the Suppression of Political and Civil Liberties." *Social Science Quarterly* **79**(2): 321–40.

(1999). "Human Rights and the Democratic Proposition." *Journal of Conflict Resolution* **43**(1): 92–116.

(2004). "The Promise of Democratic Pacification: An Empirical Assessment." *International Studies Quarterly* **48**(3): 539–60.

Davenport, C. and D. A. Armstrong II (2004). "Democracy and the Violation of Human Rights: A Statistical Analysis from 1976–1996." *American Journal of Political Science* **48**(3): 538–54.

Davenport, C. and P. Ball (2002). "Views to a Kill: Exploring the Implications of Source Selection in the Case of Guatemalan State Terror, 1977–1996." *Journal of Conflict Resolution* **46**(3): 427–50.

Davenport, C. and M. Eads (2001). "Cued to Coerce or Coercing Cues? An Exploration of Dissident Framing and Its Relationship to Political Repression." *Mobilization* **6**(2): 151–71.

Davis, D. and B. Silver (2004). "Civil Liberties Vs. Security: Public Opinion in the Context of the Terrorist Attacks on America." *American Journal of Political Science* **48**(1): 28–46.

De Swann, A. (1977). "Terror as Government Service." *Repression and Repressive Violence: Proceedings of the 3rd International Working Conference on Violence and Non-Violent Action in Industrialized Societies.* M. Hoefnagels Ed. Amsterdam, Swets & Zeitlinger.

Della Porta, D. (1995). *Social Movements, Political Violence and the State: A Comparative Analysis of Italy and Germany.* New York, Cambridge University Press.

Della Porta, D. and H. Reiter (1998). *Policing Protest: The Control of Mass Demonstrations in Western Democracies.* Minneapolis, University of Minnesota Press.

Denemark, R. and H. Lehman (1984). "South African State Terror: The Costs of Continuing Repression." *The State as Terrorist: The Dynamics of Governmental Violence and Repression.* M. S. a. G. Lopez. Westport, Greenwood Press.

Diamond, L. (1995). *Promoting Democracy in the 1990's: Actors and Instruments, Issues and Imperatives.* New York, Carnegie Corporation.

(1996). "Is the Third Wave Over?" *Journal of Democracy* **7**(3): 20–37.

Diamond, L., J. Linz and S. M. Lipset, Eds. (1995). *Politics in Developing Countries: Comparing Experiences with Democracy.* Boulder, Colorado, L. Rienner Publisher.

Duvall, R. and M. Stohl (1988). "Governance by Terror." *The Politics of Terrorism.* M. Stohl Ed. New York, M. Dekker.

Earl, J. (2003). "Tanks, Tear Gas and Taxes: Toward a Theory of Movement Repression." *Sociological Theory* **21**(1): 44–68.

Eckstein, H. (1980). *Theoretical Approaches to Explaining Collective Political Violence. Handbook of Political Conflict: Theory and Practice.* T. R. Gurr Ed. New York, Free Press.

Eckstein, H. and T. R. Gurr (1975). *Patterns of Authority: A Structural Basis for Political Inquiry.* New York: John Wiley & Sons.

Eisenstadt, S. N. (1971). *Political Sociology; A Reader.* New York, Basic Books.

Ekiert, G. and J. Kubik (1999). *Rebellious Civil Society: Popular Protest and Democratic Consolidation in Poland, 1989–1993.* Ann Arbor, University of Michigan Press.

Elliot, G. (1972). *Twentieth Century Book of the Dead.* New York, Charles Scribner.

Fein, H. (1995). "More Murder in the Middle – Life-Integrity Violations and Democracy in the World, 1987." *Human Rights Quarterly* **17**(1): 170–91.

Ferrara, F. (2003). "Why Regimes Create Disorder: Hobbes Dilemma During a Rangoon Summer." *Journal of Conflict Resolution* **47**(3): 302–25.

Fox, J. (2000). "Civil Society and Political Accountability: Propositions for Discussion." Presented at Institutions, Accountability, and Democratic Governance

Bibliography

in Latin America, The Helen Kellogg Institute for International Studies, University of Notre Dame, May 8–9.

Francisco, R. (2004). "After the Massacre: Mobilization in the Wake of Harsh Repression." *Mobilization* **9**(2): 107–26.

Franklin, J. (1997). "IMF Conditionality, Threat Perception and Political Repression: A Cross-National Analysis." *Comparative Political Studies* **30**: 576–606.

Franks, C. E. S., Ed. (1989). *Dissent and the State*. Toronto, Oxford University Press.

Freedom House (1986–7). *Freedom in the World Country Ratings: The Annual Survey of Political Rights and Civil Liberties, 1986–1987*. New York, Freedom House.

(1991–2). *Freedom in the World Country Ratings: The Annual Survey of Political Rights and Civil Liberties, 1986–1987*. New York, Freedom House.

Friedrich, C. J. and Z. Brzezinski (1962). *Totalitarian Dictatorship and Autocracy*. Cambridge, Massachusetts, Harvard University Press.

Freidrich, R. (1982). "In Defense of Multiplicative Terms in Multiple Regression Equations." *American Journal of Political Science* **26**(4): 797–833.

Gartner, S. and P. Regan (1996). "Threat and Repression: The Non-Linear Relationship between Government and Opposition Violence." *Journal of Peace Research* **33**(3): 273–87.

Gasiorowski, M. J. (1996). "An Overview of the Political Regime Change Dataset." *Comparative Political Studies* **29**(4): 469–83.

Gastil, R. (1973). "The New Criteria of Freedom." *Freedom at Issue* **17**(January–February): 2–24.

Gates, S., H. Hegre, M. P. Jones and H. L. Strand (2003). "Institutional Inconsistency and Political Instability: Polity Duration, 1800–2000." *American Journal of Political Science* **50**(4): 893–908.

Geddes, B. (1999). "Authoritarian Breakdown: Empirical Test of a Game Theoretic Argument." Presented at the Annual Meeting of the American Political Science Association, Atlanta.

Gibney, M. and M. Dalton (1996). "The Political Terror Scale." *Human Rights and Developing Countries*. D. L. Cingranell, Ed. Greenwich, Connecticut, JAI.

Gibson, J. L. (1988). "Political Intolerance and Political Repression During the Mccarthy Red Scare." *American Political Science Review* **82**(2): 511–29.

(2004). *Overcoming Apartheid: Can Truth Reconcile a Divided Nation?* New York, Russell Sage Foundation.

Giliomee, H. (1987). "Apartheid, Verligtheid, and Liberalism." *Democratic Liberalism in South Africa: Its History and Prospect*. R. E. Jeffrey Butler, and David Welsh, Eds. Middletown, Connecticut, Weslayan University Press.

Gill, J. (2001). "Interpreting Interactions and Interaction Hierarchies in Generalized Linear Models: Issues and Applications." Presented at the Annual Meeting of the American Political Science Association, San Francisco.

Gleditsch, K. S. and M. D. Ward (1997). "Double Take – A Reexamination of Democracy and Autocracy in Modern Polities." *Journal of Conflict Resolution* **41**(3): 361–83.

(2000). "War and Peace in Space and Time: The Role of Democratization." *International Studies Quarterly* **44**(1): 1–29.

Goldman, R. M. and W. A. Douglas (1988). *Promoting Democracy: Opportunities and Issues*. New York, Praeger.

Goldstein, R. J. (1978). *Political Repression in Modern America: From 1870 to the Present*. Cambridge, Massachusetts, Schenkman Publishing Co.

(1983). *Political Repression in 19th Century Europe*. Totowa, New Jersey, Barnes & Noble.

(1986). "The Limitations of Using Quantitative Data in Studying Human Rights Abuses." *Human Rights Quarterly* **8**(4): 607–27.

Greene, W. (2000). *Econometric Analysis*. Upper Saddle, River, New Jersey, Prentice Hall.

Gurr, T. R. (1974). "Persistence and Change in Political Systems, 1800–1971." *American Political Science Review* **68**(4): 1482–1504.

(1986). "The Political Origins of State Violence and Terror: A Theoretical Analysis." *Government Violence and Repression: An Agenda for Research*. M. Stohl and G. A. Lopez, Eds. New York, Greenwood Press.

Hadenius, A. (1992). *Democracy and Development*. Cambridge, Cambridge University Press.

Hafner-Burton, E. (2005a). "Right or Robust? The Sensitive Nature of Repression to Globalization." *Journal of Peace Research* **42**(6): 679–98.

(2005b). "Trading Human Rights: How Preferential Trade Agreements Influence Government Repression." *International* Organization **59**(Summer): 593–629.

Harff, B. (2003). "No Lessons Learned from the Holocaust: Assessing Risks of Genocide and Political Mass Murder since 1955." *American Political Science Review* **97**(1): 57–74.

Harff, B. and T. R. Gurr (1988). "Toward Empirical Theory of Genocides and Politicides: Identification and Measurement of Cases Since 1945." *International Studies Quarterly* **32**: 359–71.

Harrelson-Stephens, J. and R. Callaway (2003). "Does Trade Openness Promote Security Rights in Developing Countries? Examining the Liberal Perspective." *International Interactions* **29**: 143–58.

Hegre, H., T. Ellingsen, S. Gates and N. P. Gleditsch (2001). "Toward a Democratic Civil Peace? Democracy, Political Change and Civil War, 1916–1992." *American Political Science Review* **95**: 33–48.

Held, D. (1996). *Models of Democracy*. Stanford, California, Stanford University Press.

Henderson, C. W. (1991). "Conditions Affecting the Use of Political Repression." *Journal of Conflict Resolution* **35**: 120–42.

(1993). "Population Pressures and Political Repression." *Social Science Quarterly* **74**(2): 322–33.

Hibbs, D. A. (1973). *Mass Political Violence: A Cross-National Causal Analysis*. New York, Wiley.

Hirschman, A. O. (1970). *Exit, Voice, and Loyalty; Responses to Decline in Firms, Organizations, and States*. Cambridge, Massachusetts, Harvard University Press.

Hobbes, T. (1950). *Leviathan*. New York, Dutton.

Huber, E., D. Rueschemeyer and J. D. Stephens (1993). "The Impact of Economic-Development on Democracy." *Journal of Economic Perspectives* **7**(3): 71–86.

Human Rights Watch. (1998). "Human Rights Watch World Report 1998: Rwanda." *http://www.hrw.org/worldreport/Africa-10.htm*.

Huntington, S. P. (1991). *The Third Wave: Democratization in the Late Twentieth Century*. Norman, University of Oklahoma Press.

Immergut, E. (1998). "The Theoretical Core of the New Institutionalism." *Politics and Society* **26**(1): 5–34.

Isaac, J. C. (1998). *Democracy in Dark Times*. Ithaca, New York, Cornell University Press.

Jaggers, K. and T. R. Gurr (1995). "Tracking Democracy's 3rd-Wave with the Polity-III Data." *Journal of Peace Research* **32**(4): 469–82.

Kaiser, A. (1997). "Types of Democracy – From Classical to New Institutionalism." *Journal of Theoretical Politics* **9**(4): 419–44.

Karatnycky, A., Ed. (1999). *Freedom in the World: The Annual Survey of Political Rights and Civil Liberties 1998–1999*. New Brunswick, New Jersey, Transaction Publishers.

Keefer, P. (2002). *Database of Political Institutions: Changes and Variable Definitions, Development Research Group*, Washington, D.C., The World Bank.

Keefer, P. and D. Stasavage (2003). "The Limits of Delegation: *Veto Players*, Central Bank Independence, and the Credibility of Monetary Policy." *American Political Science Review* **97**(3): 407–23.

Keith, L. C. (1999). "The United Nations International Covenant on Civil and Political Rights: Does It Make a Difference in Human Rights Behavior?" *Journal of Peace Research* **36**(1): 95–118.

(2002). "Constitutional Provisions for Individual Human Rights (1977–1996): Are They More Than Mere 'Window Dressing?" *Political Research Quarterly* **55**(1): 111–43.

Kelley, R. D. G. (1994). *Race Rebels: Culture, Politics, and the Black Working Class*. New York, Free Press.

King, J. (1998). "Repression, Domestic Threat, and Interactions in Argentina and Chile." *Journal of Political and Military Sociology*. **26**: 1–27.

(2000). "Exploring the Ameliorating Effects of Democracy on Political Repression: Cross-National Evidence." *Paths to State Repression: Human Rights Violations and Contentious Politics*. C. Davenport, Ed. Boulder, Colorado, Rowan and Littlefield.

Krain, M. (1997). "State-Sponsored Mass Murder: A Study of the Onset and Severity of Genocides and Politicides." *Journal of Conflict Resolution* **41**(3): 331–60.

Kuhn, T. S. (1962). *The Structure of Scientific Revolution*, 1st ed., Chicago, University of Chicago Press.

Lamb, G. (2002). "Debasing Democracy: Security Forces and Human Rights Abuses in Post-Liberation Namibia and South Africa." *Measuring Democracy and Human Rights in Southern Africa*. Y. D. Davids, Christiaan Keulder, Guy Lamb, Joao Pereira and Dirk Spilker, Eds., London, Nordic African Institute.

Lane, J.-E. and S. O. Ersson (2000). *The New Institutional Politics: Performance and Outcomes*. London; New York, Routledge.

Levene, M. (2005). *Genocide in the Age of the Nation State*. New York, Palgrave Macmillan.

Levin, M. B. (1971). *Political Hysteria in America; the Democratic Capacity for Repression*. New York, Basic Books.

Lichbach, M. I. (1987). "Deterrence or Escalation – The Puzzle of Aggregate Studies of Repression and Dissent." *Journal of Conflict Resolution* **31**(2): 266–97.

Lijphart, A. (1993). "Constitutional Choices for New Democracies." *The Global Resurgence of Democracy*. L. Diamond and M. Plattner, Eds. Baltimore, Johns Hopkins University Press.

Linfield, M. (1990). *Freedom under Fire: U.S. Civil Liberties in Times of War*. Boston, South End Press.

Linz, J. (2000). *Totalitarian and Authoritarian Regimes*. Boulder, Colorado, Lynne Rienner.

Lipset, S. M. (1959). "Some Social Requisites of Democracy – Economic-Development and Political Legitimacy." *American Political Science Review* **53**(1): 69–105.

Liska, A. E. (1992). *Social Threat and Social Control*. Albany, State University of New York Press.

Locke, J. (1963). *Two Treatises of Government*. New York, Cambridge University Press.

Long, J. S. (1997). *Regression Models for Categorical and Limited Dependent Variables*. Thousand Oaks, California, Sage.

Long, J. S. and J. Freese (2001). *Regression Models for Categorical Dependent Variables Using Stata*. College Station, Texas, Stata Press.

Lopez, G. A. and M. Stohl, Eds. (1989). *Dependence, Development, and State Repression*. Contributions in Political Science, No. 209. New York, Greenwood Press.

Machiavelli, N. (1980). *The Prince*. Champaign, Illinois, Project Gutenberg.

Mamdani, M. (2001). *When Victims Become Killers: Colonialism, Nativism, and the Genocide in Rwanda*. Princeton, New Jersey, Princeton University Press.

Markus, G. B. and B. A. Nesvold (1972). "Governmental Coerciveness and Political Instability – Exploratory Study of Cross-National Patterns." *Comparative Political Studies* **5**(2): 231–43.

Marshall, M. and K. Jaggers (2001). "Polity IV Project: Political Regime Characteristics and Transitions, 1800–1999. Data Users Manual." College Park, University of Maryland.

Mason, T. D. and D. A. Krane (1989). "The Political-Economy of Death Squads – Toward a Theory of the Impact of State-Sanctioned Terror." *International Studies Quarterly* **33**(2): 175–98.

Matau, M. (2001). "Savages, Victims, Saviors: The Metaphor of Human Rights." *Harvard International Law Journal* **42**: 201–45.

McAdam, D. (1982). *Political Process and the Development of Black Insurgency, 1930–1970*. Chicago, University of Chicago Press.

McCammant, J. (1981). "A Critique of Measures of Human Rights Development and an Alternative." *Global Human Rights: Public Policies, Comparative Measures, and Ngo Strategies*. V. P. Nanda, J. R. Scarritt and G. W. Shepherd. Boulder, Colorado, Westview Press.

(1984). "Governance without Blood: Social Sciences Antiseptic View of Rule; or, the Neglect of Political Repression." *The State as Terrorist: The Dynamics of Governmental Violence and Repression*. M. Stohl and G. A. Lopez. Westport, Connecticut, Greenwood Press.

McCormick, J. and N. Mitchell. (1997). "Human rights violations, umbrella concepts, and empirical analysis." *World Politics* **49**(4): 510.

McFaul, M. (2002). "The Fourth Wave of Democracy and Dictatorship – Noncooperative Transitions in the Postcommunist World." *World Politics* **54**(2): 212–44.

McLennan, B. (1973). *Cross-National Comparison of Political Opposition and Conflict: Political Opposition and Dissent*. New York, Dunellen Publishing Company.

McMahon, R. (2005). "2005 in Review: Bush's Democracy Agenda Sees Mixed Results, Radio Free Europe – Radio Liberty." www.rferl.org/featuresarticle/2005/12/3c64dfdc-dc88-4f57-9b65-39e92de7bac0.html

McPhail, C., D. Schweingruber and J. McCarthy (1998). "Policing Protest in the United States, 1960–1995." *Policing Protest: The Control of Mass Demonstrations in Western Democracies*. D. Della Porta and H. Reiter. Minneapolis, University of Minnesota Press.

Meyer, W. H. (1996). "Human Rights and MNC's: Theory Versus Quantitative Analysis." *Human Rights Quarterly* **18**(2): 368–97.

Michels, R. (1962). *Political Parties*. New York, Free Press.

Mill, J. S. (1861). *Considerations on Representative Government*. London, Parker, Son, and Bourn.

Mitchell, N. J. and J. M. McCormick (1988). "Economic and Political Explanations of Human Rights Violations." *World Politics* **40**(4): 476–98.

Monshipouri, M. (1995). *Democratization, Liberalization & Human Rights in the Third World*. Boulder, Colorado, Lynne Rienner Publishers.

Montesquieu, C. d. S. (1989). *The Spirit of the Laws*. New York, Cambridge University Press.

Moore, B. (1954). *Terror and Progress USSR: Some Sources of Change and Stability in the Soviet Dictatorship*. Cambridge, Harvard University Press.

Moore, W. H. (1998). "Repression and Dissent: Substitution, Context and Timing." *American Journal of Political Science* **45**(3): 851–73.

Mosca, G. (1980). *The Ruling Class – Elementi Di Scienza Politica*. Westport, Connecticut, Greenwood Press.

Munck, G. and J. Verkuilen (2002). "Conceptualizing and Measuring Democracy: Evaluating Alternative Indices." *Comparative Political Studies* **35**(1): 5–35.

Ngowi, R. (2003). Rwandans Endorse New Constitution. Associated Press. www.mail-archive.com/ugandanet@kym.net/msg03791.html.

O'Donnell, G. A., P. C. Schmitter and L. Whitehead, Eds. (1986). *Transitions from Authoritarian Rule: Prospects for Democracy*. Baltimore, Johns Hopkins University Press.

O'Kane, R. (1996). *Terror, Force and States: Path from Modernity*. Brookfield, Massachusetts, Edgar Elgar Publishing Company.

Olson, M. (1982). *The Rise and Decline of Nations: Economic Growth, Stagflation, and Social Rigidities*. New Haven, Connecticut, Yale University Press.

(1993). "Dictatorship, Democracy and Development." *American Political Science Review* **87**(3): 650–74.

O'Neal, J. R. and B. Russett (1999). "The Kantian Peace: The Pacific Benefits of Democracy, Interdependence, and International Organizations, 1885–1992." *World Politics* **52**(1): 1–37.

O'Neal, J. R., F. H. O'Neal, Z. Maoz and B. Russett (1996). "The Liberal Peace: Interdependence, Democracy, and International Conflict, 1950–85." *Journal of Peace Research* **33**(1): 11–28.

Pateman, C. (1970). *Participation and Democratic Theory*. Cambridge, United Kingdom, University Press.

Paxton, P., K. A. Bollen, D. M. Lee and H. Kim (2003). "A Half-Century of Suffrage: New Data and a Comparative Analysis." *Studies in Comparative International Development* **38**(1): 93–122.

Penna, D. (1998). "Democratization and Pluralism in South Africa: Policy and Process in the Post-Apartheid Transition." *Democratization and the Protection of Human Rights*. P. Campbell and K. Mahoney-Norris. Westport, Connecticut, Praeger Publishers.

Pion-Berlin, D. (1989). *The Ideology of State Terror: Economic Doctrine and Political Repression in Argentina and Peru*. Boulder, Colorado, L. Rienner Publishers.

Poe, S. and C. N. Tate (1994). "Repression of Human-Rights to Personal Integrity in the 1980s – A Global Analysis." *American Political Science Review* **88**(4): 853–72.

Poe, S., C. N. Tate and L. C. Keith (1999). "Repression of the Human Right to Personal Integrity Revisited: A Global Cross-National Study Covering the Years 1976–1993." *International Studies Quarterly* **43**(2): 291–313.

Powell, G. B. (1982). *Contemporary Democracies: Participation, Stability, and Violence*. Cambridge, Massachusetts, Harvard Univerity Press.

(2000). *Elections as Instruments of Democracy: Majoritarian and Proportional Visions*. New Haven, Connecticut, Yale University Press.

Przeworski, A. (2000). *Democracy and Development: Political Institutions and Well-Being in the World, 1950–1990*. Cambridge, Cambridge University Press.

(2004). "Institutions Matter?" *Government & Opposition* **39**(4): 527–41.

Przeworski, A., S. C. Stokes and B. Manin (1999). *Democracy, Accountability, and Representation*. Cambridge, United Kingdom; New York, Cambridge University Press.

Raftery, A. (1995). "Bayesian Model Selection in Social Research." *Sociological Methodology* **25**: 111–64.

Rapoport, D. C. and L. Weinberg (2001). *The Democratic Experience and Political Violence*. London; Portland, Oregon, F. Cass.

Rasler, K. (1986). "War, Accommodation and Violence in the United States, 1890–1970." *American Political Science Review* **80**: 921–45.

Bibliography

Regan, P. and E. Henderson (2002). "Democracy, Threats and Political Repression in Developing Countries: Are Democracies Internally Less Violent?" *Third World Quarterly* **23**(1): 119–36.

Reiter, D. and A. C. Stam (2002). *Democracies at War*. Princeton, New Jersey, Princeton University Press.

Rejali, D. M. (1994). *Torture & Modernity: Self, Society, and State in Modern Iran*. Boulder, Colorado, Westview Press.

Reyntjens, F. (1996). "Constitution-Making in Situations of Extreme Crisis: The Case of Rwanda and Burundi." *Journal of African Law* **40**: 236–9.

(2004). "Rwanda, Ten Years On: From Genocide to Dictatorship." *African Affairs* **103**(411): 177–210.

Richards, D. L. (1999). "Perilous Proxy: Human Rights and the Presence of National Elections." *Social Science Quarterly* **80**(4): 648–65.

Richards, D. L., R. D. Gelleny and D. H. Sacko (2001). "Money with a Mean Streak? Foreign Economic Penetration and Government Respect for Human Rights in Developing Countries." *International Studies Quarterly* **45**: 219–39.

Roller, E. (2003). "Conceptualizing and Measuring Institutions of Democratic Governance: A Critical Review and Empirical Validation of Veto-Player Indexes." *ECPR Joint Sessions Workshop on "Institutional Theory: Issues of Measurement and Change."*

Rosato, S. (2003). "The Flawed Logic of Democratic Peace Theory." *American Political Science Review* **97**(4): 585–602.

Rothgeb, J. (1989). *Direct Foreign Investment, Repression, Reform and Political Conflict in the Third World. Markets, Politics, and Change in the Global Political Economy*. William P. Avery and David P. Rapkin. Boulder, Colorado, Lynne Rienner.

Rousseau, D. L., C. Gelpi, D. Reiter and P. K. Huth (1996). "Assessing the Dyadic Nature of the Democratic Peace, 1918–88." *American Political Science Review* **90**(3): 512–33.

Ruland, J. (2003). "Constitutional Debates in the Philippines: From Presidentialism to Parliamentarianism?" *Asian Survey* **43**(3): 461–84.

Rummel, R. J. (1997). *Power Kills*. New Brunswick, New Jersey, Transaction Publishers.

Russett, B. M. (1993). *Grasping the Democratic Peace: Principles for a Post-Cold War World*. Princeton, New Jersey, Princeton University Press.

Sambanis, N. (2004). "What Is Civil War? Conceptual and Empirical Complexities of an Operational Definition." *Journal of Conflict Resolution* **48**(6): 814–58.

Sartori, G. (1987). *The Theory of Democracy Revisited*. Chatham, New Jersey, Chatham House Publishers.

Schmid, A. P. (1991). "Repression, State Terrorism, and Genocide: Conceptual Clarifications." *State Organized Terror: The Case of Violent Internal Repression*. P. T. Bushnell. Boulder, Colorado, Westview Press.

Schumpeter, J. (1962). *Capitalism Socialism and Democracy*. New York, Harper Torchbooks.

Scoble, H. and L. Weisberg (1981). "Problems of Comparative Research in Human Rights." *Global Human Rights: Public Policies, Comparative Measures and Ngo*

Strategies. V. P. Nanda, J. Scarritt, and G. W. Shephard. Boulder, Colorado, Westview Press.

Scott, J. C. (1985). *Weapons of the Weak: Everyday Forms of Peasant Resistance*. New Haven, Connecticut, Yale University Press.

Shapiro, I. (2003). *The State of Democratic Theory*. Princeton, New Jersey, Princeton University Press.

Sherr, A. (1989). *Freedom of Protest, Public Order, and the Law*. Oxford, United Kingdom; New York, Basil Blackwell.

Shin, D. C. (1994). "On the 3rd Wave of Democratization – A Synthesis and Evaluation of Recent Theory and Research." *World Politics* 47(1): 135–70.

Sidanius, J. and F. Pratto (1999). *Social Dominance: An Intergroup Theory of Social Hierarchy and Oppression*. Cambridge, United Kingdom; New York, Cambridge University Press.

Sidel, M. (2004). *More Secure Less Free? Antiterrorism Policy & Civil Liberties after September 11*. Ann Arbor, University of Michigan Press.

Singer, J. D. and M. Small (1994). *Correlates of War Project: International and Civil War Data, 1816–1992*. Ann Arbor, Inter-university Consortium for Political and Social Research.

Sloan, J. (1984). "State Repression and Enforcement Terrorism in Latin America." *The State as Terrorist: The Dynamics of Governmental Violence and Repression*. M. Stohl and G. A. Lopez. Westport, Connecticut, Greenwood Press.

Smith, J., M. Bolyard and A. Ippolito (1999). "Human Rights and the Global Economy: A Response to Meyer." *Human Rights Quarterly* 21(1): 207–19.

Southall, R. (2001). *Opposition and Democracy in South Africa*. London; Portland, Oregon, Frank Cass.

Stam A. (1996). *Win, Lose or Draw: Domestic Politics and the Crucible of War*. Ann Arbor, University of Michigan Press.

Stanley, W. (1996). *The Protection Racket State: Elite Politics, Military Extortion and Civil War in El Salvador*. Philadelphia, Temple University Press.

Stohl, M. (1976). *War and Domestic Political Violence: The American Capacity for Repression and Reaction*. Beverly Hills, California, Sage Publications.

Stohl, M., D. Carleton, G. Lopez and S. Samuels (1986). "State Violation of Human Rights – Issues and Problems of Measurement." *Human Rights Quarterly* 8(4): 592–606.

Tilly, C. (1978). *From Mobilization to Revolution*. Reading, Massachusetts, Addison-Wesley Pub. Co.

Tilly, C., G. Ardant and Social Science Research Council (U.S.) Committee on Comparative Politics., Eds. (1975). *The Formation of National States in Western Europe*. Princeton, New Jersey, Princeton University Press.

Timberlake, M. and K. R. Williams (1984). "Dependence, Political Exclusion, and Government Repression – Some Cross-National Evidence." *American Sociological Review* 49(1): 141–46.

Tsebelis, G. (2002). *Veto Players: How Political Institutions Work*. Princeton, New Jersey, Princeton University Press.

Bibliography

U. S. State Department (2001). "The Community of Democracies." *www.state. gov/g/drl/c10790.htm.*

Van den Berghe, P. L. (1990). *State Violence and Ethnicity.* Niwot, Colorado, University of Colorado Press.

Vanhanen, T. (2000). "A New Dataset for Measuring Democracy, 1810–1998." *Journal of Peace Research* **37**(2): 251–65.

Walter, E. V. (1969). *Terror and Resistance: A Study of Political Violence, with Case Studies of Some Primitive African Communities.* New York, Oxford University Press.

Wantchekon, L. and A. Healy (1999). "The 'Game' of Torture." *Journal of Conflict Resolution* **43**(5): 596–609.

Ward M. (2002). "Green Binders in Cyberspace: A Modest Proposal." *Comparative Political Studies* **13**(1): 46–51.

Weber, M. (1946). *From Max Weber: Essays in Sociology.* New York, Oxford University Press.

Wedeen, L. (1999). *Ambiguities of Domination: Politics, Rhetoric, and Symbols in Contemporary Syria.* Chicago, University of Chicago Press.

Whyte, J. and A. MacDonald (1989). "Dissent and National Security and Dissent Some More." *Dissent and the State.* C. E. S. Franks. New York, Oxford University Press.

Wintrobe, R. (1998). *The Political Economy of Dictatorship.* Cambridge, United Kingdom; New York, Cambridge University Press.

Wood, E. J. (2000). *Forging Democracy from Below: Insurgent Transitions in South Africa and El Salvador.* Cambridge, United Kingdom; New York, Cambridge University Press.

Wrong, D. H. (1988). *Power, Its Forms, Bases, and Uses: With a New Preface.* Chicago, University of Chicago Press.

   (1994). *The Problem of Order: What Unites and Divides Society.* New York, The Free Press.

Zakaria, F. (2004). *The Future of Freedom: Illiberal Democracy at Home and Abroad.* New York, W. W. Norton and Company.

Zanger, S. C. (2000). "A Global Analysis of the Effect of Political Regime Changes on Life Integrity Violations, 1977–1993." *Journal of Peace Research* **37**(2): 213–33.

Ziegenhagen, E. A. (1986). *The Regulation of Political Conflict.* New York, Praeger.

Zimmermann, E. (1983). *Political Violence, Crises, and Revolutions: Theories and Research.* Boston, G. K. Hall.

Index

Index

socioeconomic development and
modernization. *See* repression
Solidarity (Poland), 47
Somoza, Anastasio, 144
South Africa
democracy in, 59, 65–6, 118–19
political organizations in, 46
political parties in, 57–8, 65, 119
repression in, 53–4, 57–9, 65–6, 92,
179
Veto and *Voice* in, 53–9, 65–6, 119,
179
South African Communist Party, 53
Southall, R., 59
Soviet Union (USSR), 71
Stalin, Joseph, 33
Stam, A.C., 27
Stanley, W., 28, 40
Stroessner, Alfredo, 33
Suffrage. See elections; *Voice*
Suppression of Communism and
Group Areas Acts of 1950 (South
Africa), 57
Supreme Court, 8, 188
Suzman, Helen, 58

Tate, C. Neal, 76, 79
terrorism. *See also* USA Patriot Acts;
individual countries
counter-terrorism, 14
dangers of, 5
democracy and, 28
domestic terrorism, 6, 67
repression and, 27, 39, 72
terrorism-related detainees, 7
Terrorism Acts of 1967 (South Africa),
58
Third Wave, 178
Tiananmen Square massacre (China
1989), 33
Tocqueville, Alexis de, 17
totalitarianism, 33
Truth and Reconciliation Process. *See*
South Africa
Tsebelis, G., 24, 174

Turkey, 92
Tutsi. *See* Rwanda
Twagiramungu, Faustin, 3

Umukindo (human rights review), 2
United States
blacks in, 56
civil society in, 187–8
democracy in, 7, 184–8
foreign policies of, 18–19
political conflict in, 188
repression in, 6, 9, 27, 33, 97, 184–9
repressive legislation of, 5–8, 26, 185
September 11, 2001 and, 5–7
Veto and *Voice* in, 186–8
Uniting and Strengthening America
Providing Appropriate Tools
Required to Intercept and
Obstruct Terrorism Act. *See* USA
Patriot Act (2001)
University of San Carlos (Guatemala),
46
Unlawful Organizations Act of 1960
(South Africa), 58
Uruguay, 144
US Agency for International
Development (USAID), 103
USA Patriot Act (2001), 5–8, 185–8
USA Patriot Act II (2003), 7–8, 186
USAID. *See* US Agency for
International Development
(USAID)
USSR. *See* Soviet Union

Vanhanen/Gates democracy measure,
116, 141
Vanhanen, T., 91, 102, 104–5, 111, 115,
141, 205
Verkuilen, J., 100
Veto. See also democracy; hypotheses;
research methods and studies;
South Africa
components of, 106–10, 125, 148–62
concepts of, 13, 29–30, 51, 56–7, 74,
102, 133, 177, 182

231